ART, RELIGION, AMNESIA

Art, Religion, Amnesia addresses the relationship between art and religion in contemporary culture, directly challenging contemporary notions of art and religion as distinct social phenomena and explaining how such Western terms represent alternative and even antithetical modes of world-making.

In this new book, Preziosi offers a critique of the main thrust of writing in recent years on the subjects of art, religion, and their interconnections, outlining in detail a perspective that redefines the basic terms in which recent debates and discussions have been articulated both in the scholarly and popular literature, and in artistic, political, and religious practice. *Art, Religion, Amnesia* proposes an alternative to the two conventional traditions of writing on the subject which have been devoted, on the one hand, to the "spiritual" dimensions of artistry, and on the other hand to the (equally spurious) "aesthetic" aspects of religion.

The book interrogates the fundamental assumptions fuelling many current controversies over representation, idolatry, blasphemy, and political culture. Drawing on debates from Plato's proposal to banish representational art from his ideal city-state to the Danish cartoons of Mohammed, Preziosi argues that recent debates have echoed a number of very ancient controversies in political philosophy, theology, and art history over the problem of representation and its functions in individual and social life.

This book is a unique re-evaluation of the essential indeterminacy of meaning-making, marking a radically new approach to understanding the inextricability of aesthetics and theology and will be of interest to students and researchers in art history, philosophy and religion, and cultural theory.

Donald Preziosi is Professor Emeritus of Art History at UCLA, where he developed the art history critical theory program as well as the UCLA museum studies program. His research, teaching, and writing link together cultural studies, intellectual history, critical theory, and the arts and museologies of various ancient and modern societies.

ART, RELIGION, AMNESIA

The enchantments of credulity

Donald Preziosi

LONDON AND NEW YORK

For Praxiteles, who had his hands on the problem

First published 2014
by Routledge
2 Park Square, Milton Park, Abingdon, Oxon OX14 4RN

and by Routledge
711 Third Avenue, New York, NY 10017

Routledge is an imprint of the Taylor & Francis Group, an informa business

© 2014 Donald Preziosi

British Library Cataloguing in Publication Data
Preziosi, Donald, 1941-
    Art, religion, amnesia : the enchantments of credulity / by Donald
    Preziosi. – 1 [edition].
    pages cm
    Includes bibliographical references and index.
    1. Art and religion. 2. Art and society–History–21st century. 3. Religion
    and sociology–History–21st century. I. Title.
    N72.R4P747 2013
    701'.08–dc23

                                                                    2013023608

ISBN: 978-0-415-77860-2 (hbk)
ISBN: 978-0-415-77861-9 (pbk)
ISBN: 978-0-203-12928-9 (ebk)

Typeset in Bembo
by Wearset Ltd, Boldon, Tyne and Wear

Printed and bound in Great Britain by
TJ International Ltd, Padstow, Cornwall

CONTENTS

FIGURES

ACKNOWLEDGMENTS

Any honest acknowledgment will inevitably trouble simple or singular notions about authorship or origins – a fact that applies equally to artistry or cosmology. In the most general modern sense, acknowledgments are an admission or acceptance of the truth about something. In the case of a textual artifact such as this one, I acknowledge both here and throughout the text to follow the multiplicity and heterogeneity of the sources to which and to whom this book and the labor that went into producing it is indebted. Many of these sources are cited in each of the chapters (or *Passages*) below.

But just as singularity is continually troubled or problematized, so also is its converse: Even in the case of a modest text such as this, a full listing of all my indebtednesses would be of such magnitude and extension over time and place as to wear out the patience of the reader before the text itself is read.

This being the case, and given the ephemeral nature of these words, let me say straight away that the following work is beholden to an extraordinarily rich and diverse network of colleagues, students, friends, antagonists, and collaborators. This book is truly haunted by many names and places, and by encounters in many countries over several decades: This truly has been a collaborative venture, both materially and virtually – so as to also trouble any simple distinction between those two terms, or between materiality and immateriality more broadly. In addition to Jae Emerling, to whom I am indebted in countless ways, it has been Claire Farago, whose wit and intelligence has continued to move me deeply and for so long in ways both imaginable and unimaginable, in so many places around the world where this book germinated. The text grew and took root in and between Los Angeles, New York, Santa Barbara, Boston, Cambridge, Irvine, Boulder, Denver, Oxford, London, York, Norwich, Berlin, Munich, Graz, Copenhagen, Aarhus, Stockholm, Uppsala, Amsterdam, Leiden, Maastricht, Paris, Athens, Ioannina, Thessaloniki, Istanbul, Melbourne, Monash, Brisbane, Sydney, Alice Springs, Canberra, and

Wellington, and various universities, museums, and galleries in those and other places: juxtapositions in time and space which themselves have triangulated upon and given rise to ever more unsuspected dimensions. Many of the issues pursued in this book were pursued in earnest during a Slade Professorship in Fine Art and subsequent research associations at Oxford, and more recently during a semester as Visiting Professor at Bogazici (Bosphorus) University in Istanbul, part of a Getty Institute initiative to inaugurate a new doctoral program in art history.

I want to thank the following, with whom I've been privileged to engage as colleagues, students, friends, and teachers; those who (when not now deceased) will (mostly but not always) know how and why some of the ideas staged in this book are being acknowledged here and now for their contributions to what the book has become. Traces of all of these may be found in various places below. This *hauntology* (both historiographic and personal; see also *Passage* 4) includes Roman Jakobson, Michel de Certeau, Hayden White, Hubert Damisch, Martin Kemp, Louis Marin, Michael Landzelius, Michel Foucault, Amelia Jones, Jean-Francois Lyotard, Neil Cummings, Jacques Derrida, Louise Hitchcock, Phillip Armstrong, Sam Weber, Preminda Jacob, George Hanfmann, Irene Bierman, Michael Fehr, Marysia Lewandowska, Kylie Message, Joanne Lamoureux, Lyle Massey, John Onians, Jan Bakos, Ruth Phillips, Cecelia Klein, Paolo Girardelli, Jennifer Jane Marshall, Anne Waldman, Robert Summers, Howard Morphy, Ahmet Ersoy, Judith Butler, Susan Pearce, Tony Bennett, Cigdem Kafescioglu, Henrik Reeh, Anne Sejten, David Ferris, Vassilis Lambropoulos, Nilay Ozlu, Gizem Tongo, Ian Verstegen, Linda Waugh, Giorgio Agamben, Almila Akdag Salah, Alexandros Lagopoulos, Karin Boklund-Lagopoulou, Umberto Eco, Susan Buck-Morse, Bill Germano, Annika Waernerberg, Cynthia Colburn, Kostas Ioannides, Jenny Green, Ed Bowes, Susan Manchester, Jaynie Anderson, Matthew Rampley, Mark Winokur, Eleni Sikelianos, Katherine Eggert, Terry Smith, Laird Hunt, Mary Legier Biederman, Jonathan Mane-Wheoki, Chris Barlow, Sandra Esslinger, Michael Fotiades, Rob Zwijnenberg, and Helen Hills.

PROVOCATIONS[1]

It may seem odd to start a book with a series of provocations directed at the three terms juxtaposed in the book's title. But it is not: Much of what this book has become concerns what is powerfully provoked by the relativity and contingency of each of those terms, as well as their manufactured modern reifications or ontologies, the consequences and effects of which – no less than their *terrors* – are of profound concern today in not a few parts of the contemporary world.

And part of what is of concern here in rethinking or *deconstituting* "art" and "religion" and "amnesia" (no less than the "ands" between them) is the inextricability of provocation and *evocation*. Or, to put it another way, the indeterminacy at the heart of our engagement with material things: an engagement which despite its promotion as confirming *im*materiality, can equally be taken (as I do here) as a renewed challenge to reconsider and reconstitute all that is believed to be essential about every one of these terms. But taking up any such challenge entails allying its reconstitutions to those of its precedents that have not confused rebuilding with reupholstery – a task equally epistemological, archaeological, and critical; combining some heavy labor and not a little subtle attending.

The chapters or *Passages* making up this book take up various aspects or perspectives on such a challenge, including the social technologies of believing, which as a performative activity involves what I shall call here the *enchanting of worlds and things*: the spectral rendering of experience that troubles clear or fixed distinctions between the material and the immaterial. One that *dissipates* the onto-theological binaries of life/matter, organic/inorganic, as Jane Bennett recently put it,[2] and what I explore here in terms of the kaleidoscopic fluctuations of the epistemological matrices of representation.[3]

In beginning "new" excavation projects, I often feel that I've been preparing for the actual labor forever, or rather that I've been writing a renewed version of a project that is but a continuation and extension of all those I've been working on forever. The explicit beginning of a new project is usually an implicit continuation of the same overall set of concerns and interests that have obsessed or fascinated me for a long time – the sense of being *bound*, tied, or tethered to problems, paradoxes, and conundrums whose "half-life" is fully coterminous with the one I'm apparently living. In the present case, it is the current stage in the ongoing palimpsesting of all those interests that, from the here and now of this text, appear as specters haunting what is perhaps too precipitously claimed as the present of all those pasts, and the (latest) *harbinger* (to hark back to a Benjaminian concern to be engaged with below) of a present's future. The drift of presence(s) is one of the themes to be excavated below.

Art, Religion, Amnesia: The enchantments of credulity had long been planned as an investigation of the *concordances and discordances* arising in the juxtaposition of what are commonly distinguished in (largely "Western") modernity as "art" and "religion." I've been concerned with various aspects of the problems, paradoxes, and conundrums arising in the juxtaposition of these modern social practices and institutions for some time and from various perspectives, and I've written and lectured about aspects of these problems as they affect the modern discourses on visuality and visual and material culture studies in their diverse institutional and professional manifestations for as long as I've been professionally active, so it now appears, as well as when I have been inactive or "just looking" (which is not infrequently at the "same" time).

For a work like the present study, however, I should make several things clear at the outset. First, this is *not* an attempt to articulate what might be called an "aesthetics of" religion (or of spirituality, or of faith and belief). Second, it is *not* an exploration of the religious or "spiritual" *dimensions* or aspects of art, artistry, and artifice, as much as some might hanker for such a guidebook. I will, however, consider what's entailed by the manufacturing of hankering. And while appreciating the succinctness (and some of the motivations) of Walter Benjamin's characterization of the relations between art and politics as chiasmatic – as (to put it quickly) a reading or realizing the one as the inverse of the other – what unfolds here articulates any such stagings differently, in the light of so much that has changed in the three-quarters of a century since his remarkable and nearly lost labors. But its differences are necessarily different *in the light* of his labors.

In addition, the book undertakes the redefinition and recasting of "relations between" art and religion, in contrast to what on the face of it and in advance might have seemed parallel or similar endeavors to link conventionally distinguished practices or phenomena – for example, Jacques Ranciere's on occasion insightful attempts to recast the relations of aesthetics and politics.[4] Ranciere sought to frame such a relationship *chiasmatically* – that is, each as the inversion of the other: a move seeming to resonate with Benjamin's characterization of fascism as the aestheticization of politics, vs. its inversion, namely, communism as the politicization of aesthetics. Ranciere's insights, however, have been seen (and not only by myself) as linked to fairly uncritical (parochial; Eurocentric, etc.) notions of both such reifications (*the* aesthetic; *the* political). These are notions the present study problematizes for a variety of reasons.

More directly and urgently, *Art, Religion, Amnesia* is written in the *wake* and the aftermath (different actions, as argued below) of a phenomenon coming to prominence and strongly manufactured during the last decade of the twentieth century – the discourse around what was then called by not a few commentators a "return to (or resurgence of) religion" in various countries (terms used with positive and negative connotations) – *and* it is written in the wake of what that awakening of (what is customarily referred to as) "religion" (as if that term were universal and not culturally specific and locally contingent) has *itself* simultaneously *awakened*: the increased critical attention to what the discourse on resurgence has occluded and avoided.[5] As Derrida put it in the opening of a symposium on the island of Capri in 1994:

> Why is this phenomenon, so hastily called "the return of religions," so difficult to think? Why is it so surprising? Why does it particularly astonish those who believed naively that an alternative opposed Religion, on the one side, and on the other, Reason, Enlightenment, Science, Criticism (Marxist Criticism, Nietzschean Genealogy, Freudian Psychoanalysis and their heritage), as though the one could not but put an end to the other? On the contrary, it is *an entirely different schema* that would have to be taken as one's point of departure in order to try to think the "return of the religious." Can the latter be reduced to what the *doxa* confusedly calls "fundamentalism," "fanaticism," or, in French, "integralism"? Here perhaps we have one of our preliminary questions, able to measure up to the historical urgency.

Derrida's theses on religion ("Faith and Knowledge") are considered in *Passage* 6, "Godless in Copenhagen: theses, corollaries, objections," in regard to the question of the relations between religiosity and artifice which Derrida obliquely dealt with, focusing more explicitly on religion in the light of (the artifice of) writing. Understanding the social, political, semiological, and ideological manufacture of such modern *amnesias* constitutes a primary focus of the work of this volume, seen through the lenses of what the *distinction* itself (between artistry and religiosity) *disremembers*.[6]

As the archaeological labor of this project evolved – as the blueprint of "an entirely different schema" – it became an increasingly explicit interrogation of what will be articulated here as the *epistemological dramaturgy of a double amnesia*: one manifested as a disbelief in the impossibility of representation, and another manifested *inversely* as a disbelief in the artifice of belief.

In the first case disbelief renders artistry a perpetually *paratheistic* practice, and in the second case the disbelief renders religion a perpetually *paraesthetic* practice.[7]

These perspectives have been evolving for quite some time through my engagements with a number of academic disciplines, not to speak of the *grout* between them, and were expanded and ramified in a series of lectures delivered in Oxford during a residency as Slade Professor.[8] Although several books and other publications and interviews have appeared since then, the present text is based on premises voiced and promised then as these have evolved singly and jointly over those years. As with other excavations, the present report is essentially a collective endeavor acknowledged both at the beginning of this text and in numerous places below.

In addition, what have become the *Passages* making up this book are (another) demonstration of the *porosity* of the conventional barriers seen to exist under certain conditions between the scholarly and the personal: their necessary inextricability.

FIGURE 0.1 Room No. 2 (popularly known as the Mirrored Room). 1966. Samaras, Lucas (b. 1936) © Copyright. Photo credit: Albright-Knox Art Gallery/Art Resource, NY.

As well as a manifestation (to consider that last statement from a different perspective) of the contingencies of the separation of the present and the past of one's experiences and engagements. While, as the old cliché has it, the past isn't even past but is still *present*, presence is, however, *preternaturally porous:*[9] We continue living among and in engagement with the ghosts and shadows of ever-ramifying and migratory selves, their ancestors, kin, and progeny. And it is necessary to our labor here to articulate why porosity, in this case as well as others, is "preternatural," that is, *beyond* what is taken as natural: a beyond which calls attention to the *artifice* of what is culturally and time and place specifically delimited as (the) natural. Including, of course, presence "itself."

One *Passage* (No. 4: "Specters of artifice: a hauntology") brings together some early events which might be read as stepping stones toward what this text has now become; specifically a genealogy of conundrums which might seem by hindsight to add up to an itinerary toward unweaving the *chiasmatic double amnesia* at the heart of this inquiry both then and now. A trajectory, that is, of compounded echoes and palimpsests of each other. Any "personal" hauntology will foreground the ficticity (and the contingency, complexity, hybridity, and indeed the spatio-temporal *drift*) of identity: The fact that we "occupy" not simply as *singular* bodies, but *live* and manifest in concordance with others a multiplicity of embodiments. Moreover, any codes as might be cited as governing behavior across this multiplicity themselves have no permanent stability or fixity, but are themselves adrift. All such epistemological heterotopologies will become more explicitly delineated through the *Passages* making up this book.[10]

On method

A quick note on the somewhat heterodox methodology, and the scenography and dramaturgy of this book. Readers familiar with the remarkable and remarkably diverse (and prematurely truncated) body of work of Walter Benjamin will be familiar with some of the ways in which this text presents itself to be read and responded to; its dialectical, interrogative, and *solicitous* character. At the beginning of her 2008 book on Benjamin's engagement with secularization and the manner in which he engaged (or didn't) with that exceedingly complex modern subject throughout much of his life's work, Sigrid Weigel succinctly noted that Benjamin "does not so much work with a theory of secularization, a term he seldom uses explicitly; instead his approach to language, concepts, and images involves a rhetorical and epistemological practice that presents <u>scenes</u> of secularization."[11] This is a method or practice not dissimilar to that referred to as *mythomorphic* by Derrida – as figures, formations, fabrications, or images palpably approximating or isomorphic to aspects of what they refer to or talk about. Mythomorphic mimeses constitute *one* of the rhetorical modalities of signification among the variety employed and examined throughout the text. The book does, however, work toward a perspective on secularization in its relation to artistry, which, in its own way, and in historical contexts rather different from Benjamin's, parallels his ongoing concern with language and translation insofar as it ostensifies a *dialectic* between "Adamic" language and the (bipolar or dyadic) language of signs.[12] The notion of "dialectical imagery" is a continuing concern of what follows here, for it is something with a very ancient history that tends not to be reflected in the mirrored walls of modern and contemporary "art history."

The text proceeds through a series of chapters, or what I'm calling *Passages* (with periodic pauses and asides or side-bar commentary), whose *work* normally begins with the posing/juxtaposing of texts (or images or quotations or observations or claims) often put out ("on the table") as things to think with; to think through, or *reckon with* or against. Some of these "image-pieces" or fragments ("shards") are taken ("randomly") from the present or recent past, some from personal events or encounters, and some from very distant historical or geographical horizons. Most are usefully seen as bits and pieces here and there which are staged so as to be *reckoned with* together – literally, thought with and contended or struggled with. Compound objects to be rotated in the hand – like Wallace Stevens' "palm at the end of the mind" held out for examination.

The remainder of each *Passage* works through various implications of these images for the underlying concern of the book, namely, *to rethink the profound and uniquely complex relationships of* (what are conventionally distinguished in Western modernities – though I'm not pretending to speak for all of them, just a few local ones) *as artistry and religiosity and their reifications.* And in problematizing and deconstituting that distinction, along with what is "between" the sacred and the secular, and the gap or *caesura* between politics and philosophy (to cite a few prominent dyadic conventions) the book aims to and is motivated by a need to not only foreground but to reconfigure and *recast* that discourse and its epistemological and semiological premises, but also to conceive of possibilities for an ethical or civic life starting from different premises.

The book, moreover, is a reminder (and an ostensification) of the porosity or *indiscipliniarity* of the manufactured boundaries between the personal and the scholarly (and the critical and the scientific). It is also (yet another) manifestation of the fragility and contingency of the epistemological technology of temporality and the ideologies of chronology. The book is quite frankly haunted by many specters of the past in the present and the futures haunting the previous two. And it is directed to the multiple *amnesias* characterizing contemporary discourse on artistries and religiosities. Things and events driven, perhaps, *beyond* or *beneath* the boundaries of the palpably here-and-now to occasionally re-emerge: ghostly presences outside the frames of the present.

Which brings up the important question of *how to read* this book; this re-counting of an excavation; this field report notebook. It is organized as follows.

The first three relatively short sections (called here "Avant-propos," "Preamble," and "Perambulations") introduce many of the themes of what then follows in greater depth and at length. The fourth ("Specters of artifice: a hauntology") is a fielding of memories and encounters along the way to the here and now of the book's articulation of what is at stake in excavating the spaces "between" art and religion. The fifth ("Parenthesis: art, time and the untimely") considers the artistry of modernist disciplinary time.

The sixth *Passage* is the propositional heart of the text (*Godless in Copenhagen: theses, corollaries, objections*), a spelling out of claims and implications and potential consequences. A blueprint for a matrix of manifestoes.

The following four (*Passages* 7 through 10) deal with *aspects of amnesia* from various aesthetic and theological perspectives. The text is followed by an eleventh *Passage*, the *coda* to the overall composition.

The just-outlined plan of the book may also be envisioned as centripetally/centrifugally (globally) organized – as having a virtual beginning point or center in the formally gathered set of theses and corollaries – namely, *Passage* 6, "Godless in Copenhagen." One way in which the book may be read is to start there, and then read ("outward") from the beginning and on beyond to the final coda on the perimeter.

Again, the book is more *dialogic* and interrogative than assertive, for its (usually collegial) assertions are intended to elicit dialogue, and hence may also seem from some perspectives to be marking a certain distinction between philosophy and theology, between a world of signs and an Adamic language. The latter, I will argue in detail, following up on the cumulative implications of this project, being itself the staging of a world of *artifice*. Which makes it no less open to belief. To paraphrase Wallace Stevens again, the final or *supreme* fiction is to know that "the world" is a fiction, and to consciously *believe in it nonetheless*.

Or to put it more prosaically, to acknowledge the existence of semiological determinacy within a co-present realm of indeterminacy; invariance within a field of variability.

Which is – from a related perspective – yet another *index* of the contingency of "authorship": the apparent singularity of my *role* in this text, and the genuinely *composite* nature of its composition, as will become increasingly clear as this project unfolds.

On etymology

In connection with the previous section, "On method," I should insert a caution regarding the frequent appearances of etymological references (often in parentheses) throughout the text. Those appearing here, usually "taken from" ancient Latin, Greek, and on occasion Sanskrit or Hebrew, are meant to serve as aids to thinking about/ rethinking the subject(s) at hand as themselves contingent. They are used in full awareness of Maurice Blanchot's skepticism regarding the lure and allure of the *etymon* taken to mean the true literal sense of a word according to its origins. There were two reasons for the concern of this philosopher whose influence on Jacques Derrida and other contemporaries was profound on many levels, including some of the very vocabulary and syntax often taken as singly originating with those authors.

The first has to do with a belief that the first recorded occurrence of a term, especially in German Romanticism and the philological tradition subsequent to that aesthetic movement, implies something essential about its *future* significance, which implicitly or explicitly validates the (usually nationalist or not infrequently racist) bringing together of beginnings and ends of what we would today distinguish as political and philosophical.

The second has to do with Humpty Dumpty, that character in Lewis Carroll's *Through the Looking Glass* who famously claimed that "when *I* use a word it means just what I choose it to mean – neither more nor less."[13] That is, the supposed semantic permanence or invariance of a term, which marks an ahistorical amnesia regarding etymology as the artifact or product of rhetorical and philological research into the historical evolution and migration of the meanings of words in the service of particular political ends – one of which had to do with justifying the claims of various peoples for national unity and territorial contiguity.[14]

Yet there is a deeper theological reason for the modern European development of etymological scholarship as a philological discipline, namely as an early modern version of medieval biblical exegesis and the intensely pragmatic requirement to justify proper or correct readings of sacred texts, and in particular for Western Europeans those in non-extant or foreign languages (Hebrew, Aramaic, Greek). Such a requirement is grounded in a Humpty-Dumpty kind of *faith* in the perfect correspondence between (what are conventionally distinguished as) word and thought (or reference or meaning or signification). A fundamentalist or literalist belief; that *x* means a *y* that is of a different order of being. Or, in other words, that *x* is *equated* to (what is referenced as a) *y*.

These are no small matters; indeed, they are at the heart of what is investigated variously in each of the *Passages* making up the book. To put it briefly, Humpty-Dumpty was *both* right and wrong, for if he was right in his claim, he was at the same time necessarily *incorrect* precisely because it was his language – itself – that made it not only possible but necessary for him to make the assertion in the first place.

It is also the conundrum or paradox at the heart of artistry and its relation to religiosity: the *disobedience* of things (*lacrimae rerum*) to permanently or invariantly signify what may be claimed of them. It is an issue that Blanchot was deeply concerned with throughout his work, and in particular regarding the *efficacy* or adequacy of political writing, where ideological claims *for* something are equally available for use *against*.

A poignant example of this "disobedience" was to be found in the 2010 exhibition at the Centre Pompidou in Paris, called "The Promises of the Past," displaying a collection of avant-gardist artwork from the Cold War in Eastern European countries before the dismantling of the Berlin Wall. The wall text at the exhibition entrance, reading "The idea of art is to change and improve the world," immediately evoked its opposite, manifested in – indeed ostensified by – the aesthetic claims of the (failed) societies of the "old East" (*l'art dans l'ex-Europe d'Est*) within the exhibition halls.[15]

My occasional use, then, of "etymology" (*etymon* + *logos*, *true word*) below is pragmatically to foreground the contingency and mediatedness; the historically, socially, and spatio-temporally tethered nature of *both* the artistry of language *and* the language of artistry and religiosity.

What follows immediately are a few image-pieces or *shards* to provoke and *evoke* what is to become the text below, namely, the *aftermaths* of the following direct provocations. Also, these are the beginning of a series of *questions*, both explicit and implicit, to both reader and author: *how* and in what ways do the following assertions, descriptions, and memories – there are about a dozen – relate to one another?

1 Wandering not long ago through a university library in the north of England looking for the section on art I came across a (mis-shelved/overlooked) copy of a mid-nineteenth century book by the American Transcendentalist philosopher and social critic Henry David Thoreau called *Walden, And on the Duty of Civil Disobedience*. It is a diary recounting his two-year solitary sojourn ("A Life in the Woods") in a cabin he built in the forest away from the urban distractions of Boston. He recorded this remark on May 10, 1853:

> The Man of Science, who is not seeking for expression, but for a *fact* to be expressed *merely*, studies nature as a dead language. To an art historian this immediately conjured up the phrase dead nature (nature morte) or "still(ed.) life."

Thoreau was referring to *undiluted* expression; expression not sought for its *expressiveness*. One purporting to ignore – or believing it could effectively mask – the traces of its own artistry: an art, so to speak, of amnesia taken as an activity performed on what is consequently construed or framed as the past.[16]

But what exactly could it mean for "science" to take "nature" as an artwork masking its own artistry? Science staged as a *Praxitelean* performance whose artistry consists of erasing the traces of its (aesthetic) fabricatedness; masking the marks of the sculptor's chisel? It prompted me to ask what exactly, then, do "art historians" study *merely*? What would art history as a modern social practice be amnesiac about?

Q. Have "art historians" (or historians of "visual and material culture") been in effect studying *art as a dead religion*? (*Follow-up* Q: Is religion similarly a dead or muted artistry?)

2 Thoreau's remarks reminded me of comments made in Paris half a century earlier by Richard Lenoir about Napoleon's looting of the many churches, monasteries and palaces around Europe for artworks destined to fill the recently established museum in the former royal palace of the Louvre. He framed Napoleon's actions as a campaign not of plunder but of *liberation* – the liberating of the <u>*aesthetic*</u> qualities inhering in objects long held captive by dead and dusty religions and absent, absconded, or displaced aristocrats.[17]

A veritable instance of *aesthetic cleansing*, and precisely the *founding gesture* of much subsequent (art) museology in modernity and the passionate craft or gesture of collecting.[18] Museology as *erasure*; the erasing and elimination from its corpus (honed consequently and constitutively into a *canon defined as much by what it occludes as what it includes*) of objects and phenomena not in conformity or concordance with a founding vision (agenda; ideology; canon) of what is deemed fitting or proper to include in and as the "history" or national genealogy being staged on behalf of those simultaneously situated and staged as auditors or audience; its civil public. The suppression and rendering vacant of a past by a newly commodified present. It is such amnesia; as Lefebvre once observed, such "forgetfulness – or as a philosopher might say, this mystification – [is what] makes possible the fetishism of commodities: the fact that commodities imply certain social relationships whose *misapprehension* [my emphasis]) they also ensure."[19] An enterprise, as argued below, echoed in and through the "secularization" or evacuation of the religiosity in artistry. As if that religiosity (or artistry or "embellishment") was an exchangeable condiment or flavoring added to an unadorned or *mere* meal.

And indeed a movement mirroring the *political cleansing* and de-domesticating of the former royal residence of the Louvre, through its concurrent reformatting as an explicitly *pedagogical* institution meant to expose the newly minted citizens of the nascent Republic to a new political teleology staged as a choreographic drama; a *journey* through the spaces of the evolving *aesthetic* grandeur of France; a chronological or *teleological* array of masterworks culminating in the manufactured glories of the present regime. A journey through what was staged as echoing or re-presenting the unfolding national glory. The commoditization and reification of space-time. An *explicitly Masonic* ambition[20] of reshaping space so as to transform character. In this case, to transform monarchical subjects into republican citizens.[21]

3   Here it would seem we have obversely equivalent evacuations and complementary fictions. On the one hand, Thoreau's *evacuation* of the artistry or artifice from "expression," leading to an appreciation of the "mere being" of phenomena devoid of extraneous addenda, a mere thingness of things,[22] and, on the other, Lenoir's *extraction* (abstraction) of the (*thenceforth* freestanding or reified) aesthetic qualities out of objects whose religiosity was correspondingly muted. A reminder that amnesia is no simple loss or oversight, nor a *mere* forgetting, but, as Michel de Certeau once aptly put it, *an action performed against* (what is thereby and consequently staged as) *the past*. That invisible but no less haunting *theological* elephant in the room of post-Revolutionary "secular" Europe. But then hasn't art history been a Mormonism in *mufti*, bent on "baptizing" all the dead *artistry* in all the dead artifacts that ever lived, aligning them all together in a more decorous rearrangement of space and time – a *Gleichschaltung*,[23] to use a term favored by the *emeritus* pope Benedict XVI?

4   Juxtaposing the comments of Thoreau and Lenoir evokes a palindromic palimpsest impertinently insisting itself with the words: *So: if art is one's religion, then surely religion must be one of (and indeed perhaps the finest of) the "fine arts"?* Suddenly an echo of a half-remembered phrase, the title of a notorious book published in London in 1827 by Thomas de Quincy called *Murder Considered as One of the Fine-Arts*. Is religion, then, one (or is it several) of the fine arts?

And what, then, of *politics* considered as a fine art? (What exactly would Ranciere have written about art and politics had he not omitted Machiavelli?)

5 The latter recalls the translucent subtext of Plato's (baffling to some today) *banishment of the arts* from his ideal city, as we'll also see below. But Plato was duplicitous/disingenuous about his evacuation of artistry, for while his ostensible aim was to contrast the imperfect world (the world of daily life and its confusing and duplicitous artistries) with an ideal invisible cosmic other, what he did in fact (legerdermanically) was to reframe *the city itself as a properly ordered or disciplined* <u>work of art</u>. A more *fittingly harmonious* architectonics of civil space. The *cure* for art was – as of course it always has been, and still remains today – a *better art*; the duplicity repeated by Augustine a millennium later in his dream of a "City of God" standing in opposition to the all-too deficient, all-too-lachrymose and mortal (*sunt lacrimae rerum*) "City of Man." A manufactured duplicity reinstantiated by literalists and orthodox fundamentalists or grand reifiers of every stripe ever since, whether religious, social, political, scientific, or economic. The unknowability of a transcendent divinity is the medium of the *engineering of desire*.[24]

Here we might seem to have a glimpse of the fold or *hinge* upon which swings any putative *distinction* between "art" and "religion": as if these were the two leaves of a folding screen. This very screen (seen from another angle) may be the *scrim* on which is inscribed the present inquiry/excavation, whose mythomorphic, ostensive, para-Benjaminian(?) labor is dedicated to illuminating or manifesting its configurations (as if) "from behind." Or, if you prefer, in plan, as if (again; see above) in a bird's-eye view.

Although as we'll see it was always "in plain sight," it is *we* who have been made to forget that we were *not* blind and forgetful.

6 The viability of the modern fictions of art historicism or museology were grounded in masked or obscured connections to religion, which is what makes the claim that professing such practices as "art history" or its allomorphic museology as allegedly "secular" modern practices, depends on art being staged and articulated precisely as a muted or <u>dead</u> *religion*. One, moreover, crying out (as if from an open grave, and vampirically) for explication and voice; crying out to be heard. An *evacuation* or erasure or a *rendering moot* of religious (or "spiritual") qualities and functions of cultural materials so as to bring to light or instantiate or release or liberate their "more purely" aesthetic values.

Surely a collective enterprise in *hygiene*; a veritable hygienic reductionism. The elusive charm of the "return to the (art) object" *itself* – more recently (re) vivified in contemporary attention being afforded by some to *materiality* or "thing" theory which isn't necessarily accompanied by an equal attention to the social, political, philosophical, disciplinary and historiographic contexts within and because of which any "thing" is discernible in the first place.[25]

As Protestant Christianity itself is said to have *morphed into* capitalism, it may be that at present *materiality* (or at least the recent materiality industry) is one of the allomorphs of what the metaphysical has morphed into: one of the current flip-flops of transcendence – something to be investigated at length below. Not to speak of what Jane Bennett has termed the "vibrancy" of matter and the "material recalcitrance" of cultural productions in her call for *horizontaliz-ing* the (once adamantine *verticality* of) the Great Chain of Being, a call explicitly rooted in Guattari's *transversalist ecology*, Spinoza's theory of bodies, and (what is currently being called) post-environmentalism.[26]

There is, of course, no materiality as such, no *mere* materiality, divorced from its "immaterial" co-determinates in given times and places. Matter is invariably not a mere *what* in many cultural environments, as we'll discuss in some detail below, in many cases problematizing or troubling familiar distinctions (not only "Western") between *subjects* and *objects*.[27] Indeed, power (as in the power of sovereignty or of the state) is a performative fiction deriving (as I will argue) from an *elision* – itself a reification with obvious links to the processes of the political manufacture of space amenable to capitalism – of its "fictional" origins and its "real" effects. A twinning and troubling, which is to say a *spectral*, construct.

7 There is a *vice versa* to the notion of art as *dead religiosity* just suggested above, namely *religion as dead art*: as the practice or profession of deadening or muting or erasing (as, again, the operation of a *Praxitelean hygiene*) the traces of its own contingent artistries; its *facture*, in art historical terms. What I might call a dis-facturing. Yet in fact the masquerading of the immaterial gods simultaneously reveals (unmasks) the *artistry of divinity*, a process W.B. Yeats gave voice to in his poem "Sailing to Byzantium" regarding *the artifice of eternity*.

8 Unmasking the artistry of "art's history" simultaneously reveals the (or "a") "truth" of art or artistry as the (an) *unmasking of the impossibility of re-presentation*. So, then, it might be asked, what was being done in staging yet again (virtually annually it has seemed) the endless carousal of art historicism's teleology? The mythology of disciplinary progress and the ceremonies of monitoring the "state" of that progress are grounded and fixed in the fiction of art being staged, articulated, and construed *as* a sign; as a re-presentational practice. Yet no amount of progress toward a properly "globalized" or a more decorously respectful or properly *rounded* "world" art history (should that be desired) – that final fiction of the fully and sumptuously stocked and appointed museum at the end of (the time of) the mind which stages and decorously distributes all possible artistic objects and their subjects (the dangerously alluring yet politically essential fiction of "art" as a pan-human, pan-regional, and pan-temporal phenomenon) purporting to *account properly for* the artistry of all peoples and places – will do anything more than dust and lightly vacuum the tacky upholstery of corporate museology. Could there be a *mere* museology uncoupled from (what I will argue below seems to be) the Mormonism of art historicism/ historiography/museology? Or, less parochially, its *messianicity* – regarding which there's a lot to be said below.

The art of art history was a circumstantial product or effect of certain historically specific frameworks of evaluation.[28] The (not so) curious modernist/

reductionist fiction of seeing art as if it really were a *kind* of thing (rather than construing artistry as a way of/skill in using (m)any things – a commercially not unproblematic endeavor – is *itself* an artifact or effect of how knowledge was produced so as to be of service to the early modern European nation-state as itself a representational artifact: the *polis* tethered to its translucently transcendent *commedia*.[29] We could hear echoes of what Thoreau claimed to be facts susceptible to being "*merely* described" in various recent "returns to the (art) object" once crowed about by some art marketers and historians to replace rampant critical thinking which just doesn't know its proper place.

Yet any such reification such as art or religion is itself an artifact of historical *struggles* over the meaning or significance of phenomena which only appear to be external to what is seen as being susceptible to alteration or transformation. In this case, art as an *evacuation* of something which from another perspective is intrinsic and *non*-detachable.

As, for example, a living relationship to an image, object, or icon that entails the acknowledgment by an individual or community of different presumptions about the nature and function of connectivity. But if politics or aesthetics or religiosity are framed as removable qualities or inflections of some *mere* other, commodities like coriander or chiaroscuro or gender or even aura, then such *merenesses* are themselves the *effects* and aftermaths of specific historical contestations and (de)contextualizations. What we may isolate as artworks or as phenomena with aesthetic uses and effects are fundamentally and at base mutable and contingent. Reductionism may be functionally useful in certain contexts (social, scientific, or epistemological) but counter-productive and even destructive in others, as recent examples from the "new biology" suggest.[30]

9   This requires closer attention to the historical and cultural circumstances within which attending to the *artistry of the invention of art as a kind of thing* arose, and the functions served by the very *form* of asking "what *is* (art)?" in the first place.[31] As opposed to the more nuanced and substantive question *when* and under what conditions and for whom is (something) art(istic). And what would society, religion, or politics *un*reified be if framed processually as interleaved or intercalated functions or activities? As the residue, relic, or remainder of specific historical negotiations and contestations in a certain time and place invariably tethered to palpable social consequences?

In asking "what is" religion, Derrida, for example (as noted above), addressed the concept or "idea" or essence (*quiddity*) *abstracted from* all particular religions (*haeccity*), as itself not only a mark of a very specific (Western, modernist, etc.) cultural perspective, but also the mark of an elision of the language itself of asking such a question – in this case what is implied by (the silhouetted shadow of) the Latin *religio*. Which must at the same time raise the co-determinate question of all that "religion" is *not*.

The conundrum of the "it." If your confrontation with an image, *object*, or icon involves acknowledging that your very identity is inextricably entailed with what I might call *a transcendental (dis)possession*; that is, with an acknowledgment that you do *not entirely* "own" your identity but that you (and it) are in effect multiply intertwined with each other, so that while it may be "proper" to you, it's not solely your *private* property, nor necessarily is your depriving others of that "it" yours alone either, so then consequently these cannot be (mere) *eachs* then, either. Your individuality is tethered to and exists with respect to your divisibilities or multiplicities; your *dividuality*[32] and the "contingencies, complexities, and hybridities" of your not necessarily always similar selves.

I've been fielding a few provocations about a very ancient and enduring problem I unexpectedly stubbed my toe on in Thoreau's *Walden* and its echoes widening out elsewhere − that is, the problem of the relations between what in many times and places are distinguished as *art* and *religion*. Or − as is the case in not a few contemporary communities − as art, religion, and *politics*. Or not at all so distinguished, for in many places and times, what I've just now voiced as distinct are in practice or by preference properly *in*distinguishable, something sharply highlighted in both recent and ancient murderous contestations between what we might distinguish correspondingly as theocratic and democratic polities.

10 These are issues emblematic of the fundamental indeterminacy (itself contingent) or the *indisciplinarity*[33] of signification or meaning-making processes across a wide range of social situations, and not least in and as the discourse on artistry. Emblematic, that is, of a gap between construction and construal − a semiological, epistemological, and theological conundrum that lies at the very heart of what we are still not infrequently asked to consider today as "the state of" the discipline of the history of art; of the afterlives of that state. As David Ferris has put it in relation to the state of the modern academic "disciplining" of comparative literature, it was a field whose

> history registers an essential indiscipline at the very core of its concept, but not an indiscipline that can be simply accorded the value of alterity with respect to the Enlightenment and modernity − as if the "rationality" of the Enlightenment and the modernity that it inaugurates could be confined to the exclusion of alterity. But to bring the force of indiscipline, this impossibility we would know as alterity, out of its confinement by modernity − is this not already the still most essential gesture of modernity? Let us not forget that modernity is itself founded on *impossibility*, as Winckelmann put it, the impossibility of imitating an inimitable antiquity.

If, for many, an artwork appears to embody or elicit a certain *politics*, does it not or indeed has it not always *also* demanded or evoked a certain *theology*? Isn't *embodiment* a theological artifact, product, or effect, and not only as the foundational and instituting claim of one of the three major extant monotheisms (and its suppression and transference in and by the other two)?

Moreover, when Derrida provocatively claimed that *a divine teleology secures the political economy of the fine-arts* (see below), isn't the *obverse* of his assertion both equally cogent and mutually entailed – namely, that it is a certain divinely tethered *artistry that* secures (indeed, makes possible in the first place) *the political economy of religion?* And of course the religious economy of the political. What (or who) is "securing" (tethering) whom or what, and for what reasons? Who benefits from prolonging what I might now call (and not entirely facetiously) the *bipolar disorder* of representation – that is, the metaphysical faith in fixed and palpable distinctions between signifier and signified – if not of religiosity "as such"? But then, as I discuss here, there are significant and substantial problems with any such "as suchs."

11 What exactly would constitute cogent or compelling criteria for judging when and how a religion is *purely* religious? *Mere* religiosity from which has been *evacuated* (abstracted, extracted) all (purely) aesthetic or "expressive" qualities? The artistry or fiction of a facticity from which fiction has been *evacuated* – that impossible desideratum of not a few religious practices over the centuries (was Protestantism *not* the ultimate Jesuitical trick of believing that one has stepped, or could step, or is stepping right here and now *outside* the forest of religious symbols, ceremony, and "expression" to a *mere* [pure] literalism); a "true" confrontation with the god(s)? The very catalyst of not a few theo-genocidal confrontations and more than a little ethnic and ethno-theological *cleansing.*

Q. How is it that the cure for non-literal religiosity seems invariably more (and more decorously disciplined) artistry purporting to be *merely* religion?

12 These shards/image-pieces here seem to be caught (like flies in a piece of prehistoric amber) in the double-bind of Thoreau's (and Plato's) perpetually unresolved conundrums, whose *uresolvedness* is not (merely) a failing but a successful political artifice of hegemonic power, as we'll see in more detail as we proceed.

And what of the discursive practices of art historicism? When we claim to be considering the "state of" art history or visual or material studies we so frequently disremember that art history's history is truly a dumb-show or masquerade: the ventriloquism of the endless metamorphoses of the history of capital. The history of art is (coterminous with) the history of capital. That is: *it does not engage with or confront artistry except* as a *sign*; as a "representational" phenomenon: a reification tethered, moreover, to a transcendent immateriality: the divine reproduction/praxis of capital. The point was very well made many years ago that art history was never actually or precisely *in* crisis, but was itself *the mark of a crisis in thinking about art* because it was founded in *denial* of the impossibility of representation – the fiction that "artworks" *really do* adequately (and inadequately) echo, reflect, embody, or express mentalities, identities, beliefs, social mores, etc. But then is this not a "religious" move? (to be continued...)

Art historicism as the practice of a *manufactured amnesia* about the historical circumstances of its fabrication as an *evacuated theology*; the simulacrum of a secularity which – as explored at length and tantalizingly by Talal Asad, Wendy Brown, Judith Butler, and Saba Mahmood in a recent Berkeley symposium[34] – is a continuation or perpetuation of religiosity in (what is thereby co-constructed as) a "post-religious" age.

Every word in the last sentence is a twig in a thickly entwined nest of conundrums, reminding us of their collective strength as well as the fragility of the machinery of the language of what is retroactively constituted as transparently indexical with respect to its sense or significance; the "content" of its "form."

Historically, these have been *no mere* metaphors but at the very same time and consequently real catastrophes for the unwary. But art history, theory, and criticism are hardly unique in falling into the venus fly-trap of semiological fixity or epistemological literalism: what I called above the bipolar disorder of the representationalism of religiosity. Indeed, they were ushered into that stickiness by a host of theocrats of every denomination.

Which may give some pause when dogmatically insisting on drawing a hard and fast "distinction between" art and religion. Not that there *isn't* such a distinction (a "fact on the ground" as some hard-line politicians are wont to insist), but it's one that draws its spectral strength from the efficacy of the glue or *elision* of the material and the virtual; a twinned amnesia.

Art history's amnesia is twin to the obverse amnesia known as theology, suggesting that institutional religiosity functions above all as a mode of artistry in denial of the artifice of its own expression: amnesiac, ambivalent, or duplicitous with respect to its foundations and origins as a product and effect of art; with respect to the fabricatedness of its own fabrications, and with respect to the artifice of what is promoted by many religions as "real," "true," "natural," or as "revealed" or "authored" or *"designed"* by unaccountable immaterial forces, spirits, gods, entities, or beings.[35]

13   In fact, as I suggest here and will elaborate upon below, artistry and religiosity constitute alternative (and not merely or *simply* antithetical) and *fractal perspectives* on the fundamental philosophical problem of representation or signification. (Neither "art" nor "religion" exist independently of each other except as (marks of) differential intricacy or variable modalities of semiosis. Which also and not incidentally may lead to a keener awareness of the status of philosophy as a collective, dialogic endeavor (Lacoue-Labarthe, Badiou, Plato, etc.).

It is at that more fundamental *in*disciplinary level that substantive critiques of religiosity and of artistry (or all of its allomorphs such as art history, theory, criticism, museology, aesthetics, or the industrial light and magic of the ceremonial praxes of fashion, tourism, and heritage-manufacture and marketing), have proven to flourish more productively than within the spot-lit stages of disciplinarity alone, which necessarily leave dark what is "outside" any spotlight. But again it is well to recall the *modernity* (and cultural specificity) of such disciplinary distinctions, including particularly the evolving oppositions and porous boundaries between art, science, and technology – a development linked to the emergence of capitalist commodity production in the nineteenth century, prior to which art, artist, and artistry (and more) were (in the Western tradition) terms denoting a common domain of human skill in many domains (Greek *tekne*, Latin *ars*).[36]

Time to move forward. The next five *Passages* are prequels to the core theses comprising *Passage* 6 ("Godless in Copenhagen"), and the following four (*Passages* 7–10) are sequels, ramifications, and consequences of the central theses and corollaries. The book ends with *Passage* 11, a short *coda*.

Notes

1 An earlier version of the following remarks was part of the opening address to the Caucus of the Art Historians of Southern California, organized and chaired by Prof. Sandra Esslinger, at the 100th annual convention of the College Art Association of America (CAA) in Los Angeles, February 24, 2012. It was delivered when early drafts of what was becoming this book were being written, and what follows is a synopsis of what is being pursued at length and in detail below.

2 See Jane Bennett's poignant study *Vibrant Matter: A Political Ecology of Things* (Durham, NC and London: Duke University Press, 2010), pp. ix–x. Although I'm not quite convinced about the efficacy of Bennett's "dissipations," I am encouraged (as may be seen below) by her tweaking of developments in the once prominent "thing theory" industry, regarding which I take an oblique perspective: see below, n. 9.

3 An exploration or, more accurately, a field excavation down into the levels of the dirty nuts and bolts of the manufacture of modern signifying processes: an industrial archaeology, if you like.

4 Jacques Ranciere's attempts to recast the relations of politics and aesthetics are usefully seen in his *The Politics of Aesthetics: The Distribution of the Sensible* (London: Continuum, 2004) (*Le partage du sensible: esthetique et politique* [Paris: La fabrique, 2000]), where he argued for the aesthetic dimension (of social activity) as inherent to any emancipatory politics. Not the least of the problems with such a view, of course, is that the aesthetic dimension is equally ("inherently") *anti-emancipatory*. For a discussion of the ambivalence of the term, in connection with a recent exhibition at the Parisian Centre Pompidou (*Les promesses du passé*, 2011), see D. Preziosi and Claire Farago, *Art Is Not What You Think It Is* (London: Wiley-Blackwell, 2012 [Blackwell's *Manifestoes*], ch. 1 [hereafter cited as *AINT*]. In his later and more subtly argued *Malaise dans l'esthetique* (Paris: Galilee, 2004), p. 39, he staged these relationships chiasmatically, apparently echoing the structure (if not the "spirit") of Walter Benjamin's characterization of fascism in relation to communism. The problems with both perspectives continue to be voiced; for example, David Ferris' 2009 essay on relationships between literature and politics: "Politics after Aesthetics: Disagreeing with Ranciere," in *Parallax* Vol. 15, No. 3, 37–49, which critiques Ranciere's (mis)reading of Benjamin's notions of the relationships between aesthetics and politics. As I argue below, the topology itself needs to be fundamentally rethought *in its essence*; the juxtaposition of artistry and religiosity marks (as I argue below) what is more accurately a *double and reciprocal amnesia*. For a useful collection of key texts of the classic debate on aesthetics and politics within European Marxism, see *Aesthetics and Politics: Ernst Bloch, Bertolt Brecht, Walter Benjamin, Theodor Adorno*, with an Afterword by Frederic Jameson. Translation Editor Ronald Taylor (London: New Left Books, 1977 [Verso edition, 1980; 2nd printing 1986]). I will have occasion to comment on Ranciere's perspectives at various points below.

5 An excellent critical introduction to Jacques Derrida's reckoning with the "idea" or "essence" of religion is Michael Naas, *Miracle and Machine: Jacques Derrida and the Two*

Sources of Religion, Science, and the Media (New York: Fordham University Press, 2012). The book is a detailed exegesis of the *theses* comprising Derrida's 1994–95 essay "Faith and Knowledge: The Two Sources of 'Religion' at the Limits of Reason Alone," Trans. Samuel Weber. In *Religion*, ed. Jacques Derrida and Gianni Vattimo (Stanford, CA: Stanford University Press, 1998) pp. 1–78 (*La religion*. ed. Jacques Derrida and Gianni Vattimo. [Paris: Editions du Seuil, 2996]). The text was published again four years later in *Acts of Religion*. ed. and introduced by Gil Anidjar (New York: Routledge, 2002), pp. 40–101. Hent de Vries, in *Philosophy and the Turn to Religion* (Baltimore, MD: Johns Hopkins University Press, 1999), argued that "Faith and Knowledge" is Derrida's most explicit discussion of the theme of religion and may be seen as bringing together numerous threads of his other, earlier writing as well. See also de Vries' excellent and important essay, " 'The Two Sources of the Theological Machine': Jacques Derrida and Henri Bergson on Religion, Technicity, War, and Terror," in Creston Davis, John Milbank and Slavoj Zizek, eds., *Theology and the Political: The New Debate*, with an Introduction by Rowan Williams (Durham, NC and London: Duke University Press, 2005, 366ff). In the latter (pp. 367ff.), de Vries, discussing "the somewhat tired concept of secularization," claims (as I do here) that concepts and practices presumed to be antithetical to acknowledged forms of religiosity "remain tied to the very traditions [they] tend (or intentionally seek) to subvert or substitute" (a not unfamiliar phenomenon). On the presumed "secularization" of religious practices in the evolution of modern disciplinary formations, such as the history of art, see *AINT* 2012, first four chapters.

6 At the Capri symposium, Derrida claimed (op. cit., p. 4) that

> now, if today, the "question of religion" actually appears in a new and different light, if there is an unprecedented resurgence, both global and planetary, of this ageless thing, then what is at stake is language, certainly – and more precisely the idiom, literality, *writing*, that forms the element of all revelation and of all *belief*, an element that ultimately is irreducible and untranslatable – an idiom that above all is inseparable from the social nexus, from the political, familial, ethnic, communitarian nexus, from the nation and from the people: from autochthony, blood and soil, and from the ever more problematic relation to citizenship and to the state. In these times, language and nation form the historical body of all religious passion.

7 I borrow the neologism *paraesthetic* from David Carroll's coining of the term in his seminal comparative critical study of Nietzsche, Lyotard, Foucault, and Derrida, *Paraesthetics: Foucault, Lyotard, Derrida. The Displacement of Theory and the Question of Art* (New York and London: Methuen, 1987). My own neologism, *paratheistic* is its mirror-image. More on these terms and their use as the text unfolds.

8 Those lectures (delivered under the title "Seeing Through Art History" were published two years later as *Brain of the Earth's Body: Art, Museums, and the Phantasms of Modernity* (Minneapolis and London: University of Minnesota Press, 2003) – hereafter cited as *Brain*. I am grateful for the hospitality of All Souls College during my term as Slade Professor, and to the Department of the History of Art at Oxford and Professor Martin Kemp and his colleagues for subsequent research associations.

9 I'm using the term *porous* in a manner not unlike its use by Stanley Tambieh, in his *Magic, Science, Religion, and the Scope of Rationality* (Cambridge: Cambridge University Press, 1990), in contrasting Western and Ayurvedic medicine in the treatment of mental illnesses: "the empirical individual is … seen as porous and open to outside influences all the time" (p. 134). See also "Bulwarks of Belief," in Charles Taylor, *A Secular Age* (Cambridge, MA: The Belknap Press of Harvard University, 2007), pp. 25–89; and Stephen Wilson, *The Magical Universe* (London: Hambledon & London, 2000), esp. pp. xvii ff. See below on discussions on *materiality* and "thing theory," *passim* and esp. *Passage 7*.

10 On which see Arthur Kroker, *Body Drift: Butler, Hayles, Haraway* (Minneapolis and London: University of Minnesota Press, 2012), and on the entailments of individuality and dividuality see especially Karl Smith, "From Dividual and Individual Selves to Porous Subjects," *The Australian Journal of Anthropology* (*TAJA*) 23, 2012, pp. 50–64.

11 Sigrid Weigel, *Walter Benjamin: Images, the Creaturely, and the Holy* (Stanford, CA: Stanford University Press, 2013 [*Die Kreatur, das Heilege, die Bilder*, Frankfurt am Main: S. Fischer Verlag, 2008]), p. 2. I'll have occasion to discuss (and put into perspective) some of Weigel's own perspectives on Benjamin, on secularization, and on artistry, at various points below. On the "tired old idea" (the artifice) of "secularization," see Hent de Vries, *Philosophy and the Turn to Religion* (Baltimore, MD: Johns Hopkins University Press, 1999), and for contrary perspectives on the contemporary lives of "the" secular in relation to practices of critique, see the discussions by Judith Butler, Wendy Brown, Saba Mahmood, and Talal Asad, in the Berkeley Townsend Papers volume cited below (n. 36).

12 Weigel, op. cit., p. 18 and references to Benjamin's "The Task of the Translator," etc; a subject (or rather a matrix of issues) to be addressed multiple times explicitly and implicitly in many of the *Passages* below.

13 Lewis Carroll, *Alice's Adventures in Wonderland and through the Looking-Glass*, ed. Roger-Lancelyn Green (Oxford: Oxford University Press, 1971), p. 190.

14 These issues are finely discussed by Leslie Hill, who mentions Humpty-Dumpty in her "The World is not Enough," *Angelaki: Journal of the Critical Humanities*, Vol. 7, No. 2, 2002, pp. 61–68; this is a special issue: "Inventions of Death: Literature, Philosophy, Psychoanalysis." Hill's essay concerns Blanchot's book *The Writing of Disaster*, trans. Ann Smock (Lincoln, NE: University of Nebraska Press, 1995 [*L'ecriture du distastre*, Paris: Gallimard, 1980]). Blanchot's skepticism about etymology is grounded in his observations that the quest for truth (the "true, literal" and original meanings) is never safe from dogmatism.

15 *Les Promesses du passé: une histoire discontinue de l'art dans l'ex-Europe de l'Est*. Centre Pompidou, April 14–July 14, 2010; *Exh. Cat.*, ed. Christine Macel and Joanna Mytkowska (Paris: Centre Pompidou, 2010). Discussed in relation to the subject of manifestoes in Donald Preziosi and Claire Farago, *Art Is Not What You Think It Is*, pp. 5–10.

16 Henry David Thoreau, *The Journal of Henry David Thoreau*. Vol. 2. ed. Bradford Torrey and Francis H. Allen (New York: Houghton Mifflin, 1949). See also *The Writings of Henry David Thoreau: Walden*, ed. J. Lyndon Shanley (Princeton, NJ: Princeton University Press, 1973) and *Walden and Resistance to Civil Government*, 2nd edn., ed. William Rossi (New York: W.W. Norton, 1992). On Thoreau's critique of scientism and his notions of the *non-mereness* of things, see Jane Bennett's thoughtful *Vibrant Matter, passim*, and below, as well as her earlier *Thoreau's Nature: Ethics, Politics, and the Wild* (New York: Rowman & Littlefield, 2002).

17 On which, see Jean-Louis Deotte, "Rome, the Archetypal Museum, and the Louvre, the Negation of Division," in Susan Pearce, ed., *Art in Museums* (London and New Jersey: Athlone Press, 1995), pp. 215–232. Reprinted. in Donald Preziosi and Claire Farago, *Grasping the World: The Idea of the Museum* (London: Ashgate, 2004), pp. 51–64, with commentary, pp. 17–19 (hereafter cited as *Grasping*).

18 I've commented upon this phenomenon in some detail in connection with other "hygienic" enterprises, such as the foundation of late nineteenth- and early twentieth-century museums in Egypt (see *Brain*, 2003) by separating out from the original Egyptian Museum certain cultural materials to be associated with what were being distinguished (by colonial European art historians and archaeologists as different "ethnic" strains within (what had been) a multi-ethnic and polyglot society throughout Egyptian history. The Pharaonic-period materials being kept in "The" Egyptian Museum, "Greco-Roman" materials in a new museum of that name in Alexandria, "Coptic" materials in another separate museum, and a museum of "Arab art." In not a few cases, the identical materials in the latter three institutions were labeled as examples of "distinctly" (Arab or Coptic) artistry. This project of ethno-aesthetic "cleansing" was at the same time echoed in the reconfiguration and rezoning of the city of Cairo itself into a "new, modern, Western-style city" west of the Citadel, and an older "native" ("Arab") city to the east. In a number of cases, whole buildings (mosques, fountains, madrassas, etc.) were moved wholesale to more *appropriate* (ethno-historical) zones or parts of the city. Urban theme-parking on a

grand and fine scale; urban deconstructing and reconstituting as fundamentally co-determinate. The decorum of (what is thereby distinguished *as*) décor.

19 Henri Lefebvre, *The Production of Space*, trans. D. Nicholson-Smith (Oxford: Blackwell, 1991), p. 113.

20 On the Masonic philosophy shared by (apparently most of) the founders and designers of many of the new public museums of the eighteenth and early nineteenth centuries (Lenoir, like Bernard Ashmole in England, was a prominent Freemason), see the discussion in *Brain*, especially pp. 63–91, "The Astrolabe of the Enlightenment."

21 Such Masonic ambitions clearly resonate with a variety of semiological – or more accurately *semio-religious* processes and postulates – as considered below, including in particular the question of *indexical* relationships between what under certain conditions are distinguished as signifiers and signifieds. Such relationships invariably are fielded as variant facets of multidimensional meaning-making strategies – an issue explored in detail in *Passage* 6.

22 Recalling Wallace Stevens' last poem, "Of Mere Being," to be looked into below in the next section. See the very fine recent discussion of Stevens' work by Simon Critchley, *Things Merely Are: Philosophy in the Poetry of Wallace Stevens* (London and New York: Routledge, 2005), notably ch. 6, "The Thing Itself and its Seasons," pp. 61–84, and esp. pp. 73–74, "The Mere Thereness of Things," and also the more prosaic – though not less insightful – discussion of Stevens by Harold Bloom, *The Poems of our Climate* (Ithaca, NY: Cornell University Press, 1977). What all this also reminded me of was a phrase of David Finn, the author of the book *How to Visit a Museum* (New York: Abrams, 1985), p. 10:

> There is no right or wrong way to visit a museum ... You have a feast in store for you and you should make the most of it. Stay as long or as short a time as you will, but do your best at all times to *let the work of art speak directly to you with a minimum of interference or distraction.* [my emphasis]

Recalling as well the mantra of some fundamentalist Protestant Christian sects with respect to sacred scripture and the rejection of the (consequently extraneous, hence impure) non-verbal trappings of (Catholic and other non-Protestant) Christian worshipping practice. Trust *only* in the *words* of the Lord (discussed below in *Passage* 7, "Semiosis and its Discontents"), leaving open the question of who or what could definitively *guarantee* what is claimed to be the *truth* of those "words" – an endless regression and postponement, "cured" or secured through (the artistry of) linking contingency to what can only be (in)securely tethered at a transcendent point ("word") beyond the horizons or boundaries of the here and now, off away in some brighter air.

23 The German term refers to alignment and ordering and was often used in the writings on art and religious ritual of Joseph Cardinal Ratzinger, the recent Pope Benedict XVI, to be discussed below in *Passage* 10. See George Cardinal Pell, "The Concept of Beauty in the Writings of Joseph Ratzinger," in D. Vincent Twomey SVD and Janet E. Rutherford, eds., *Benedict XVI and Beauty in Sacred Art and Architecture* (Dublin and New York: Four Courts Press and Scepter Publishers, 2011), pp. 24–36. See also next note here.

24 See Marc de Kesel, "Religion as Critique, Critique as Religion: Some Reflections on the Monotheistic Weakness of Contemporary Criticism," in *Umbr(a) 2005: The Dark God*:

> Religion, the second kind of sublimation that Lacan distinguishes [the first being science], has a more accurate truth value. At the very least, it does not simply deny the unknowable kernel toward which human desire points. Placing an unknowable God at the locus of this kernel, religion *keeps desire consciously unfulfilled and thus ongoing* [emphasis mine]. It operates as a first recognition of the primacy of desire, but remains immature insofar as it lacks the clarity of an artistic sublimation, the third sublimation that Lacan distinguishes ... art is the most explicit presentation of the impossibility of desire gaining access to its final object.

(p. 133)

See also below, *Passage* 10, on the theological desire for transcendence and Benedict XVI's views on artistry.

25 See the special issue on "Things" in the journal *Critical Inquiry*, Vol. 28, No 1, 2001, pp. 1–22, edited by American literary historian Bill Brown. "Thingness" continued for a while to be the subject of academic discussion and debate. For example, in September 2006, the Open University in the UK hosted a "New Cultural Materialisms" Workshop organized by Tony Bennett and with panelists such as Bill Brown of Chicago, John Frow of Melbourne, and several others including myself. My contribution dealt with the blind spots or *specters* being brought to light by the revivified intense interest in materiality and "things," and in particular the (repressed) specters of *immaterialism* haunting these debates. Compare this to the (posthumously published) work of anthropologist Alfred Gell, particularly his *Art and Agency: An Anthropological Theory* appearing two years earlier (Oxford: Oxford University Press, 1998). Of the many critiques of the latter, see Howard Morphy, "Art as Mode of Action: Some Problems with Gell's *Art and Agency*," *Journal of Material Culture*, Vol. 14, No. 1, 2009, pp. 5–27; Ross Bowden, "A Critique of Alfred Gell on *Art and Agency*," *Oceania*, Vol. 74, 2004, pp. 309–324; and also *Grasping* 2004, esp. "Deconstructing the Agencies of Art," pp. 74ff., and pp. 102–109. For a different perspective on "thingness," see Peter Schwenger, *The Tears of Things: Melancholy and Physical Objects* (Minneapolis, MN and London: University of Minnesota Press, 2006).

26 Jane Bennett, *Vibrant Matter*, 2010. Bennett's call for a vibrant and vigorous materiality echoes the concern for modes of agency in the non-human in Freya Mathews, Bruno Latour, Donna Haraway, N. Katherine Hayles, Gilles Deleuze and Felix Guattari, and literary critic and art theorist W.J.T. Mitchell (p. 111, and n. 4., pp. 152–153).

27 Nor, obviously, are there mere things. One of the explicit origins of "thing theory" (see above) was the slippage between Western notions of things and objects, a subject of particular interest to Heidegger, according to Brown, op. cit., p. 1ff. But thingness, as we'll see later, didn't seem to extend to the circumstances within which "things" appear *as* things, which surely qualify as things themselves, and thing theory was largely innocent of the essential problem of *reification* as memory disorder, on which see Michael Landzelius, "Spatial Reification, or, Collectively Embodied Amnesia, Aphasia, and Apraxia," *Semiotica: Journal of the International Association for Semiotic Studies*, Vol. 175, 2009, p. 39; and Richard Terdiman, *Present Past: Modernity and the Memory Crisis* (Ithaca, NY: Cornell University Press, 1993), pp. 12ff. For a different perspective, see Allan Pred, *Making Histories and Constructing Human Geographies* (Boulder, CO: Westview Press, 1990), and the discussion below in *Passage* 7, "Semiosis and its Discontents."

28 On which, see D. Preziosi, *The Art of Art History* (Oxford: Oxford University Press, 2nd edn., 2009). Hereafter cited as *AAH* 2009.

29 See also *AINT, passim*, for an explication and expansion on this idea.

30 A useful discussion of such issues may be found in recent debates on the "new biology" in Hilary Rose and Steven Rose, *Genes, Cells and Brains: The Promethean Promises of the New Biology* (London and New York: Polity Press, 2012), who present a lucid case for the *interpenetration* of biology and culture in many discursive dimensions (what some may phrase as discrete or semi-autonomous "levels"). A classic case of a fundamentally mistaken reductionist project was mid- to late-twentieth century "IQ" measurement that originated as a project by French psychologist Alfred Binet (1857–1911) to find effective ways to teach learning-disabled children, but eventually resulted in the reification of IQ scoring as an absolute measure of intelligence – a fantasizing of one biological element in the multiple coexistent facets of behavior. A *Praxitelean* rather than "Promethean" Promise of the New Biology. Or of various other "new" disciplines, such as neuro-art history.

31 On which see Naas' discussion of Derrida's reckoning the "what is?" religion (*ti esti?*) as the founding or "instituting question of philosophy": Derrida, *Of Grammatology*, trans. and with a preface by Gayatri Chakravorty Spivak (Baltimore, MD: Johns Hopkins University Press, 1976 [*De la grammatology*. Paris: editions de Minuit, 1967]), p. 19. These and related issues are explored in various places below. See also Preziosi and Farago, *Art*

Is Not What You Think It Is, passim, and compare Jacques Derrida, *The Truth in Painting,* trans. Geoff Bennington and Ian McLeod (Chicago, IL and London: University of Chicago Press, 1987 [*La verite en peinture,* Paris: Flammarion, 1978]. The "*what is* religion" as we elaborate here is inseparable from the "truth in art," and *vice versa.*

32 See *Passage* 4, "Specters of artifice: a hauntology."

33 The term *indiscipline* was first used in a somewhat different way by David Ferris in relation to the state of the modern academic field of comparative literature: David Ferris, "Indiscipline," in Haun Saussy, ed., *Comparative Literature in the Age of Globalization* (Baltimore, MD: Johns Hopkins University Press, 2006), p. 92. Ferris' citation of Winckelmann's assertion about modernity being *founded in an impossibility* recalls my own statement at the beginning of this book regarding artistry and religiosity as grounded in a double amnesia – and, as discussed below in connection with my 2001 Oxford Slade Lectures and the *grounding* of the field of art history, in a *denial* of the impossibility of representation. See *Brain,* 2003, pp. 1ff. I will return to these issues periodically throughout the book.

34 See Talal Asad, Wendy Brown, Judith Butler, and Saba Mahmood, *Is Critique Secular? Blasphemy, Injury, and Free Speech* (Berkeley and Los Angeles, CA: University of California Press, 2009). Also, Vincent P. Pecora, *Secularization and Cultural Criticism: Religion, Nation & Modernity* (Chicago, IL: University of Chicago Press, 2005). As Pecora put it regarding secularity:

> What is important is that the static and totalizing concept of secularism – connoting an already achieved and reliably reproducible intellectual standpoint – be supplanted with a dynamic understanding of secularization, that is, with a process that has remained, at least up to the present, in some ambiguous relationship with religious tradition, neither translation and transformation, nor radical overturning and forgetting.

This recognizes, as I'll be elaborating upon here, that any "religious tradition" itself exists primarily as the manufactured reification of an ambiguous relationship to what is socially co-fabricated as its antithesis. Our concern in this book is with the mechanisms of the (manufactured) amnesia regarding such artifice. And see again, De Vries, op. cit.

35 See *Passage* 6, "Godless in Copenhagen," for an elaboration of these claims.

36 Raymond Williams, in *Keywords: A Vocabulary of Culture and Society* (London: Flamingo, 1983), pp. 40ff., traced the semantic shifts in such terms from the thirteenth to twentieth centuries. See also David Tomas, "An Identity Crisis: The Artist and New Technologies," in Jody Berland, Will Straw, and David G. Tomas, eds., *Theory Rules: Art as Theory: Theory and Art* (Toronto: YYZ Books & University of Toronto Press, 1991), pp. 195–222.

1

AVANT-PROPOS

We are living in a time marked by exponential expansions of autocratic power and its devastations and destructions across the globe, in its many guises *hell-bent* (a phrase apt in more ways than one) on derailing, dismantling, and erasing democratic civic institutions, professions, customs, and aspirations, more often than not masquerading and marketed as advances or improvements in spiritual and religious value and enhancements of economic worth and individual "freedom." The recuperation and rejuvenation of democracy, critique, and consensual politics has never been more urgent. The Empire has indeed (already) struck back, with penetrative powers undreamed of in the past.

As Michael Landzelius lucidly observed

> The transformative powers of global capitalism presently dispossess and unsettle millions of people, as well as comprehensively reshape the built environment on previously unseen scales of creative destruction. When the world is constantly dis(re)membered in ever new ways, remembrance as both [an] individual and trans-generational complex of experience, memory, and knowledge loses significance in everyday life. Confronting rapidly transforming neo-liberal landscapes across the globe, critical scholars no less than dispossessed migrants find themselves in a memory crisis akin to the one observed as part of the context of the French Revolution and the profound transformations of European modernization.[1]

And yet: the essential fragility and contingency of the *artifice* of those (as argued below) para-theocratic powers may also be construed as a *sign* that living through these times may *also* afford the ways and means to live *through them toward* their dissolution and resolution. Even recognized and enacted by hindsight.

What this book investigates and attempts to articulate are some methods of realizing such resolutions as some of the grounds for the restitution and regeneration of democracy.

While there are diverse motivations for composing and publishing any text, there is, among the several in the present case, one that remains foremost. It may be plainly stated: to play however modest a role in rolling back, containing, and re-channeling neo-feudalism (globalization) and its amnesiac reifications on any front.

In the case of what follows here, this will entail the disruption of certain seemingly minute or obscured parts of the *technical apparatus or machinery* of theocratic imperialism: the mechanisms or the nuts and bolts of signification, discourse, and meaning-production. That is, the epistemological technologies of presentation, representation, expression, communication, and fabrication.

It is on just such a level that the *inextricability* and intimate intricacies of the art-and-religion conundrum or matrix are staged and naturalized – or more specifically, *simultaneously justified and troubled*. And it is precisely there – at the "intimate *conjunction* of classification, interpretation, and subject formation," in the succinct words of Karen Jacobs,[2] that the labor of this book unfolds. That investigative or archaeological labor is concerned with foregrounding the ongoing fabrication of various kinds of manufactured *memory disorders* such as amnesia and reification and commodification as these have been realized in and by such practices as artistry and religiosity; "art" and "religion" that is, by the artifice of religiosity and the religiosity of artifice. And in and by certain dyadic or *bipolar disorders* such as the logic of representation as embodied by practices such as the history of art or theology.

In a very real sense, what follows here is an exfoliation or *unwinding* and laying out (in the form of a multiply-layered narrative) of the dense package of insights, or the multidimensional and multi-temporal puzzle-piece (conundrum, if you prefer) hinted at in the *Provocations* above and strung out in plain sight below. If, for example, "antiquity" became the mirror[3] on which was written European modernity's invention of itself as a *re*invention of a longed-for lost antiquity (with different valences for the British, the French, the Germans, the Italians, the Greeks, the Scandinavians, the Spaniards, etc.), it was in effect a kind of mirror-reversed Leonardesque mirror-writing, in which modernity came to be scripted as the *reversal of a reversed writing* (which of course and inevitably laid traps for unwitting literalists). Similarly, this text is in a sense an unpacking of a multi-dimensional puzzle package: a (hetero)topological conundrum unpuzzled; or perhaps a Borromean knot severed.[4]

But first a few stage-setting thoughts (image-pieces), after which the book is introduced in a more orderly fashion in what I'll call a *Preamble*.

> Any history of "art and religion" does well to acknowledge the deeply modern and Western character of the subject. Although all cultures have fashioned artifacts for use in ritualistic practice, it remains problematic to call the artifacts "art" and the rituals "religion" without critical reflection of the modern character of the categories.
>
> *(David Morgan)*[5]

The question is thus not only how to talk about religion without generalization or perhaps even profanation but how _not_ to talk about religion when the language we use is perhaps already and from the beginning a language _of_ religion, that is, ... a _Latin_ language that will have informed so many of our words and concepts, beginning with the word or concept _religion_ itself. To ask the question of what religion _is_ by using the term _religion_ is thus perhaps already to have provided a kind of response.

(Michael Naas)[6]

At the end of the nineteenth century, religion in Europe had for all appearances become, at least for those who wanted to gather the history and build the science of religion, something so strange and indecipherable that they had to seek the key to it among primitive peoples rather than in their own tradition: but the primitive peoples could only return as in a mirror the same extravagant and contradictory image that these scholars have projected upon them.

(Giorgio Agamben)[7]

The representation of language as "expression" is not an accidental prejudice, but rather a kind of _structural lure_, what Kant would have called a transcendental illusion. The latter is modified according to the language, the era, the culture. Doubtless Western metaphysics constitutes a powerful systematization of this illusion, but I believe that it would be an imprudent _overstatement_ to assert that Western metaphysics _alone_ does so.

(Jacques Derrida)[8]

FIGURE 1.1 Preparation of Eruv between Oz Zion and Givat Assaf, Israel. 2012. © בקעי/Wikimedia Commons.

Consider the previous comments as delineating the *margins* of the domain or "space within which" the archaeological labor of the book unfolds: where the *concordances and discordances* of the act of juxtaposing "art" and "religion" are most intensely played out; or perhaps as the domain of an eruv (Figure 1.1)[9] that delineates and distinguishes between the possible and impossible, the permissible and impermissible, thresholds intersecting and crossing the field of the palpable. Speaking metaphorically, of course. Which is to say (of course) literally – to continue the self-problematization of the literal/metaphorical dyad.

Notes

1 Cited above in *Provocations*. Landzelius' notion of amnesia as "a situation of enforced irrelevance of memory in which previously gained knowledge is no longer applicable, and in which continuity also in terms of emotional states amounts to being inflexible in relation to a constantly changing environment" resonates with the perspectives on amnesia elaborated below (*Passage* 10), which are also closely linked to the mystical processes and practices of *reification* and commodification.
2 The phrase is from a review essay by Karen Jacobs, "Aesthetic Currencies: Ranciere's Critical Art and Cummings and Lewandweska's *The Value of Things*," *The British Journal of Aesthetics*, forthcoming. Recall the work of Raymond Williams, the purpose of whose *Keywords* was to show that "some important social and historical processes occur *within* language, in ways which indicate how integral the problems of meanings and relationships really are." See Raymond Williams, *Keywords: A Vocabulary of Culture and Society* (London: Flamingo, 1983), p. 22.
3 See "Tragedy and Modernity: The Logic of Affect," by Todd Kesselman, an interview with Simon Critchley, March 2011, in Carl Cederstrom and Todd Kesselman, eds., *Impossible Objects: Interviews with Simon Critchley* (Malden, MA: Polity Press, 2012), pp. 139–163.
4 On "Borromean knots" in Lacanian psychoanalytic theory and practice see Ellie Ragland and Dragan Milovanovic, eds., *Lacan: Topologically Speaking* (New York: The Other Press, 2004), esp. part III, "Topology of Knots," pp. 249–384. Lacan's focus on topology as an alternative *mapping* (and as homologies, not metaphors or analogies) of the psychic apparatus and of sense production, began to appear in his seminars of the early 1960s, intensifying in his later work (1972–77) ("Borromean knots," op. cit., 368ff.). Briefly, a Borromean knot (named after the coat of arms of the aristocratic Borromeo family of Milan) is defined by two or more rings knotted by another (each ring representing one of the three *orders* of the Lacanian psyche: the imaginary, the symbolic, and the real), such that if one is cut, all disentangle. The knot (technically a *ring*) depicts (i.e. is homologous to) the interconnectedness of the psychic apparatus: a hypothesis about how the psyche maintains its constancy. As Ragland and Milovanovic argue, Lacan's notions of space bore resemblances to later chaos theory and the fractal, and inspired theorists such as Deleuze and Guattari in the 1980s: see Gilles Deleuze and Felix Guattari, *A Thousand Plateaus* (Minneapolis, MN and London: University of Minnesota Press, 1987). See also the critical anthology, *Art: Sublimation or Symptom?* ed. Parveen Adams (New York: The Other Press, 2003), exploring, among other related issues, Lacan's relation of art to the symptom (*le sinthome*) in his work in the mid-1970s, suggesting a new theory of artistic creation. We'll have the opportunity to address this later in the book.
5 David Morgan, "Art and Religion in the Modern Age," in James Elkins and David Morgan, eds., *Re-Enchantment* (London and New York: Routledge, 2009), p. 25. That volume, the outcome of a one-day symposium (an "art seminar") held at the Art Institute in Chicago in 2007, was an assembly of what one evaluator correctly termed "a salient confusion of voices and a retreat to one's own turf" (anthropologist Jojada

Verrips, "Missing Religion, Overlooking the Body," op. cit., p. 288). Issues raised in and by that symposium that have a bearing on the questions raised in this volume will be dealt with in detail as this book unfolds. Morgan also observed in his introduction to the volume of the Chicago art seminar, p. 40, that

> Moving through the discourse of Modernism in art was a dominant conception of the sacred, one which distanced art from institutional religion, most importantly Christianity, in order to secure the freedom of art as an autonomous cultural force that was sacralized in its own right – in Hegelian terms, the manifestation of *Geist*, Mind, Spirit, or Genius, the essence of an age or nation (*Zeitgeist*). To this end, the discourse appropriated a variety of histories and cultures, transforming artifacts into "art" and sacred ritual and story into "religion," especially from . . . primal cultures [*sic*.].

6 Michael Naas, *Miracle and Machine: Jacques Derrida and the Two Sources of Religion, Science, and the Media* (New York: Fordham University Press, 2012), pp. 47–48.
7 Giorgio Agamben, *The Sacrament of Language: An Archaeology of the Oath* (Homo Sacer *II*, 3), trans. Adam Kotsko (Stanford, CA: Stanford University Press, 2011 [*Il sacramento del linguaggio. Archeologia del giuramento*. Milan: Gius, Laterza and figli, 2008]), p. 15.
8 Jacques Derrida, "Semiology and Grammatology," an interview with Julia Kriseva, in *Positions*, trans. and annotated Alan Bass (Chicago, IL: University of Chicago Press, 1981 [*Positions*. Paris: Les Editions de Minuit, 1972]), p. 33.
9 In some Jewish communities an eruv (pl. eruvin or eruvim) is a ritually delineated area within cities (often marked by translucent wire on raised poles and/or along building walls so as to enclose space where domestic activities such as carrying or transferring items can occur. Within the delimited (and ritually "domesticated") space, certain practices otherwise forbidden on the Sabbath may be allowed. Two useful articles discussing aspects of distinguishing, constructing, maintaining, or expanding eruvim are Ethan Wilensky-Lanford, "Ritual Fences Set for Jews in Manhattan is Extended," *New York Times*, June 16, 2007; and Sewell Chan, "A Translucent Wire in the Sky," *New York Times*, June 15, 2007. *Wikipedia* open-source online pages contain useful introductory information and multiple references.

2

PREAMBLE

Very early in my life I took the question of the relation of art to truth seriously:
and even now I stand in holy dread in the face of this *discordance.*
(Martin Heidegger, quoting Nietzsche)[1]

Very early on I began taking very seriously the *discordances and concordances* between
what I later learned to call *art* and *religion*, and increasingly over time have been
fascinated by the astonishing *inextricability* of what these two terms mark and how
that mark is made and sustained. This book is a critical meditation[2] on that conundrum – that very ancient and enduring oscillating inverse interrelationship or
chiasma and its variations or allomorphs, with their multiple social, political,
epistemological, aesthetic, and ethical implications and consequences. It is concerned equally as noted above with the *amnesia* endemic to *both* the modern discourses on artistry and on religiosities – although within the former discourse there
has been of late an increase in critical attention to the historiography of aesthetic (or
art historical) *amnesia.*[3] The foregoing quotations are some thoughts to keep in
mind as we begin; many more will follow.

While this book may have been advertised as an investigation of the *relationships*
between what have been conventionally distinguished and set apart from each other
(as presumably different in kind, essence, nature, concept, or idea) as *art* and *religion*,
in point of fact that is *not* exactly (or not only) what the following is doing. Among
other things, it is directly concerned with problems that arise when imagining actually making comparisons and contrasts between phenomena presumed in advance
(prior to explicit justification for the distinction) as not only existing in their own
right – marking contrastive ontological phenomena – but manifesting a special
interrelationship that would merit bringing the two terms together and then investigating what each has to do with the other. A manifestation and acknowledgment

of an *ideological assertion*, as we shall see and as articulated in diverse ways by various modern and contemporary commentators, including Gilles Deleuze, Philippe Lacoue-Labarthe, Michel de Certeau, Jacques Derrida, Giorgo Agamben, Theodor Adorno, and others.[4]

For example, in a lucid and finely succinct articulation of relationships between psychoanalytic practice and the writing of history, art historian and theorist Hubert Damisch commented upon what he termed the "false simplicity" of such conjunctions ("two uncertainly defined terms are coordinated in service of a demonstration, usually of an ideological nature"), linkages which depending upon the circumstances, might signify union as much as opposition, adjunction as much as exclusion.

Of course, it could be argued that each (art, artistry, artifice; and religion, religiosity, immateriality, spirituality) is and has been so inextricably a part of what constitutes the other as to profoundly *trouble* the idea of each as distinct or ontologically autonomous. Social and cultural phenomena marked by each of those terms do indeed exist (in modernity) as relative positions or nodes (*loci*) within the matrices of phenomena or behaviors constituting any society. But are the connections between what we designate as art and what we refer to as religion uniquely different than any others that may be juxtaposed (art and science, or religion and politics)? Is any such marking of an ontology *deponent*, and significant mainly insofar as it reflects upon the entire set of phenomena which may be claimed to be more than circumstantially or randomly connected? What would justify a claim – such as that made by this text – that artistry and religiosity have a uniquely special relationship?[5] With politics the dramaturgy for the stagecraft of this *chiasma*.

One of the chief arguments being developed here is that not only does such a special relationship exist – and with regard to which the *political* may seem, as we will see below, *epiphenomenal* (or rather tactical rather than strategic *vis-à-vis* an artistry–religiosity matrix), but it exists in such a manner as to fundamentally problematize the autonomous existence of each *except in relationship to its other*. Each as each other's ghost.

Moreover, there's a key semiological dimension to the question that evokes and appears to echo or form the *silhouette* of phonematic phenomena in language wherein significance is a mark of *difference* from other phonemes; other *markers of difference*, that is, which in combination build or "ground" more directly significant phenomena (morphemes, words, syntactic structures, sentences, discourse, etc.).[6]

More directly, addressing the nature of the relationship between religiosity and artistry entails, for this investigation, articulating and reckoning with a relationship of *differential intrication* in which the involvement of terms with each other constitutes their only identity, their *quiddity*, recalling Philippe Lacoue-Labarthe's meditation on what he called the "double discursive economy" of the relation of philosophy to literature.[7]

This is a way of saying in shorthand that "art" and "religion" are manifestations of more fundamental phenomena: that each is a facet or dimension of some common underlying (semiological, epistemological, ideological) phenomenon. It is the work of this text to account for what might ground and justify this initial sweeping and perhaps at the moment somewhat counter-intuitive (i.e., more accurately, counter-orthodox) hypothesis, to anticipate the conclusions of the investigations recounted below. The claim, succinctly and on one level, is that what (may be termed) artistry is *is not* (what is not uncommonly termed) *religiosity*[8] – a radical redefinition of relationships that are articulated in what follows: a *topological epistemology* elaborated in consort with investigations and analyses not unfamiliar in a number of other areas of critical inquiry.[9] What is implied here is the need to articulate precisely what each consists of in the light of its deponency and contingency, as well as – what are routinely ignored in much contemporary debate – the *spaces* (topological and other) in which and with respect to which these practices and processes emerge.[10]

To arrive at such conclusions requires intensive detailed excavation. While such an investigation as the one begun here is very technical in nature, it impacts immediately upon widespread, pressing social and cultural problems, for these distinctions and connections – not to speak of the amnesia both within and between these – are strongly echoed in current social and political disputes and upheavals, and are marked by frustratingly unresolved discussions and debates over various politically manufactured artistries (in some contemporary communities) of "secularization," blasphemy, fetishism, idolatry, iconoclasm, iconophilia, and what are staged and promoted as fundamental *incompatibilities* of democratic and theocratic polities. The problem of how these relationships have been framed, articulated, and investigated has been a subject of deep concern in many societies since antiquity – both in communities where investigation is sanctioned and in those where critique is invisible, muted, prohibited, or punished.

A not unimportant aim of this investigation is to clarify and delineate why exactly in various religious or theocratic traditions art, artistry, or artifice are not uncommonly seen as *dangerous*, destabilizing, or even *terror-inducing* to individuals and communities, unless closely managed and disciplined. This is an issue that has returned to prominence in recent years as a chief catalyst for ostracism, banishment, violent confrontation, ethnic "cleansing," mass murder, and genocide. A large part of delineating the *why* is in attending closely to the *how*: the manner, means, or artifice of meaning-production. The artistries of religiosity.

It may already be gathered that this is an *impatient* text. But it is by no means a hasty one, for it has in fact been germinating for some time both within and between the various discussions and debates, and the academic disciplines I've been practicing and engaging with over the years, often feeling that I was living and working in or even as the *grout* between them all: I will tell you shortly when, where, and how that sensation arose, for that auto-archaeological exercise has a direct bearing both on *what* is unfolding here and on *how* it is unfolding. The impatience that has propelled the writing of this book has been growing over the years of my engagement with the erstwhile claims of various disciplinary fields, which for many years have come to seem (on the ground) as thoroughly deponent and inextricably interdependent.

In addition, while this is a short book, it is not a "straightforward" narrative account nor is it (as a text) like a unicursal maze (something that appears to be a labyrinth from only one angle but is in fact a single, if convoluted, line): it moves forward on more than one front and dimension. Furthermore, it is *haunted* throughout by experiences and situations which may perhaps be read as stepping stones through the several streams leading to (*hankering* after, in one light) the present book, should that be of interest. My concerns over the production and practice of artistry and religiosity date, as it does for many others, from well before my/(y)our formal, institutional, or professional connections to (lashings to the mast of) those questions. All of these engagements (and not least my very earliest) *haunt* the questions I am trying here to reckon with; that is, to think through *and* wrangle with. The fourth chapter or *Passage* of the book constitutes just such a *hauntology*.

So the following remains (like all works, even posthumously or indeed even anonymously) a work in progress: it is a porous or *open work*[11] not unlike a *mashrabiya* or lattice screen beyond which is the light of what it multiply frames and, in framing, renders palpable (and thus modulated and mobile) to sense. Questions are raised by any sustained engagement with the most daunting and fundamental problems of artistry, religiosity, and politics in our time. A very great deal is at stake (really, *everything*) in how the issues articulated below will be dealt with; what worlds these *enchantments* (I take this *etymologically* and also do not use this word lightly) will *sing into existence* and of whom (and for whom) they sing.

The question of relationships between artistry and religiosity are no *mere* "abstract" subjects and their investigations and explications over the centuries in not a few societies have had profound and very palpable consequences for individuals, communities, and nations. And while the discussions between the author and the publisher which led specifically to an invitation to write this book took place several years ago, at a time when the international furor over what was being framed as a conflict between religious "blasphemy" and "freedom" of artistic expression was still at its height, in the immediate aftermath of the Danish "Mohammed cartoon controversy" of 2005–06, and in the wake of subsequent violence, destruction, and death in several countries, this was *also* a time when what has been marketed as a putative "return to religion" both more generally and within a variety of disciplinary discourses (see above) was at its height, not least in its being staged and articulated in some quarters as a reaction to (what had been framed as) "secular" or "humanist" or "materialist" mores and political correctness.

While it may be the case that certain religiosities have indeed returned to plain(er) sight, it is important to note that (1) they are not what they may have once been (despite wishing it were so in some sectarian or theocratic quarters), and (2) in fact they have not returned alone but in concert with parallel and comparative movements and counter-movements. Nothing as culturally and politically complex as "a" religiosity ever existed in a vacuum but was always essentially tethered to *what it stood for* stood *against*. What has come along with them (on the side, in the margins, and/or parenthetically) is a new (or renewed) awareness of the *artifice* of the very promotion of the trope of return. This has been manifested variously as a renewed attention to semiosis (in the form of a focus on indexicality in fields such as art history, visual studies, or anthropology) and a critical attention to materiality and even *mere* "things," regarding which I alluded to above and will attend to in several places below.

I'm equally concerned with what recent and current debates have ignored or have appeared amnesiac about, including not least of all the great antiquity in a number of traditions of the essential (rather than circumstantial or ancillary) "roles" of artistry in religion if not in all aspects of social life, and the long history of managing and disciplining artistry as an essential component of how societies should be conceived, organized, and function. Such *managerial* solutions not infrequently masquerade as more suitable (in fact, *aesthetic*) solutions to theological conundrums.

The dilemmas evoked by these social and political developments are a distant but no less strong echo of those with which Plato wrestled two and a half millennia ago; but what I will refer to here as "Plato's dilemma" has reverberations elsewhere in both the East and West. Indeed, as I will argue, the problem of what artistry *has to do with* religiosity and *vice versa* is so central to the fabrication of communal life no less than to the constitution of individualities as to constitute a core property of human behavior. For Plato (and the previous pope), the resolution to the problem of the *disrespect* of artistry for hegemonic power was *more better artistry*, as discussed below: for the former philosopher, the polis as a more decorously (fittingly) managed or disciplined art work.

While it may be that no single book or author could fully articulate, let alone adequately reckon with, the great complexity and diversity of these issues in all of their ramifications and implications, one factor in their investigation that has been equally important (and which is one of my chief concerns here) has been a widespread failure to frame sufficiently productive questions about what justifies and maintains conventional distinctions between art and religion in those times and places and societies where such distinctions are significant. No small factor in that failure has been the fact that such questioning is invariably linked to what is perceived by disciplinary formations as legitimate − the contingencies of Foucault's speaking *dans le vrai*.[12] And while *Art, Religion, Amnesia* is singly authored, it carries with it, links to, and indeed is powerfully haunted by (and consequently deeply indebted to) the work of not a few other observers whom I've been privileged to know, work with, and learn from, both in person and at a distance − all of whom are cited throughout this book as well as in the acknowledgments section.

It must be stressed (again) that what follows is *not* a general history or historiography of art or religion, but is rather a recounting of a longstanding and ongoing reading project undertaken by myself partly in dialogue with others on the problem of what artistry and religiosity have to "do" with each other on various levels. While it is not a history of the modern disciplinary discourses on and of aesthetics and theology, references to a considerable amount of recent and older critical and historical literature on those subjects is found throughout the text. Nor is it focused except obliquely upon the historiography of the discourses and institutions of art history, theory, and criticism, and visual and material culture studies – about which much current and recent work, including much of my own (both singly and jointly) has long been devoted.

But above all the following is an attempt to recast, refashion, and reorient the discourses on art and religion *otherwise*, and to provide criteria for reconstituting these anew on foundations that incorporate what has been hidden, suppressed, ignored, unacknowledged, and marginalized in our various concurrent modernities. To begin anew in the light of their deeper co-determinations. It is written in the light of recent attention to the ironies of spatializing past and present alongside each other rather than as coexisting, and of the social, political, and theological effects and consequences of *historicism*, a subject of not a little attention by authors as diverse as Deleuze, de Certeau, Derrida, and Benjamin.[13]

It is also written in light of the *matrix* of practices and processes that are the spatial, visual, and architectonic complement to historicism, which includes reification and commodification, as well as topology. One manifestation of the confluence of these is explored below in *Passage* 9 in relation to the spatial topologies of manufacturing *gender* as parallactic performance/ostensification.

With respect to what has become an enormous body of writing on the historiography of religion, religiosity, and (for want of better terms) the "spiritual" or virtual or immaterial aspects of many social institutions and practices, including what have been called artistries, this book is not intended to summarize, synopsize, critique, and thereby extend that corpus in a linear or cumulative fashion. It is not a history of religions with or without respect to art, nor a history of art's entanglement with one or another religious system – though it is written in the light of the ironies and paradoxes of the historicist-realist rhetorical tradition and its penchant for comprehensive surveys of genres, as Tomoko Masuzawa astutely noted in her book *The Invention of World Religions*[14] in relation to the nineteenth-century invention of a modern religious "scientific object" designed to foster the fiction of the superiority of European Christianity relative to other versions of theism (whether mono-, poly-, or a-).

I'm concerned here with what it is that the reified object, the artifact *art*, and its putative co-constructed and co-determined *enchantments-and-disenchantments*[15] was designed and manufactured to establish and foster. What it is that artistry *desires* – if not (*a la* Benjamin) pure religiosity or messianicity.

Although what follows does build upon and extend a fair amount of what for these purposes has been the critically relevant available literature on both fields – namely, religious perspectives on art, artistry, and artifice, and engagements of the current discourse on art and aesthetics with ostensibly or implicitly religious questions and problems – the particular interests of this book are considerably more modest, as well as of a more personal nature. The book is (to repeat what was said at the beginning) another manifestation of the inextricability and porous boundaries of the scholarly and the personal, and is to a large extent concerned with problems encountered in my own engagement with these issues through the *lenses* of the various professional and institutional contexts within which I have worked over the years. These have principally been art and architectural history, museology, archaeology, critical theory, semiology, anthropology, and neighboring disciplinary formations (as currently staged). Moreover, while the book is grounded in and springs from my own history of engagements, its assertions – and in particular the theses and corollaries about to be staged below – are intended as provocations and potential catalysts *for* conversation and collaboration.

Art, Religion, Amnesia is thus more interrogative and dialogic than categorical (that is, it is oriented more toward the "philosophical" than the "theological," to again draw a faulty yet conventional distinction, and again "for the moment"), while at the same time working to trouble any fixed contrast between these and the artistries with which they both have engaged and from which they draw sustenance.

More simply still, the book is, among other things, an excavation account of my own wranglings and encounters, and with what and with whom they have long been and remain *haunted*; their penumbral domains or silhouettes. The silhouettes of evacuated ontologies. It has been an opportunity to clear a space (or the palate) in the morass (goulash) of contemporary (circular) discussion and debate with the aim of reframing some of what I have come to be convinced are more fundamental and pressing questions and conundrums about art and religion and their auras and shadows.

The book tries to pose some very direct questions about what art and religion have to do with each other, whether distinguishing them is generally or specifically and contextually justifiable, and whether or not their distinctions or differences have been an artifact and product of relations with what has been voiced as their antitheses. Whether, in fact each is a *what* or a *when*: a kind of thing or phenomenon, or a process or method of using (some or many) things, a subject central to a co-authored investigation immediately prior to this one.[16]

It will become evident fairly quickly that even the most gentle probings or proddings (as those here, so far) of things taken for granted about either art or religion brings to the surface some enduringly knotty conundrums about our understanding of much more than either of these terms, and about what has kept or continues to keep them *at bay* as well as in abeyance.

Notes

1 Martin Heidegger, *Nietzsche*, v.1, *trans.* David Farrell Krell (New York: Harper and Row, 1979), p. 142. Heidegger's section 19 of *Nietzsche* is in fact entitled "The Raging Discordance between Truth and Art." On this, David Carroll, *Paraesthetics: Foucault, Lyotard, Derrida. The Displacement of Theory and the Question of Art* (New York and London: Methuen, 1987) p. 5, noted that

> Heidegger shows how Nietzsche's position of the question of art at the center of his interrogation of being leads not to harmony between truth and art, or the dominance of one over the other, but to a "raging discordance" ... This in itself, however, is not enough to ensure that art will not constitute such a reversal.

That is, a (re)making of art *as truth*; as (a) religion. The present text is concerned with interrogating the various facets of that conundrum and works in a direction which both runs alongside and veers away from Nietzsche (and Heidegger's Nietzsche and Derrida's Heidegger and his and others' Walter Benjamin). As well as away from a number of recent wranglings with the issue of artistry-and-religiosity that, by and large and across a number of contemporary disciplines, have managed to avoid directly addressing the origins, effects, and motivations of such discordances.

2 It is inevitably tethered to a book appearing a quarter-century ago with "meditation" in its subtitle: *Rethinking Art History: Meditations on a Coy Science* (New Haven and London: Yale University Press, 1989, 1991), hereafter *RAH*. The latter is through this writing eligible and available to be re-read as a *prolegomenon* to the present (rather less decorous) meditation/excavation.

3 See *AINT*, 2012, where the question of the religious roots of modern Western art historicism is directly addressed, as are the renewed disciplinary interests in indexicality and other modalities of semiosis. As regards the former, see Claire Farago, "Towards an Archaeology of the Index," in *Taidehistoriallisia Tutkimuksia/Konsthistoriska Studier/ Studies in Art History, 44: Tiedeidenvalisyys ja rajanynnylitykset taidehistorissa Annika Waernebergin juhlakirja* (Helsinki: Society for Art History in Finland, 2012), pp. 35–48. See again Hent de Vries, *Philosophy and the Turn to Religion* (Baltimore, MD: Johns Hopkins University Press, 1999), pp. 374f. on equivalences between the "mystical" and the "mechanical," in reference to Henri Bergson, *The Two Sources of Morality and Religion*, trans. R. Ashley Audra and Cloudsley Brereton with assistance of W. Horsfall Carter (Notre Dame, IN: University of Notre Dame Press, 1986) (*Les deux sources de la morale et religion* [Paris: Presses Universitaires de France, 1997]), on the universe as a machine for the making of gods.

4 Among numerous discussions in many fields regarding the notion of *relations between* (what are staged or reified or taken to be) distinct phenomena, three are of immediate pertinence here: Hubert Damisch's *Semiotics and Iconography* (Lisse, Netherlands: Peter de Ridder Press, 1975); Michel de Certeau's "Psychoanalysis and its History," in de Certeau, *Heterologies: Discourse on the Other*, trans. Brian Massumi (Minneapolis, MN: University of Minnesota Press, 1986) ("Histoire et Psychanalyse," in *La nouvelle histoire*, ed. J. Le Goff, R. Chartier, and J. Revel [Paris: Retz, 1978]), pp. 3–16. Damisch noted the "false simplicity" of such conjunctions ("two uncertainly defined terms are coordinated in service of a demonstration, usually of an ideological nature"), linkages which depending upon the circumstances, might signify union as much as opposition, adjunction as much as exclusion. His investigation of semiotics and art (painting) (*Huit theses pour [ou contre?] une semiologie de la peinture. Macula* 2, 1977) was cited by Derrida at the very beginning of his 1978 book, *La verite en peinture*, to be referred to on occasion below. De Certeau argued that the relationships between psychoanalysis and history are two distinct ways of "distributing the space of memory … conceiving the relation between the past and the present differently." Psychoanalysis recognizes the past *in* the present; history-writing – what de Certeau calls historiography, positing a clean break between past and present – places them one *beside* the other (succession staged as "cause and effect" as in teleology. (What mnemic traceries has art historicism (dis)placed?) What configurations emerge in other topological formations? On the general problem of relationships between entities and phenomena, see the essay by Saba Mahmood, cited below, with references to Ammonius' commentary on Aristotle's *Categories* and various kinds of *schesis*. See in addition the series of essays by Stephen Melville, *Seams: Art as a Philosophical Context*, ed. and introduction by Jeremy Gilbert-Rolfe (Amsterdam: OPA Press, 1996) esp. ch. 8, "Notes on the Reemergence of Allegory, the Forgetting of Modernism, the Necessity of Rhetoric, and the Conditions of Publicity in Art and Criticism," pp. 147–186. With regard to psychoanalysis, see ibid., "Psychoanalysis and the Place of *Jouissance*," op. cit., pp. 89–110. These and related problems are discussed at length by Philippe Lacoue-Labarthe in his *The Subject of Philosophy*, ed. and foreword by Thomas Trezise (Minneapolis and London: University of Minnesota Press, 1993) (*Le Sujet de la philosophie* [Paris:

Flammarion, 1979]), ch. 6, "The Unpresentable," pp. 116–157 and esp. pp. 120–125, on the distinction between "aesthetic religion" (i.e., "fine art") and "revealed" ("true") religion (i.e., the *Christian* version of monotheism). See also Giorgio Agamben, *The Signature of All Things: On Method*, trans. Luca D'Isanto with Kevin Attell (New York: Zone Books, 2009) (*Signatura rerum* [Milan: Bollati Boringhieri, 2008]), esp. part III, "Philosophical Archaeology," pp. 87ff., and also Martin Jay's discussion of art and aesthetics in Adorno and Kierkegaard in their relationship to Hegel, in his *The Dialectical Imagination: A History of the Frankfurt School and the Institute of Social Research, 1923–1950* (Boston & Toronto: Little, Brown & Co., 1973).

5 The enduringly unfixed or constantly drifting boundaries between these domains are constantly of deep concern for many, particularly in societies like the United States, where the politically manufactured maintenance of theological or scientific anxiety is financially remunerative. In January 2013 it was reported in the US media that a California religious business corporation called "Christian Century" had brought suit against a local public school system for *not* explicitly confirming that the school's offering of classes in *yoga* was a tacit condoning of the latter's non-Christian (Hindu) religious roots (www.christiancentury.org/article/2011–05/yoga-religious), while at the same time seeing no contradiction in the school system's permitting Christian fundamentalist "Bible study classes" (http://reigiondespatches.org/archive/8643/protesting_yoga_in_school_ but_allowing_bible_study). As of this writing, the outcome of that legal protest remains unclear. Such "protests" (so obviously invented and promoted by political demagogues) are very much related to the problems addressed in these investigations. See Michael Landzelius, "Spatial Reification, or, Collectively Embodied Amnesia, Aphasia, and Apraxia," *Semiotica: Journal of the International Association for Semiotic Studies*, Vol. 175, 2009, pp. 39–75, for a discussion of the sustained contemporary promotion of (to paraphrase Proust), "the *dis*-remembrance of things past" as well as of the (dis)configured totalities of capitalist space – both of which are addressed here in *Passages* 8–10.

6 The relationship between such linguistic entities is only circumstantially one of scale or the material (acoustic) size of such units, but is primarily a marker of levels of organization. Thus, the acoustic mark "*i!*"[ee!] (*go!* [2nd person singular] in Latin) marks a phenomenon on multiple levels: the acoustic mark is *simultaneously* a phoneme, morpheme, single word, and a complete sentence. A seeming "syntactic paradox": for one spatial (architectonic) semiological homology, see D. Preziosi, *Architecture, Language and Meaning: The Origins of the Built World and its Semiotic Organization* (hereafter cited as *ALM*) (The Hague, Paris, and New York: Mouton, 1979), esp. ch. 2, "Tool Use, Object Manipulation, and Spatial Behavior," pp. 18–46 (to excavate a bit deeper in the personal/professional hauntology to be staged in the next *Passage*).

7 Philippe Lacoue-Labarthe, op. cit. See especially the Foreword ("Persistence") by Thomas Tresize, pp. xiii–xx. For Lacoue-Labarthe, the *double mimesis* concerns the relation between a "restricted economy" in which meaning is founded on the principle of identity, where language "means what it says" (the Humpty-Dumpty effect; see above) and a "general economy" whereby *every* term is also *non*-self identical, or "outside" itself – an excess over the closure of meaning: where meaning is always *a venir*, "to come." Such a distinction closely resembles what I have elsewhere articulated (and will elaborate further in the *Theses* chapter) as resembling the ancient rhetorical/semiological distinction between *equation* and *adequation*. Lacoue-Labarthe's distinction places in question – as I do here – the ontological difference itself, "displacing the bar," as he writes in ch. I ("The Fable [Literature and Philosophy])" p. 9, "that symbolically separates literature and philosophy ... such that both are crossed out and cancel each other in communicating." In this, Lacoue-Labarthe refers (op. cit., n. 16) to Nietzsche's problematizing the distinction itself between "truth" and its "other," a recurrent theme of the present volume.

8 I will be using these terms on many occasions in preference to "art" or "religion" to foreground the idealist reification of the latter – very much to the point of these investigations. On the mysticism of reification, see Landzelius, op. cit., and Richard Terdiman,

Present Past: Modernity and the Memory Crisis (Ithaca, NY: Cornell University Press, 1993), and the remarks above on mysticism.

9 There will be methodological parallels in what follows to some of the topological investigations of Jacques Lacan regarding the constitution of the subject in society, although this book does not claim to directly "apply" Lacanian theory to my subject matter. A useful recent introduction to Lacan in the context of self–other interrelationships may be found in the anthology *Lacan: Topologically Speaking*, ed. Ellie Ragland and Dragan Milovanovic (New York: The Other Press, 2004). In her biography *Jacques Lacan* (New York: Columbia University Press, 1997), Elisabeth Roudinesco recounts the influence of topological mathematics on Lacanian psychoanalytic theory and practice from as early as 1950. Lacan, as Ragland and Milanovanovic note (op. cit., p. xx) formed a study group with linguist Emile Benveniste, mathematician Georges Guilbaud, and anthropologist Claude Levi-Strauss to explore connections between the social sciences, mathematics, and topology so as to more fully understand the multidimensional and multimodal production and maintenance of social realities – an aim shared by the present investigation (and interestingly echoing *avant le lettre* the critical issue of the interpenetration of social and biological behaviors; see the previous *Passage*. A lucid investigation of the intersections and relationships between psychoanalysis and deconstruction is Steven Melville's "Psychoanalysis and Deconstruction," ch. 3 of his *Philosophy Beside Itself: On Deconstruction and Modernism*, with a foreword by Donald Marshall (Minneapolis, MN: University of Minnesota Press, 1986), pp. 84–114. See, in addition, Parveen Adams, op. cit., ch. 7, "Art as Prosthesis: Cronenberg's Crash," pp. 147–164.

10 A concern of *Passage* 7 ("Semiosis and its Discontents"). See there the first illustration.

11 The phrase echoes the title of an early and widely influential book by Umberto Eco, *The Open Work*, trans. Anna Cancogni (Cambridge, MA: Harvard University Press, 1989) (*L'opera Aperto* [Milano: Bompiani, 1962]).

12 Michel Foucault's "The Discourse on Language," where the phrase occurs, was delivered as a lecture at the College de France on December 2, 1970, and published under the title *L'ordre du discours* (Paris: Gallimard, 1971). The English translation by Rupert Swyer was published the same year in *Social Science Information*, April 1971.

13 See, for example, Deleuze's "Memory as Virtual Coexistence," ch. 3 of Gilles Deleuze, *Bergsonism* [*Le Bergsonisme*], trans. Hugh Tomlinson and Barbara Habberjam (Paris: PUF, 1966; Cambridge, MA, 1988), pp. 51–72, as well as de Certeau, "Psychoanalysis and its History."

14 Tomoko Masuzawa, "Writing History in an Age of Theory: A Brief Discourse on Method," in *The Invention of World Religions, Or How European Universalism Was Preserved in the Language of Pluralism* (Chicago, IL: University of Chicago Press, 2005), pp. 29–33.

15 See, for example, Rainer Rochlitz, *The Disenchantment of Art: The Philosophy of Walter Benjamin*, trans. Jane Marie Todd (New York: The Guilford Press, 1996) (*Le desenchantment de l'art: La philosophie de Walter Benjamin* [Paris: Gallimard, 1992]), especially Rochlitz's introduction, pp. 1–10 and in Benjamin's ch. 1: "The Philosophy of Language," the section "The Magic of Language," pp. 11–20.

16 *AINT*, 2012.

3

PERAMBULATIONS

This *Passage* resonates with the story told above in *Provocations* about a chance encounter with a misplaced text in a university library[1] that evoked a cascade of memories of other texts and experiences. Juxtaposed as palimpsests of each other, they projected shards or image-pieces of the *margins* or boundaries of the core conundrums motivating the writing of this book.

The present section consists of a perambulating or a walking-through of several short texts scattered on my desk, forming a virtual ambulatory: a space like a colonnaded cloister or ambulatory[2] the sighting of whose contents or objects evokes (thereby serving to *place* or "store") memories of other things and places and notions – a mnemonic geography – to *relate* things in the dual sense of that word (positioning together and speaking of texts for others).[3] What setting them out together seems to stage as potentially related. An exercise staged as a kind of *sortes derridiana*,[4] echoing what ancient or medieval writers did with passages in books (like a Virgil or a Christian Bible) pointed to at random so as to *provoke/evoke* a prophecy. Or what was done at so many pilgrimage sites throughout Christendom, re-creating sacred sites and spaces, not infrequently with full-scale religious figures depicted at particularly salient moments of a religious story, such as shown in Figure 3.1.

Here are a few image-scenes or shards to reckon with:

1   *Art strips us bare to clothe us in threads of enchantment . . .*
2   *In his poem* A Note on Moonlight, *Wallace Stevens speaks about the surface of things being the purpose of things seen.*[5]
3   *If the Greek thought the sea lovely in color and form, the color and the form remain. The imaginary being in whom the phenomena were embodied could only be known through the phenomena. . . . Why not love the sea instead of loving Proteus, who is but the sea personified? . . . The sailor, imagining a treacherous deity lurking beneath the waves, saw*

FIGURE 3.1 The Sacramonte of Varese. 2010. Photograph taken by the author.

[therein] *new cause for dread, and would often have been glad enough to learn that Proteus was a figment.*[6]

4   *I remember that when the first week of the trial* [of Andres Behring Breivik in Oslo, 2012] *was over, and I'd finished my reporting, I dashed off to the airport to fly back to Moscow. Everything that day had been such a rush, there hadn't really been time for me to digest the full horror of what Breivik had been saying. I'd transcribed his words, of course, and reported them. But oddly enough it was only once I'd made it to the airport, passed security and paused, that I was hit by a sickening feeling about what I'd been listening to. Suddenly I spotted a children's shop with a beautiful display of colored pencils outside. I walked up to the display and stood there, it must have been five minutes – just looking at this little island of color and beauty. Anyone watching me must have thought I was mad. But at that moment I just wanted to experience something nice, something positive, to restore my faith in the world.*[7]

What exactly is going on in these passages? What seems at stake for each author and why? And what *space*, what regime, what economy, what architectonics, are delineated by their juxtaposition and superimposition?

1   The first is an assertion about what artistry can do or appears to be doing. With regard to this, I'd want to know (among other things) what constitutes the power of art (any artwork?) to strip us of what clothes and protects us *from*

enchantment (was "it" there all along, just hidden, unremarked or unfelt?), and which re-covers us then with – *what*, exactly? A magic that was "really" there all along? Can magic or art's magic keep you dry and warm? Or safe? So what is "enchantment" in the first place? Etymologically, the term refers to song or *a singing*: the singing of a/the world into being. But then what exactly is *replaced* when a world is conjured into being: was it nothingness? And must one be a divine "designer" to be such a conjuror? Isn't every poet divine? Is divinity the absolute perfection of poesis? Is reality that which (some) god produced by this planet (a planet that produces gods as Bergson noted), has sung/is singing into existence? The "artifice of eternity," as in Yeats' poem *Sailing to Byzantium*.[8]

2   The second is a passage from a poem by Wallace Stevens, *Notes on Moonlight*, about the relation between appearance and purpose; between an object and its significance: the relation between what one sees and what one understands *in*, *through*, *by*, and *with* what is seen. Is "purpose," then, palpable or visible? Does *speaking of* render something legible? How can you be sure? If you pray to(ward) a wall is it to affirm *or* deny the existence of something (god, spirit, force, person, heaven, hell, etc.) behind it? Is the function of walls to conjure otherness as palpable? Where or in what does purpose (meaning, function, idea, etc.) reside? And where (among other things) does such a distinction come from? Who or what is benefitted by making or believing in such a separation in the first place? Is purpose or significance or meaning not fixed and determined by its formation or manifestation? Is it inherent to a thing? And if the appearance of something (the "surface" of being) *is* being's "purpose," does *every* thing in the world therefore have a distinctive purpose? Should every thing (as the old Woody Guthrie song put it) "have a purpose under heaven"? Whose heaven, which purpose, for whom, and who gets to decide to join in or has leave to decline to do so?

3   The distinction between a phenomenon and its personification or embodiment; between a physical form or feature and the attempt to render, re-present, or translate it. I'd like to know what is entailed in embodying or personifying a phenomenon – giving "airy nothing," as Shakespeare once said, "a local habitation and a name"? And what (among other possibilities) is the purpose of doing so or claiming to do so, if, so it would seem, the force or power of the embodiment can be ignored, muted, or mooted in such a way that it can be *avoided*? Or modified and transformed? If the universe is imperfect and things fail? Don't think about Proteus but just those threatening (*im*personal) waves. But if it *can* be avoided then does that mean that "it" is contingent; susceptible to having been crafted or fabricated in the first place? If you can escape its power, did it (the power) ever "really" exist? Is a "figment" of the imagination, a figuration or a rendering of it as a figure or formation? A making *legible* what is visible? Is this the converse of the old art historical dream/desire of *making the visible legible* – namely, a making of the legible *visible*?

4   The fourth is a news reporter's reaction to a massive contemporary act of terrorism. What exactly is (a) faith if it can be lost and/or regained? Does "wishing"

ever really "make things so"? And what exactly is the relation between something "nice and positive" and the (presumably positive) psychological state of its user or viewer? Is there a correspondence, homology, similarity, or *concordance* between certain forms and certain meanings, to the extent that wellwrought urns would be more likely to have good contents or have good effects on the psyche or spirit or mentality or well-being of their users or viewers, with ill-wrought ones having an opposite impact on those encountering them? What exactly *is* the "relation between" aesthetics and ethics? Is there a certain *decorum* or fittingness involved in "mere" perception or apperception? Or (to put it otherwise) is perception not fully distinct from interpretation? Is interpretation a *slant* on or a slanting of perception? Is something deemed (for some) more beautiful, more true, or more fully believable, such that, for example, the economic pronouncements of a handsome finance minister appear truer and more worthy of attention than those of plainer political rivals? Aren't politicians and their handlers more or less effective *artisans* of decorous personhood? Suggesting, of course, as noted by not a few and not only recently, as we shall see, the artifice and fabricatedness (and hence, perhaps, the inevitable mutability and contingency) of selfhood as such. That the "as such" is no less contingent and mutable: a *construction* or constituting.

a Commentary

Enchantment seems to be dragging its threads everywhere, transforming every nowhere into some palpable *thing*. Including, as this book argues, *credulities* themselves.

So it would seem that the four texts' juxtaposition delineate an overlapping and intersecting domain: as much as these texts concern artistic or aesthetic matters, they also concern and ostensify the *inextricability* of art, politics, ethics, and religion, as well as the memory of (and/or amnesia about) their relationships.

Perhaps they may comprise a *severed* "Borromean knot" that calls or cries out for a *mending*: a re-sewing of what (as disciplinarity) has been rent asunder – more on such knots, chains, strings, and their spaces below. What indeed do artistry and belief *do with* one another? What keeps or has kept them *at bay* from each other? What indeed does beauty (but whose?) embody, represent, express, mirror, echo, communicate, give back, or *render*? Was it only Edna St Vincent Millay's "Euclid" who "alone looked upon *beauty bare*" (*mere* beauty?) or can we all see it, with proper (artistic, scientific, theological, psychoanalytic, legal, military, economic, etc.) training? Under what conditions do beauty and truth have to *do* with each other, assuming them to be different, at least "for the sake of argument."

But then it is this *for the sake of argument* that the book addresses, and it is written or composed the way it has been because its form (to take a cue from Stevens) has everything to do with its purpose(s). Its form "bespeaks" its purpose; it is *mythomorphic*. That is, this book assembles its purpose from the surfaces on which that purpose simultaneously appears, has appeared, and will continue to do so, so that the process resembles a jigsaw puzzle of those pieces or surfaces of purpose. All of which appear to have distinct and unique shapes and colors and dimensions.

I initially imagined that I would be composing this text as if it were a puzzle of pieces or passing surfaces (passages) whose overall purpose or aim was to make/ see all those surfaces fitted together (from the various directions from which *I've* been coming), *as if* – in making a smooth transition; that *smoothing* – the overall *figure* on the surface would "appear" in its fuller dimensionality. The "figure of its truth," so to speak. The book would have been rendering what by hindsight (foresight's differently complexioned, perhaps more contemplative twin) was now visible as having been rent apart, as if from (some presumed or desired) unified surface-purpose. A rendering – that is, literally, a *giving back* what is taken (jointly by hindsight and foresight) as (if) previously a single or singular *surface*. The surface of a (the) completely composed jigsaw puzzle, now unpacked with its component parts laid out on the table. And the rendering, returning and giving back, what is "its" imagined unity or wholeness; a com-position or an assemblage (<*ad* + *simul*, to(ward) the-same) of an "overall" purpose: that "surface ... the purpose to be seen," as Stevens put it. The "form (itself)" as the figuration of its truth.

What follows assembles, poses, composes, and juxtaposes the *traces* of where I've been coming from, both myself individually and partnered and jointly – that is, what I'm joining here as if it were to be observed; as if its overall purpose were the merging and synthesis of what might by hindsight be *construed/constructed as* places and surfaces and times nudged together into one surface/place/space/time. For the book is also about time, memory, chronicity, anachronism; about the past that lies *in as well as beside* the present (remember de Certeau) all *in regard to* what may be projected; a "future" as if in resolution of the puzzle; a post – the post that is again the shadow of the past. A past coterminous with its present.

A central conundrum for systems of theistic ideology or faith, which almost invariably site or locate the resolution of the inadequacies of mortal signification *elsewhere* – in an immateriality or noumenal realm unapproachable by reason, as the previous pope well understood, when he argued that divine perfection is the *cure* for the painful inadequacies of art; its secularity (i.e., its temporality). The better or more perfect artistry of artistic perfection. As we shall see, the perfection of a tran-scendence. Where we come up against having to imagine or mind the (artifice of) the gap or bar between imperfect mortality and divine perfection. Is artistry, then, an instrument or machinery for producing divinities? There's no simple *but* here, just the (un)bridgeable gap between art and god. It wasn't only Pascal who cast doubt on the medieval "ladder" connecting the lowest of phenomena up to the god(s); who in effect saw in the artifice of the unbridgeable gap the fabricatedness of the bridge: that unbridgeability indeed breeds bridges.[9]

This book at the same time troubles and problematizes the structural system of chronology in foregrounding its contingency; its culturally specific (Indo-European linguistic syntactic) ideological assumptions. The fifth *Passage* ("Parenthesis: art, time, and the untimely") addresses (ana)chronism (taken here as *not* an it).

Archaeologically/genealogically the book composes greater and lesser pieces with varying degrees of visibility beneath the surface of the here and now; varying vectors and directions and narrative directional threads. I've been unearthing many memories of events and phenomena and objects suspended, it might seem, in mnemic space at oblique angles to each other, all of which are seen from the surface of the here and now *as if from* the here and now of (what is thereby) the above. Consider a view of the universe where all the spiral galaxies are askew to each other.

As if, as you will see, the assembled image that is the surface of this book were a two-dimensional rendering-surface plane of its multidimensional and multitemporal *beneaths*. As if this here and now is the future anterior of what it shall have been for what it was in the process of becoming in piecing together those pieces. Again, this is an archaeological project rather than a historiography of the art–religion matrix.

Even the most gentle prodding of a "plain description" or mere reportage seems quickly to evoke philosophical, theological, and ethical problems, paradoxes, and cul-de-sacs of very great antiquity in not a few traditions. The foregoing remarks do indeed mask centuries of intense inquiry, discussion, and debate, and may evoke virtual, psychological, and corporeal empowerment and charm, violence, and coercion, even terror, genocide, and ethnic "cleansing" – one should pay attention to that locution: this is Grand Hygiene being alluded to. What is much less remarked upon or investigated, in other words, is the *aesthetic* dimension underlying both comments, which is what equally concerns this book. Genocide is of course no less (an) aesthetic (in) practice.

The following is about what links the comments (image-pieces) just set out about the terrifying Greek personification – the "god" – Proteus and the terror-producing Norwegian racist/anti-multiculturalist/Christian terrorist Anders Breivik. Many of its puzzle-pieces are recountings of my reckonings with juxtapositions of ethics and aesthetics and the intricate interpenetration of what in modernity are conventionally in modernity kept at bay[10] as *art* and *religion*. Kept – sacredly – at bay and apart. The sacraments of art history, theory, and criticism and their discordances and discontents. It is equally concerned with what has buried and keeps covered and unacknowledged their intimate intricacies. Is ignorance of such connections willful or accidental or manufactured – or all of these under particular circumstances? And is *amnesia* about the mutual entailments of artistry and religiosity, ethics and aesthetics, proactively fostered, or an artifact or effect of lapsed attention?

After all, the death and destruction wrought by Anders Breivik was no less motivated by a desire for a proper, fitting, or *decorously* ordered world than those conjured up by other militant literalists such as the Afghani Taliban or the American "Tea" Party. *The ficticities of facticity as idolatry.* Decorum, as we will see below, is a mode of idolatry – which raises some very difficult questions about how we would deal with both art and religion (and politics) today.

This book develops in the course of its investigations of these and related conundrums a number of distinct perspectives which at first glance may appear unusual and unorthodox. And possibly at later glances as well, although many of its observations concern issues reckoned with over many centuries in not a few traditions in not all that dissimilar a manner. Part of what this book addresses is the paradox of just that concordance: truly a romance, as we shall see, of unknown siblings. Within the Western tradition, especially notable has been a resurgence of interest in the *materiality* of signification by medieval art historians and historians of religion and the return to prominence of the scholarship of Frederick Ohly as a welcome antidote to the narrow verbocentrist "iconography" of his contemporary, Erwin Panofsky.[11]

b Aside

Sometimes I've been tempted to respond to those periodically asking (for much of my adult life, if not before) what I'm "working on now" by saying that I'm writing a book on the metaphysics of the colander, so shot through is it with ghosts and specters – such a hauntology – as to raise serious questions about the viability of distinctions between the material and the virtual. The ghost/specter paradox. Or "optical illusion" (but there's no illusion since it's all illusory). Investigating conundrums (as below) as a series of matches in a squash court fitted out like a Necker Cube (a very nice design problem for beginning architecture students). Or a perpetually long distance running forward on a (literally, etymologically) subversive Moebius strip whose underside is not underneath but the fiction or artistry of the beyond-belief.

But we would make a serious mistake if we were to situate these questions (and their discussion, investigation, and reckoning) as either invented in or by contemporary theoretical discourse on the visual arts. And we should take very seriously indeed the (manufactured) historical amnesia of disciplinary formations such as art history regarding the aforementioned questions, an amnesia that is itself the product not only of parochial ignorance but of the nature of (especially Anglophone) contemporary art historical (mis)education.

This was always to have been (and so must now continue as) a book on the topology of knots: how otherwise could one reckon with the artifact embodying/personifying the bizarre space-time where art and religion play together while tied back-to-back seeing opposite views; facing elsewhere and otherwise? And, moreover, each facing a wall of mirrors (like a Lucas Samaras mirror room) reflecting those gazes back and forth, simulating both non-divisibility and immortality. Immortality as an artifact of mirrors. An amnesia whose amnesty is right there in the mirror, as if in plain sight.

Insertion: an admission. It may be startling (bad form; impertinent; starting with an apology, etc.) for an author to admit that s/he would have preferred *not* to write the book its readers are beginning to read; in the case of this text this is to some extent the case. I'd have much preferred this were an extended conversation, dialogue, workshop, or seminar, with ongoing and unpredictably unfolding engagements with other views, visions, and voices: where things under discussion or "on (and under or even off) the table" were engaging multiple perspectives and expectations of the passage(s) or journey(s) ahead. Which is how I've been conducting/composing my professional life for many years, with considerable pleasure and energy, and arguably to more often than not some good effect both for myself and some others. Whether this has been an artifact of a personal taste/inclination (see below) for paradox and the ironic rather than the canonical or categoric (more precisely, much of the time, for the irony of the categorical [which recalls the lament by the protagonist of Leonard Bernstein's 1956 comic operetta *Candide* I saw as a child, based on Voltaire's novella of the same name] longing for the certainties of his master's voice), you may be better positioned than I to comment as the peculiar composition/disposition unfolding here continues to open out, and its implications and consequences multiply, broaden, and impinge on understandings that will have been brought to this textual surrogate for (or simulacrum, perhaps, of) a dialogue. Odd things happen along the way to where this text finally pauses, as you will see.

This book exists not in a vacuum but is tethered to, references, and entails about a dozen or so others I've been involved with, although it is the case that none of those (cited above and elsewhere) ever actually opened with anything like the "admission" just made, although I suspect some readers may have intuited the simulacrum of dialogue just out of sight/off the page of what was legible elsewhere. The specter of a side-bar. Which is not to say that this is in any way a disavowal of those other works and their apparent effects and impacts upon myself/ourselves/others.

In fact, this book is offered up (as mentioned earlier) as a *vow* to the *promises* of those books' *premises*, voiced and unvoiced.

And I should say again and in advance of what you will be reading below that what is to be found here is shot through and haunted by not a few ghosts, some of whom/of which are not a little strange – half-remembered cadences of this or that essay or lecture; palimpsests of power-points; echoes and mirror-reversed images of syntaxes knotted together in ways so temptingly easy to do in this age of performing "to write" by sitting at a screen hammering-out (on a laptop) or touching-out (on an iPad) vowels and consonants that can be whisked around between continents, dragged and dropped with merest finger-flicks. Maybe the memory of sitting through a long "seminar" (in fact, a three-hour monologue) by Michel Foucault one hazy, sweaty summer month in Toronto, mesmerized by the choreography of the words made from his body, conscious of all those points where you came to know in advance (it was in the leftward motion of his right arm) where he was about to change direction in his argument and breeze into a new space; one more heterotopic than topical (but then – his point – there were no heterotopias because all spaces were latently or palpably heterotopical, thereby problematizing that very distinction itself). But there have been and still remain with me many teachers, many colleagues, many students, all of whom continue to teach and advise, of course, for they are *still here*. This book is no less a *vow* to all of them. As it is to the material sites and circumstances which equally have engendered what is here now.

This book swims with/is haunted by ghosts that do on occasion bob up *as if in plain sight* and sometimes these are sign-posted in advance with many of the usual warnings; that is, with pauses in the passages of texts (the punctuated pauses often signal change of passage, which is why developments chaptered here are called *Passages*. Which as you will see are not necessarily uni-directional, and are sometimes caught up only to reverse course and take a closer look at something seen before or remembered having seen – hence a certain redundancy[12] about the text. Moebius Strips and Necker Cubes and Borromean Knots abound. This book has memories tucked into its pockets (and occasionally peering out, as you'll see along the way below) of encounters in many times and places.

Much of what follows (and what it is built upon; its shadowy elsewheres) is about time and memory, the temporary and the untimely, and it is in close touch at many points with the palpable thingness or *quiddity* of space-time – its material unyieldingness; its calling attention to itself by insisting itself to sense (an enchantment, surely) even and especially when it all seems transparently apparent. But things that may be there are there in many ways, like alternating facets of a complex solid rotated in air. Or points pointed to on a floor below the sweep of a Foucault pendulum,[13] a mechanical movement haunting the whole book's composition from beginning to ending, as these Perambulations will have been ostensifying.

This text (along with some of those others) had multiple origins in time, space, and place, and it is in and through the excavation or unearthing of those beginnings that the purposes and possible prospects of this book/excavation unfolded and are unfolding. In other words, the subject of this book and its object of study is the very conundrum(s) generated in and for me by very particular events – a linked series, a matrix or archipelago of events which I will now try to recount – the *hauntology* just below – along with recounting my sense of what that has to do with the intractable problems that have been grouped under the heading of the connections or (inter) relations between those enchanted fictions, those enchantments named as *art* and *religion*, as well as their co-implicative or co-determined *allomorphs* such as artistry and artifice on the one hand, and religiosities or spiritualities (and more) on the other hand. Of course, both of these hands wash each other simultaneously, and only together do they constitute handedness.

I will afterward discuss what this matrix of issues has to do with relevant aspects of the institutional(ized) and at the moment quite moribund (not to say *morbid*) discourse on the arts ostensifying a commonplace postmodern amnesia) and on pertinent social and political questions (to use a conventional locution wherein distinctions are both maintained and problematized) between art, religion, politics, ethics, and community. Part of that addresses some of the ways in which *the separation between art and religion have permeated, justified, and problematized these other distinctions.*

That is basically what this book will in large part be doing. And while I might perhaps have preferred (while talking things through here in this *Aside)* to have *merely pointed to* (ostensified; only shown) some of the texts I've authored and co-authored to date as fulfilling (i.e., as a *QEDing)* what (2) above said "will also discuss," I *will nonetheless* in fact and in effect synopsize all that below. I'll try to do that with dispatch, as they say, and pass on – one of the other reasons why the "sections" of this book are being called *Passages* – interspersed with *Pauses* of varying duration – because they pass on. Passages and pauses and peterings-out as pieces that the jigsaw mentioned above has seen, sawn, and rendered.

A later *Passage* (10, "The tears of thingness and the amnesty of amnesia") will address some salient consequences of the foregoing, both the wanted and the unwanted – though it's not always easy to predict in advance which is which and when. It will reckon in part with the amnesiac aesthetic theology of emeritus-Pope Benedict XVI. As will become increasingly evident throughout the following, a lot of others have been wrangling in the Scylla and Charybdis of this art–religion chiasmatic matrix before as well (often unknowingly or unbeknownst to their ostensible aims), and were no less deeply and passionately engaged with and committed to investigating and/or explicating the conundrum whose pieces or *surfaces* are shortly to be set forth here. Different melodies and choreographies with their own peculiar and also in some cases still evolving scores and labanotations.

A few general remarks now by way of a brief capsule genealogy. Why does that word conjure up images of cookbooks? As if a genealogy were a thing to think with; *to factualize through use.* Like a menu or a calendar or a city. To *render*, to reduce to a simmer and let solidify or gel. And a word about the method and flavor of the writing here (its "cuisine," in the words of some, or perhaps its "economy" for some others). Along with what was said earlier about what I would have preferred to be doing than having written (what is now becoming/ escaping my grasp *as*) this text, and my preference for dialogue – which is a collaborative (that is, in essence, precisely, a *philosophical* practice, as Deleuze and Guattari cogently argued[14]) – rather than for *monologue* and the categorical (which has and knows its place in and as *theology* or the theological – where exactly was "art" in *that* distinction?), I'll discuss such claims and distinctions as this proceeds, and in doing so will consider ways in which what I've been doing in other works couldn't necessarily be reduced to the "philosophical" (theoretical) *or* the "theological" (categorical). Nor to the distinction, captured in the work of some, between the "historical"/historiographic and the "psychoanalytic"/ethical: that old romance of unknown (twin) siblings.[15]

But then the history of such distinctions *is* a key part of the story being unfolded, composed, and excavated here, in and as this book, which is less a history, as you will be more and more aware now, than an archaeology (historicism's three-dimensional relative). And a specific part of that is the immediate evolution of the text you are reading: a series of *Passages* and *Pauses* and *Hauntings* (the *worm-holes*) tracing through the overt and covert connections between the implications of the quotations at the top of this opening text: that journey from Proteus to Breivik, which began with an impatience with the commentary about the Mohammed cartoon controversy in Denmark and elsewhere in the middle of the last decade.

Notes

1 Morrill Library, University of York, UK, undergoing massive reorganization through autumn 2011 during a residency as honorary visiting professor, a position generously granted me to continue this research and engage with a most collegial community of scholars and students in an extraordinary city.

2 Our concern in this book with amnesia and its allomorphs will deal with some of the issues famously addressed by Mary Carruthers in *The Book of Memory: A Study of Memory in Medieval Culture* (Cambridge: Cambridge University Press, 1990), as well as with those addressed by Frances Yates, *The Art of Memory* (London: Routledge & Keegan Paul, 1966). These two books, plus Carruthers' *The Craft of Thought: Meditation, Rhetoric, and the Making of Images, 400–1200* (Cambridge: Cambridge University Press, 1998) and Yates' "Architecture and the Art of Memory," *Architectural Association Quarterly*, Vol. 12, 1980, pp. 4–13, dealt with issues close to many taken up here. Other aspects of the medieval European attention to the functions of material things *in situ* are reviewed in Aden Kumler and Christopher R. Leakey, "*Res et significatio*: The Material Sense of Things in the Middle Ages, *Gesta*, Vol. 51, No. 1, 2012, pp. 1–18. The latter is of particular interest here for its insights into what from a contemporary perspective Jane Bennett has termed the "vitality" of matter (*Vibrant Matter: A Political Ecology of Things* [Durham, NC and London: Duke University Press, 2010]), which is not a vitalism.

3 As noted by Carruthers, op. cit., p. 194.

4 The allusion is to the medieval practice of *sortes virgiliana* – the random opening of a page of Vergil's *Aeneid* so as to *evoke* (provoke, fabricate) a prophesy.

5 Wallace Stevens, "A Note on Moonlight" from his *Collected Poems* (New York: Knopf, 1955), p. 531.

6 Leslie Stephen, *Selected Writings in British Intellectual History* (Chicago, IL: University of Chicago Press, 1979), pp. 14–15. Cited in Vincent Pecora, *Secularization and Cultural Criticism: Religion, Nation, & Modernity* (Chicago, IL and London: University of Chicago Press, 2006), p. 178.

7 Steve Rosenberg, "Anders Breivik Trial: A Ten-week Ordeal," *BBC Online News Magazine*, June 24, 2012: www.bbc.co.uk/news/magazine-18558319 (accessed June 25, 2012). Steve Rosenberg went to Utoeya in the aftermath of the attacks.

8 See Karl Parker, *Yeats' Two Byzantiums* (accessed July 10 2012): www.mrbauld.com/yeats1bz.html. Yeats' "Sailing to Byzantium," stanza III reads: *O sages standing in God's holy fire/As in the gold mosaic of a wall,/Come from the holy fire, perne in a gyre,/And be the singing masters of my soul./Consume my heart away: sick with desire/And fastened to a dying animal/It knows not what it is; and gather me/Into the artifice of eternity.* Compare this to Graham L. Hammill, "History and the Flesh: Caravaggio's Sexual Aesthetic – Spectatorship and the Queering of Form," in Parveen Adams, ed., *Art: Sublimation or Symptom?* (New York: The Other Press, 2003), pp. 49–74, on Lacan's proposal that "the social value of an icon is that it allows for the fantasy that the god whom it represents *is also looking at it. The icon is there to please God*, to 'arouse the desire of God' " (p. 61).

9 See Virginia K. Howe, " 'Les Pensees:' Paradox and Signification," *Yale French Studies*, Vol. 49, 1973 [special number "Science, Language, and the Perspective Mind: Studies in Literature and Thought from Campanella to Bayle"], pp. 120–131, esp. pp. 128–129:

> For Pascal, the absolute destroys gradation in the domain of the relative, and no combination of elements can constitute a ladder to infinity, for each is equally insufficient.... The natural order is no longer an ascending scale of values leading from the material to the spiritual.

10 Much of what follows deals equally with the circumstantial and culturally specific and temporal nature of what is here distinguished as "art" and "religion." On that question in general, see *AINT*.

11 An excellent recent introduction to the complexities of medieval signification and its implications for materiality studies and 1980s new-historicist "thing theory" is Aden

Kumler and Christopher Lakey, op. cit., and in particular essays by Christina Normore ("Navigating the World of Meaning," pp. 19–34) and Beate Fricke ("Matter and Meaning of Mother-of-Pearl: The Origins of Allegory in the Spheres of Things," pp. 35–54). See also in the same volume, Herbert L. Kessler, "'They preach not by speaking out loud but by signifying': Vitreous Arts as Typology," pp. 55–70. As all of the contributors to this landmark volume make quite clear, the medieval understanding of how material objects or artifacts (including words) signify was considerably more complex, open, and polyvalent than early modern and modern paradigms of meaning-making, particularly in their art historical aspects. For an earlier consideration of multi-modal signification in the history of visual studies, see *RAH*, esp. ch. 4, "The Coy Science," pp. 80–121, and part 7, "Archimedes am Scheideweg," on Panofsky's verbo-centrism and its innocence of concurrent developments in semiology. For a different understanding of Panofsky and semiotics, see Michael-Ann Holly, *Panofsky and the Foundations of Art History* (Ithaca, NY and London: Cornell University Press, 1984), critiqued in *RAH*, pp. 112–114, and notes 166 and 170.

12 From Latin *re-(d)undare*, the repeated action of waves (*undae*). In the case of this text, the wave after wave of *specters*.

13 The name refers to a device named after the French physicist Leon Foucault as a palpable demonstration of the rotation of the Earth. The device consists of a tall pendulum free to swing in any vertical plane. The plane's actual swing appears to rotate relative to the Earth; in fact, the plane is fixed in space while the Earth rotates under the pendulum once every sideral day (32.7 hours). Its first public exhibition was in February 1851 in the Meridian of the Paris Observatory. An exact replica of the original pendulum has been swinging permanently since 1995 under the dome of the Pantheon in Paris. History and technical discussion with diagrams and photographs at http://en.wikipedia.org/wiki/File:Pendule_de_Foucault.jpg.

14 Gilles Deleuze and Felix Guattari, *What is Philosophy?*, trans. Hugh Tomlinson and Graham Burchell (New York: Columbia University Press, 1994) (*Qu'est-ce la philosophie?* [Paris, Minuet, 1991]), esp. pp. 1–12.

15 Michel de Certeau, "Psychoanalysis and its History," in M. de Certeau, *Heterologies: Discourse on the Other*, trans. Brian Massumi (Minneapolis, MN: University of Minnesota Press, 1986).

4

SPECTERS OF ARTIFICE

A hauntology

By disinterring past representations that silently inhabit present expression, the student of culture reorients standard facts of history for political ends. The past is not used to establish a confirmation of the present, but [is] a form of displacement that mobilizes critical perspectives.[1]

A decade ago I gave a series of public lectures during Hilary Term at Oxford collectively called "Seeing Through Art History" that were published two years later under the title *Brain of the Earth's Body*. The ostensible aim of those Slade Lectures was to "see art history *through*" and to "see through" it to where its innermost and obscured knots and conundrums lurked, not uncommonly *as if* in plain sight. Each of the eight lectures was addressed to laying these bare *as* unresolved conundrums. My thought was that keeping these tensions and paradoxes in play might better enable a more candid reckoning with the very strange contemporary discourse on art, artistry, and artifice and its inextricable entanglements with philosophy, ethics, theology, and statecraft: the discursive practice and institution still commonly called "the history of art," or sometimes "the history, theory, and criticism of art."[2]

The tensions staged in and by my lectures signaled a tactical refusal to avoid confronting head-on both the more glaring as well as some of the less apparent dilemmas pervading modern writing about *art* and *its* alleged "histories" – in particular the familiar and simultaneously very deeply problematic academic discipline of "art history." I argued in part that what became "art history" was perhaps better approached holistically for what "it" had pragmatically evolved *as and into*: a multidimensional network of deponent and diverse theoretical, critical, and historical (sub)fields, linked to various practices and institutions with specific genealogies – archival, legal, critical, heritage, fashion, and other industries. I claimed in an opening hypothesis/provocation that the modern discourse on art was grounded in *a denial of the impossibility of representation*.

The lectures took the semi-gelled set of deponent and interdependent practices of "the history" of art as themselves variable modern inflections of very ancient philosophical and religious debates about the charms and terrors of representation, collectively *grounded in* (an often masked, though as I argued, very plain in a certain light) *a denial* of the *impossibility* of "representing" – a development with immediate and enduring socio-political effects in early European modernity. The Oxford talks were triggered by a long-simmering impatience with the status and intellectual evolution of a contemporary discourse on the visual arts that seemed at the time to be measuring its critical and theoretical progress by avoidance (changing the subject – an entire academic discipline at some American universities) or by *kicking its conundrums further down the road*. Or over the fence into someone else's garden (anthropology, archaeology, sociology, material culture studies, visual culture studies, etc.) in the faint hope that someone else might pick it up and run (away) with it. Leaving us in (a) peace that nonetheless never really seemed to arrive.

But the present book is not a direct descendent of those Oxford talks,[3] nor is "about *art history*" *per se* (which never had a *per se* it couldn't easily wriggle out of). But it does come in the immediate wake of yet another text just published, the co-authored book with Claire Farago called *Art Is Not What You Think It Is* (2012), commissioned by Wiley-Blackwell for their series of "New Critical *Manifestos*" in various contemporary disciplines ("The Idea of" [X, Y, or Z]), the first in that series being Terry Eagleton's (alas, egregiously amnesiac) *The Idea of Culture*, appearing around the time of my Slade lectures. But the book you are reading here is not a sequel or follow-up to the latter, nor is what follows here (having recently articulated what art *isn't*) an accounting or final reckoning of what art now really *is* or isn't (it isn't – and wasn't – an *it* but more of a when and a how. I'll be tackling the *why* later).

Instead, what follows is a recounting, longish in places though rapid elsewhere, of encounters – both singular and in the wake of many personal collaborations, conversations, and debates – with the problems, promises, challenges, and terrors of the recognition and acknowledgment of the materiality/facticity/*quiddity-haeccity*/ *ding-an-sich-ness(es)*[4] of what today is commonly collected under the disingenuously benign (but then that's one premise of this whole series of *Passages*) *rubric* of art. But as we'll see, rubrics often rub against the grain.

In his *Ordinatio*, (John) Duns Scotus (1265/66–1308) observed that

> Because there is among beings something indivisible into subjective parts – that is, such that it is formally incompatible for it to be divided into several parts each of which is it – the question is not what it is by which such a division is formally incompatible with it (because it is formally incompatible by incompatibility), but rather what it is by which, as by a proximate and intrinsic foundation, this incompatibility is in it. Therefore, the sense of the questions on this topic [namely, of individuation] is: What is it in [e.g.] this stone, by which as by a proximate foundation it is absolutely incompatible with the stone for it to be divided into several parts each of which is this stone, the kind of division that is proper to a universal whole as divided into its subjective parts?

I should say right away that what follows is not another thrusting tractatus nor yet another historiographic manifesto (though of course it *is*, placed here on the cusp dividing and separating hindsight and foresight [the shadow presence of an *eruv*'s dangerous thresholds, maybe], the very *idea* of a manifesto, at the fold on which swing the material and immaterial). As you will see, what this is (or literally what it's becoming as it's being written, here before [y]our eyes) is best envisioned/choreographed as the *field report of an excavation* campaign into unknown or more accurately, an unbeknownst territory: a domain unbeknownst to itself.

But in this case it is a topological archaeology; an excavation of what my juxtaposition of seemingly random events and phenomena might lead to or add up to or suggest or project as (in this case) an itinerary or trajectory or archipelago or jigsaw puzzle of *passages* into and through the multiply compounded spaces that those relationships themselves might embody. A deep dive down toward Proteus (and away from Breivik and his monotheistic monomania manufactured in the virtual theme-park of ethno-aesthetic purity).

I referred earlier to the space/time origin(s) of my engaging with the problem of "art in relation to religion" etc. It concerned, in fact, a series of simultaneous dislocations, dis-orientations, and imminent re-constitutions and reorientations: the moiré pattern of the concordance-and-discordance I mentioned at the beginning of the *Preamble*; my response to Heidegger's Nietzsche.

Others will come into view, but let's start back *then and there* with these specters; this ghostly or spectral string, this archival staging of spectrality:

> In an enigmatic sense, which will clarify itself *perhaps* (perhaps, because nothing should be sure here, for essential reasons), the question of the archive is not, we repeat, a question of the past. It is not the question of a concept dealing with the past that might *already* be at our disposal, *an archivable concept of the archive*. It is a question of the future, the question of the future itself, the question of a response, of a promise and of a responsibility for tomorrow. The archive: if we want to know what it will have meant, we will only know in times to come. Perhaps. Not tomorrow but in times to come, later on or perhaps never. A spectral messianicity is at work in the concept of the archive and ties it, like religion, like history, like science itself, to a very singular experience of the promise. We are never far from Freud in saying this. Messianicity does not mean messianism.[5]

And similarly, as Derrida also notes, we are never far from Marx:

> The commodity-form, to be sure, *is not* use-value, we must grant this to Marx and take account of the analytic power this distinction gives us. But if the commodity-form is *not, presently*, use-value, and even if it is not *actually present*, it affects it in advance the use-value of the wooden table. It affects and bereaves us in advance, like the ghost it will become, but this is precisely where haunting begins. And its time, and the untimeliness of the present, its being "out of joint."[6]

As is indeed the archival monstrosity here; this desynchronizing hauntology, this ghost of a genealogy.

Specter No. 1

(Worm-hole.[7]) During the summer, between ages four and five, my family and I moved to a new apartment in New York City, one not in another neighborhood or borough but rather one visible across a small grassy terrace in front of our imminently previous apartment, and in advance of the birth of my sister, and prior to my entering my first grade of grammar school (having been rescued (*saved*) from kindergarten thanks to the results of a just-instituted city-wide testing program (see n. 9) which steered some to the latter to kindergarten and some others directly to first grade). During that time between the old flat and the new, between being an only child and being siblinged, between childhood and school,[8] and between not having my own room and the prospect of having one, my father (sometimes with his twin brother, Remus, but that's another story) and I periodically would visit the new empty flat, talk about furnishings needed, carrying boxes over there, and in my case mostly looking out the window back across the park and over the trees to the old apartment. Seeing it plainly, fully faced, across the way: stunned.

The new one was on the fifth floor and the old one on the third, in newish red brick buildings that were eight stories high (nine including ground floors, each quaintly, though not in New York, where – in my limited experience – every ground floor, every O, was called M). All the 12-paned mullioned windows of the old apartment now seen at a distance could be framed within and uncannily *by* one of the 12 mullioned frames of the window of the new apartment – for someone *exactly* of my height standing peering over the forest-green colored metal windowsill conveniently just supporting my elbows. Mesmerized/enchanted by the distance-yet-closeness. The *building itself* zoomed in and out, not just the eye(s). But the light within the two apartments was oddly, unaccountably different, the older one being somehow more greenish, the newer more bluish.[9] A homey yet unhomely place.

A dis-location re-oriented by a re-location to a new world which given all the time I spent in both flats during that endless summer was a *palimpsest* on the old. Both apartments were made of identical mid-twentieth century fittings (post-war "moderne" with the merest hint of pre-war New York deco-nostalgia), though the new was a mirror-reversed image of the old (*not vice versa* it seemed, oddly), and the new an additional room larger, a room where no room had gone before. The proportions of perspective; a child's game of anamorphosis and juxtaposition. Not quite a Freudian *fort-da*, but a perspectival relative of that ilk: I'll call it perhaps a *nunc-tunc*.[10]

Specter No. 2

On my first day of grammar school was a second dislocation/dissonance/discordance: entering into my first school classroom suddenly and obviously *not* the one

I was supposed to be in, but one where a group of kids my age were standing and reciting. Reciting in a sing-song, syncopated way what I was later told was a prayer practice, in oddly put-together words whose meaning was opaque to me. Stunned, dropped onto an alien planet, dumbfounded, at a loss to understand what was being recited when after a few minutes it was clear that this was a *per-formance*, a charade, make-believe, and all that was visible was its *surface*: it's opacity; its artifice.

Bursting out laughing at the oddly nasal twang sing-song didn't merely call attention to myself; it resulted in being physically *spirited away* to what was in fact my properly assigned non-sectarian classroom where all the other kids were prac-ticing spelling, something not laughable at all given the bizarre history of English orthography, but really hard – i.e., interesting. Or maybe just as funny as the military-religious performance next door but not a *performance* as such (or so it seemed at the time). I had been disoriented by the labyrinthine spaces of the new school building: all the rooms had green and white tiled floors with thin brown moldings around the blackboards. Astoundingly attracting/distracting. Eventually finding my way around the labyrinth, so at odds with the squared lines of the school building seen from outside. Not only different spaces but distinct times, the school building's doorway a magical multidimensional transfer-point, switched on, oper-ated by the twist of a door handle....

Specter No. 3

Watching a presentation by a visiting video artist at the University of York in 2012, the camera panning over the rubble-strewn floor of an abandoned house with a person sifting through the rubble in search of something identifiable, coming upon a dusty misshapen thing resembling a knuckle-bone or a button, something identi-fiable only in a particular, fleeting, raking light, resembling an upholstery button from a piece of furniture once part of this empty ruin of a house (a *pointe de capiton*: M. Lacan would be proud), a relic of (some) life. A tiny object for contemplation (<*templum* – a cut from/out of the quotidian, a temple), for the weaving together of a story, histories, disappeared worlds.

The screening evoked memories of a children's "excavation" sandbox-game display a decade or so ago at the Skirball Museum of Jewish culture and history in Brentwood, west Los Angeles (on the terrace of a hill above and looking down upon the Getty Centre Museum), where children could dig with small shovels and trowels into the sand to "retrieve" (imitation) "relics" of Jewish history, identity, and culture; literally an ethnically cleansed sandbox of time; a religiously cleansed historicity.[11] A local west-side scandal rendered invisible by being staged as a chil-dren's game.

This hauntology is, among other things, a roving reliquary, and I'm paying my respects in and by what follows. What this is becoming in part is a *sifting through and piecing together, composing and voicing* memories of positioning and inhabiting along with their antitheses. Again, places suspended between hindsight and foresight: the artifice of living-in so as to learn to live on (giving to not-quite "airy-nothing a local habitation and a name").[12] My subjects (the objects found in the course of composing this book, as you are seeing), are often material things, sometimes certain (immaterial, virtual, notional) relations between and among things, and constantly things left behind or overlooked. Looking is simultaneously an *overlook-ing*, discriminating and incriminating.

Like the two mirror-reversed apartments across a small park in the first specter, itself echoed and amplified much later by another, namely the following.

Specter No. 4

The non-aligned, divergently placed street entrances onto Central Park from the latter's west and east sides in Manhattan. A disorienting transformation that was linked to my father's east side world of (hands-off) art museums and art galleries he haunted (the Metropolitan Museum on the eastern edge of the park) and my own (hands-on) west side stuffed-with-children, haunted-with-kids, the every-surface-sticky-with-fingerprints-world of the Museum of Natural History and associated Hayden Planetarium (on the western edge of the park).[13] The paved path between art and science/anthropology a meandering and rarely straight-forward line. Mr. Olmstead knew what he was about; knew what should fittingly be where, his terraforming and *sculpting into being* of the topologies of a certain mid-modernist disciplinarity. No direct or straight pathway from "art" to "science." To walk through the spaces between, through that vast enchantment of a park (no longer a small local square as earlier between two ages of apartment-dwelling) was like a passage through space-time machinery; a Lacanian parallax-machinery for manufacturing morphologies (morphoses) and their anamorphoses. Akin to the parallactic morphology discussed below in *Passage* 9 ("Art, religion, and the parallax of gender"), itself an aftermath and ruin or mowing-over of these specters.

Often the *Passages* staged by this book are things and events unearthed and re-excavated and put into new combinations with things once forgotten but, now conjured, no longer fully absent. And sometimes also there are recurrences of pat-terns emerging over the time it takes to compose these words; things not fully known until the excavation is *underway* – as now *in earnest*. This writing a script itself evoking ghosts both absent as well as non-present, but no less real.

I'll continue with another, and then proceed to gather others, so that eventually there will be a field of such things strewn about, the rocks and boulders in a flowing stream. A constellation or a gathering together of stars, perhaps, whose form is now emerging by hindsight at the far end of a journey projected by foresight. Like Isaac Asimov's fictional planet *Tazenda* (= Star's End), the back-projection from a van-ishing point to what may be visible from there in that far region of interstellar space, where (from "here") the stars (appear to) "end."[14] In short, a story's secret hidden in a stellar anamorphosis.

The latter conjuring up....

Specter No. 5

The palpable feel of a low, soft breeze on a small, skinny body standing petrified a couple of trembling inches from the south bank of the immeasurably wide St. Lawrence River just east of Quebec, toes on the edge of the high, brimming surface of that strong, swollen water, within which – over to the right just a few feet away but untouchable without drowning – lay a few half-submerged slippery stones, around and partly over which the rushing water never stopped. Over and around their individual tenacities (*haeccities*) through the flood. A vow to transcend the mortality of the right bank of the St. Lawrence on whose high left-bank bluffs stood and still stands the towers of Quebec itself, in direct alignment across the river from the line of half-submerged mossy stones being seen by a body on the edge of the right bank.

Evoking. . . .

Specter No. 6

The orientations and alignments of buildings on the Aegean island of Crete *circa* 1500 BCE, where Minoan Bronze Age planners, designers, and builders laid out and constructed immensely complex labyrinthine (a pre-Greek Minoan word) urban structures coordinating solar orientations with landscape alignments so as to fix the sacred civic building correctly in place and in harmony with the Earth and the stars, discovered 18 years after Quebec.[15]

What are strewn about in, as, and for this book's *Passages* and hauntings are stones to step with across what may seem (but only at a distance, that is, "in the abstract") a flat, calm surface. Stones to think with and wrangle with to measure the *distance* between the observations you read above. (How do you wrestle with a water stone?) Like *Proteus and Utoeya*, the two "poles" of a visual "illusion"; a Necker Cube, a Mueller-Lye Illusion and other paradoxical objects. Or as with the juxtaposition of two mirror-reversed apartments' viewing angles: had we been living backwards over there? The revelation of a new world across the square transforming what was back across there into a mummy, alive in and by its achronicity.

Afterwards, of course, we always live/are living backward and forward in the same space. Like those opposite/opposed habitations: old and new home-viewing forest-green metal windowsills, one imminently abandoned; about to be vacated yet still always visible across and over the trees through the rest of early and middle childhood). Stones to emerge from streams to be followed here.

Border-lines between complexity and contingency, as eloquently discussed by Arthur Kroker in his description of/homage to the complex bodies of Donna Haraway:[16]

> the notion that today more than ever, we no longer inhabit, if we ever have, a solitary body of flesh and bone but are ourselves the intersection of a multiplicity of bodies, with life itself as a fluid intersection of humans and

plants and animals and minerals. Of course ... perish the thought that such intersections will inevitably result in romantic naturalism.

My recounting of these very early encounters here (I've just begun: the spirit or ghost of this hauntology "colors" and inhabits *in advance* what is to come) to the (future) accounting emerging like water stones (below) or points in a stellar constellation (above) all appear to entail topological attention to the local differential intricacies of (by hindsight, but not only) certain (and certainly not only *my*) enduring fascinations and recurring engagements that, accumulated and juxtaposed here and now, may project traces of (the artifice of) an erstwhile evolution in sensibility.

Not exactly a diving down after old Proteus, but rather a deep diving into *what desynchronizes time itself.* That sequestered sibling of jarred inhabiting just encountered. Which some may have called art or artistry, or artifice (which I won't collapse together just yet, but will keep at bay, that is, in tense abeyance(s)). What has been strewn together above and held so far in tense abeyance is the (uncanny) problem of time, toward which I must now (parenthetically and not so incidentally) pass.

Notes

1 Tom Conley, in the Afterword to de Certeau's *Culture in the Plural*, introduced by Luce Girard and translated and with an Afterword by Tom Conley (Minneapolis and London: University of Minnesota Press, 1997) (*La culture au pluriel* [Paris: Seuil, 1994]), p. 156.

2 There is an interesting contrast in naming such academic departments between the United States and United Kingdom: in the former, these are called departments of art history, while in the United Kingdom they are called "departments(s) of history of art," omitting the definite article, almost as if the phrase were a Germanic compound noun. An *As If* that bears reckoning with.

3 The Slade talks, staged in the auditorium in the Museum of Natural History (where Darwin debated a religious notable about evolution in 1860), by tradition were given without a discussion period afterward. A situation frustrating to those (both speakers and audiences) used to having discussion annexed or added to lectures. In my case, audience members and especially postgraduate students lobbied the program to add on a special discussion workshop after the end of the lecture series. Prior to that, the discussion that followed Slade lectures took place elsewhere, at a nearby pub, with those few who knew which one, where it was, and didn't mind the noise.

4 Or the *haeccity* of art, cf. Duns Scotus on this Aristotelian distinction between the essential quality of, e.g., dogs in general (quiddity) and the particular qualities of a specific canine creature named Abby. Scotus, *Ordinatio* II, d. 3, p. 1. q. 2, n. 48 7:412–413; Paul Vincent Spade, *Five Texts on the Mediaeval Problem of Individuation: Porphyry, Boethius, Abelard, Duns Scotus, Ockham* (Indianapolis, IN: Hackett, 1994), p. 9.

5 Jacques Derrida, *Archive Fever: A Freudian Impression*, trans. Eric Prenowitz. (Chicago, IL: University of Chicago Press, 1996) (*Mal D'archive: une impression freudienne* [Paris: Editions Galilee, 1995]). The text was originally presented at a lecture on June 5, 1994 in London, which was followed by a visit by those of us present to the Freud Museum in North London. See also Derrida's *Specters of Marx: The State of the Debt, the Work of Mourning, & the New International*, trans. Peggy Kamuf, with an Introduction by Bernd Magnus and Stephen Cullenberg (New York and London: Routledge, 1994) (*Spectres de Marx* [Paris: Editions Galilee, 1993]), esp. ch. 5, "Apparition of the Inapparent: The Phenomenological 'Conjuring Trick'," pp. 125–176.

6 Derrida, *Archive Fever*, p. 161:

> To haunt does not mean to be present, and it is necessary to introduce haunting into the very construction of a concept. Of every concept, beginning with the concepts of being and time. That is what we would be calling a hauntology. Ontology opposes it only in a moment of exorcism. Ontology is a conjuration.

7 The term *worm-hole* derives from the 1960s US science-fiction television series *Star Trek*'s solution to bypassing the immense distances between planets and star systems; a *desynchronization* of (Euclidean) space-time. *In theory*, stellar or cosmic worm-holes allowed passage in both directions, both forward into "the future" and back into "the past" as well as "simultaneously" in different stellar coordinates. A desynchronization of both time and space, of space-time. A spectral machinery.

8 Not yet being "in" school meant for my generation of New York City kids being intensely "schooled" by parents in reading and writing and the like in preparation for formal grammar school if not for the postgraduate and professional education assumed to be one of our generation's eventual goals. A now virtually vanished world since the onset of the class war begun in earnest under US president Ronald Reagan: How does one properly mourn/reverse the (obviously manufactured) evaporation of a civil polity? A time when being "schooled" at home was a foretaste of community school rather than recently, where in North America "home schooling" is a code word for protecting one's kids from encountering kids of other colors, classes, and different (non-fundamentalist) religiosities by teaching them using "textbook" materials vetted and manufactured by theocratic institutions and anti-democratic corporations.

9 My left eye when closed reveals the world as more reddish in hue from my right eye, while the right when closed leaves what the left sees as bluer. Even today.

10 ("Now–then"). A few years later an older boy on my floor, about to go off to Harvard College, gave me his copy of a great heavy Latin dictionary (*Andrews' Freund*). A very dangerous present, as may be evident in this book and its often Latinate diction. Years later that same boy was to become one of the three authors of the notorious 1973 report on "the crisis in democracy" by the "Trilateral Commission" that diagnosed a crisis in governability of the developed world as a consequence of an "excess of democracy." Or a disobedient world order, to return to what was noted in the *Passages* above. As Jeremy Gilbert noted in a Paris symposium along with Jacques Ranciere on July 13, 2012 "Moving on from the Market Society: Culture (and cultural studies) in a Post-democratic Age," published online as www.opendemocracy.net/ourkingdom/jeremy-gilbert/moving-on-from-market-society-culture-and-cultural-studies-in-post-democratic-age (accessed July 15, 2012):

> the term "neo-liberalism" simply names nothing more or less than the strategy subsequently adopted by capital … to the democratic challenges posed at that moment, and its objectives today must still be understood not only in terms of the facilitation of capital accumulation, but also in terms of the inhibition of the emergence of any form of potent collectivity whatsoever.

What democracy challenged in fact was the fixity and determinacy of signification and also the difficulty of controlling the ways in which any group of people (in a factory, a school, a mall, or a city) would be collectively productive to produce something from which you can easily make a profit.

As discussed throughout this text, the "challenges" ostensified by the indeterminacy and contingencies of signification are interlinked at every level. Undoubtedly the view from *his* (boyhood) window at his end of our fifth-floor corridor was very different than mine. But I suspect that both of his eyes were always true-blue.

11 Evocative of the notorious description by the late Israeli politician Golda Meir of the Palestinian landscape being colonized ("settled") as "a land without people for a people without land." An image of the sandbox with children "discovering" lost Jewish relics can be seen in *Brain*, p. 122 and fig. 34, p. 123.

12 Shakespeare: *Midsummer Night's Dream*, Act 5, scene 1, lines 1844–1847: (Theseus): "And as imagination bodies forth/The forms of things unknown, the poet's pen/Turns them to shapes and give to airy nothing/A local habitation and a name."

13 The latter to be the very space-time coordinates of the onset of a last farewell to pre-adolescence, where, standing in the dark with a crowd of boys and girls one Saturday morning viewing a 360-degree presentation/projection (pre-Imax days) from the famed Zeiss Ikon Projector of all the heavens, all graspable knowledge snapped into perfect clarity: all things in place and thus knowable. A *cosmic decorum*. To be detached and deconstructed and set adrift by adolescence; to be(come) that object of theo-aesthetic desire set in perpetual motion, to be regained archaeologically, art historically, anthropologically, historically, politically.... A veritable Lacanian *objet oetit a*:

> little marks (that are) the things one drops of oneself into the world in order to be a subject forever desiring their irretrievable return ... In "What is a Picture," Lacan (1963–64) asks "If a bird were to paint, would it not be by letting fall its feathers, a snake by casting off its scales, a tree by letting fall its leaves?"
>
> (Parveen Adams, ed., *Art: Sublimation or Symptom?* [New York: The Other Press, 2003], p. 99)

14 Isaac Azimov's 1950s sci-fi trilogy of *Foundation, Foundation and Empire,* and *Second Foundation* (New York: Street & Smith, 1951, 1952, 1953), first read on a Delaware and Hudson Railway train between New York, and up along the western banks of Lake Champlain, and Montreal, and finished in the Chateau Frontenac Hotel in the city of Quebec.

15 Discussed in D. Preziosi, *The Semiotics of the Built Environment* (Bloomington, IN: Indiana University Press, 1979); D. Preziosi, *Architecture, Language, and Meaning* (The Hague and New York: Mouton, 1979); and D. Preziosi, *Minoan Architectural Design: Formation and Signification* (Berlin: Walter de Gruyter, 1983). See also, more recently, D. Preziosi and L. Hitchcock, *Aegean Art and Architecture.* (Oxford: Oxford University Press, 1999).

16 Arthur Kroker, *Body Drift: Butler, Hayles, Haraway* (Minneapolis, MN and London: University of Minnesota Press, 2012), ch. 4, "Hybridities: Donna Haraway and Bodies of Paradox," p. 15: "Haraway privileges the intersection, the knot, the intermediation, not as utopian imaginaries but as ways of deepening her epic story of domination." See also pp. 101–136.

5

PARENTHESIS[1]

Art, time, and the untimely[2]

The *hauntology* of the last few pages was an exercise staged as a necessary cleansing of the historiographic palate or a clearing of the throat before speaking further. The kind of gesture that often comes in advance of and usually immediately prior to composing a new work (but is here and now *in medias res*) and which, inescapably, builds upon acknowledging and paying homage to what is being cleared out/cleansed. Those ghosts encountered above. An *orientation* session and a *mode d'emploi* for the text is being assembled here, incorporating things which are now no longer present/visible except as the shadow or specter of the transformations you're reading here. Insofar as they have a direction they mark a launching which (in connection with the distances marked by the opening *Passages*) will send us not only back much further in time, but outward to other spaces. Heterotopically.

Walking recently (once again) through the British Museum (one seems always in the BM *again* even if visiting for the first time), for in fact we have never really *left behind* the very first museum we ever visited; a semi-permanent hovering *museological specter* (like that *Cloud* where all your digital events and traces are *said* [but by whom exactly: Google, Pentagon Mossad, Microsoft?] to be safely stored for future retrieval) and passing through the Egyptian galleries past a wall-text (or seeing over the shoulders of another visitor, reading in his brochure, or both), words calling attention to the museum's *timeless treasures*.

I was reminded/haunted in my visit by another poem by Wallace Stevens, "The Palm at the End of the Mind." The one that speaks of what is outside of and beyond the reach of human time and mind – that animal otherness whose voice is without human meaning or feeling, and thus also outside of human time itself.[3]

Echoing the eternity or achronicity accorded the Otherness of the non-human world in (to take one example) ancient Egypt. Those gods, like every dung beetle, being thereby *immortal* in being immutably identical and unchanging; appearing *as if* timeless. (So is the idea of god that of a truly one-celled organism, endlessly multiplying itself *ad infinitum*?) That otherness on which one cannot get a hand(le), for the "palm" (ambiguously *hand* or *tree* in the poem) is totally outside the furthest extension of the (immaterial) mind's (material) hand, which is nonetheless also somehow inside that mind; a kind of Lacanian *Real*. A transcendent otherness, out beyond a *gap* whose claim to being is secured by being forever mindful of the difference, the *discordance* (or it will close up in the blink of your eye).

Such otherness or alterity exists as such only through its *palpability to sense*. Like our divine sea-friend deep Proteus. Steven's poem is one articulation of extreme *anachronism*; even anarchy. Is otherness *anachronic* (literally without time) instead of being *achronic* (time-less)? Does exhibiting (or explicating or perhaps even merely viewing) a Poussin or a Velazquez here and now, this year (or, maybe, that Nefertiti over there elsewhere in Berlin, whom you could not photograph in 2012 and perhaps never will) *abuse* their space-time propriety or the *decorum* of their secularity;[4] of "their" historicity – because we, viewing here today, are not "of" their time and place? Anachronism as an *abuse* of time, of history. As a ghost is an abuse of space.

An abuse more generally of what is taken (manufactured) as *natural*, usually defined as part of a duality, juxtaposed to what is *unnatural*. As Heidegger put it,

> Whatever the power and the reach attributed to the word "nature," in the various ages of Western history, each time this word contains an interpretation of being as a whole – even where it seems only to be taken as an antithetical notion. In all these distinctions (natural-supernatural, nature-art, nature-history, nature-mind) nature not only acquires its signification as an oppositional term, but is in fact primary, to the extent that *it is always initially by opposition to nature that the distinctions are made*; consequently, what is distinguished from it receives its determination on the basis of nature.[5]

But isn't history always a story *for* some end or purpose? Is any use abusive if vision or sense is out of joint, skewed, misaligned, improper? But no: it's much more; it's about (a) the distinction between fact and fiction, and (b) *respect*: the fittingness, propriety, and appropriateness of a fabrication. About decorum. Why exactly *should* an (art) object *respect* its time, place, and the contexts of initial construal and usage by "knowing: (signaling, marking) its (time and) place"? What would be a *non*-abusive, proper, decorous, or correct and non-disrespectful use of history and (art) history's time? The politics, economy, and ethics of *chronology*. Chronism and its (his) cronies. It's been quite some time since the fundamentally ideological and political nature of *chronology* in cultural and historical studies has been well marked, and any talk about the potential *abuse* of historical time today seems, well, rather anachronistic, not to speak of being old hat.[6] There is no proper "use" in the abstract (except in ways we'll see later); use is entailed with, twin sibling and shadow puppet of, abuse.

The historical development of the institution and profession of art history and of the academic and critical discourses on artistries more generally in visual (and material) culture studies, has, over the past couple of decades (in our increasingly and explicitly corporatized university environments) articulated itself according to a series of successfully marketed and circumstantially timely and fashionable critical *turns* or even *re-turns*: the time of art history articulated as a meandering, even at times cyclic, temporality; a continual opening up to new frontiers by (perhaps every academic generation or so) turning to some other projection-point/photo-op in the road while opening some window onto something "new," each with a dedicated shelf-life. Again, kicking the conundrum further down the road of marketability. As one recent art journalist put it:

> The avant-garde penchant for rupture was carried over into the rhetoric of critical theory, structuralist, poststructuralist, feminist, queer, and postcolonial, which effectively became its own avant-garde after the artistic one has dissipated, an avant-garde that wanted put paid to metaphysics, humanism patriarchy, and racism. The worm has turned of late: today there is a preoccupation with stories of survival and models of persistence across a range of discourses, especially … in art history. The *grands recits* of modernity might be gone, but there is now a fatigue with the rhetoric of rupture. What this shift portends, intellectually and politically, it is too early [namely, November 2012] to say.[7]

What might be termed the worm-flipping theory of art history. But the worm has been run over and overrun and laid flat out quite some time ago; what the shift has portended was always already there, in plain sight for indisciplinarity at any rate.

Recall the *visual turn* in critical theory and literary studies a couple of decades ago. Or the *after* of that visual turn, for some; even for others voiced as yet another "after the new art history";[8] or the earlier and transparently disingenuous *return to the object* (abandoned in some left-luggage cupboard at LAX or JFK or LHR, perhaps). Waiting for the proper person to claim it, or the afterlife of the returns to somebody's idea of what now constitutes a worthy "object," invariably the same old object in a new frock, and now, of course, seen more clearly or starkly against somebody's no-longer-other-than-white (Necker?) Cube. What could be more expected (*un-anachronistic*) than revving up yet one more epiphenomenal "turn" (even a "turning toward" anachronism) so as to maintain and perpetuate the discipline's self-distraction away from the catastrophic political, social, and economic (un)realities of today's world?

Pay attention, please: The "History of Art" is the *history of capital*. End of story. End of (hi)story(?)

Well, we all really knew that, surely. How, then, to provide a "handle" or "method" for reckoning with the ways in which artworks somehow *transcend* (the fiction; the artifice of) their "own" time and place without moving beyond history altogether? But if time is potentially transcendable, is there consequently no transcendence? Or no history? If, as Gertrude Stein claimed, there is no there there, wasn't there also a *no then then*? How to provide a hand(le) without, to repeat, turning artistry over into the ominous "Dark Side of the Force" of Artifice, namely, religiosity? The (dead) hand(le) of (a)n absent god (but here I anticipate the point[s] of the following *Passage* ["Godless in Copenhagen"] with its trimmer theses, corollaries, and consequences).

But then again, this *is* the point, though by no means the whole *story*, which trails on below, in and out of the Clouds. The only living god is a good-and-dead god, obviously, because only a dead entity could have *real* power (the artistry of transcendence) over the living, precisely because any *living* god would be merely mortal and hence not divine, etc. The invisible god behind the wall has greater power than the one you can see (e.g., Proteus), reverberating with that faintly remembered old *midrash* about praying being a turning toward the wall not so as toward a god behind the wall but in order to remember that the god is not material *at all*. Which (personification, that is, but not only) is what this text is pursuing. Understanding how Proteus is a personification of the chaotic powers of the ocean is half of what we're aiming for and at here, as we compose a trajectory delineated by the swarms of cited hauntings being sited along the way to *the be(ing) continued* of the (more) final *Passages* below.

Moreover: the following is admittedly "anachronistic" (or achronic) in its fielding some re-readings of a series of older critical texts, and (in its insertion of old and often forgotten citations into the body of this new text, including some of my own); its playing with time; its taking to heart Benjamin's proactive, performative anachronism of using pieces of the past to *nudge* and disturb the present terms of (for one thing at least) what appears to be "contemporary" art historical debates about anachronism, all so as to move the discussion on not only historiographically but politically and ethically more effective ways.

The present tense of any text – or any object world – is always already disturbed by its *ghosts*: mine as you can see throughout the book are haunted by permeable boulders deeply and lightly etched and scattered in the landscape with many names[9] and others to be encountered, both by design and toe-stubblingly, in the rest of what follows below – in their wake of what these names awaken. A *congerie* (a conga-line dance, surely) or a heaping up together of specters, set in motion and in dialogue with each other in the ghostly play, the dramaturgy, of the present puzzle-text. Anachronistically, to be sure but no less *present*. But surely being present requires a firm knowledge of one's (proper) place? Are we off the Moebius strip yet?

The past is constituted within the present (Deleuze, on Bergson). A consideration of anachronism (and its implied others such as diachrony, synchrony, and historicism) within the orbits of a discourse on artistry and artifice also evokes the name of Michel de Certeau – for whom, in a remarkable articulation of what he mooted/ostensified *as* (as if) "two strategies of time" and "two spaces of memory" confronting each other in and as; as what (in a certain light) constitutes a certain modernity. Consider this:

> there is an uncanniness about the past that a present occupant has expelled (or thinks it has) in an effort to take its place. The dead haunt the living. The past "bites back"; history is cannibalistic, and memory becomes the arena

of conflict between two contradictory operations: *forgetting*, which is not something passive, a loss, but an action against the past; and *the mnemic trace*, the return of what was forgotten, in other words, an action by a past that is now forced to disguise itself [*in anonymity, like a soldier in formation*]. More generally, any autonomous order is founded on what it eliminates; it produces a residue condemned to be forgotten.... But what was excluded re-infiltrates the place of its origin – now the present's [*neat, tidy, decorous...*] clean place.... It turns the present's feeling of being at home into an illusion, it lurks ... within the walls of the residence, and behind the back of the owner (the ego), or over its objections, it inscribes the law of the other. (Psychoanalysis) Historiography, history-writing, on the other hand, is based on a clean break between the past and the present. It is the product of relations of knowledge and power linking two supposedly distinct domains: *On the one hand*, there is the present (scientific, professional, social) place of work, the technical apparatus of inquiry and interpretation, and the operation of describing and/or explaining; *on the other hand*, there are the places (museums, archives, libraries) where the materials forming the object of this research are kept, there are the past systems or events to which these materials give analysis access. There is a boundary line separating the present institution (which fabricates representations) from past or distant regions (which historiographic representations bring into play).... Psychoanalysis recognizes the past *in* the present; history-writing places them one *beside* the other.[10]

Not a few introductions to the disciplining of "art's history"[11] state explicitly or implicitly that their aim is to gain an understanding of *the historicity of art*. But what is history if it can be *told*? *If it can be told, then it's always a fable*: fabulous; a fiction; another of those fictions of factual representation, which, being a (re)presentation, must perchance be (un)true to the presumed original; the fiction of the origin, the *archontic*, as Derrida once put it.[12] So to develop methodological tools that give a handle on the ways in which artworks somehow *transcend their own time and place without moving beyond history altogether*. Or being *over the top*, for the more timorously orthodox. History is metaphorized as a space with fences that can be jumped over by the audacious (or indecorous; those who don't know their place). The motivation for such an exhortation (or extortion) are often quite explicit, siting *crises* in contemporary historical culture, seen by some as the product and effect of a (promiscuous, indecorous) *eclecticism* of postmodern consumer culture and the *multiculturalism* of contemporary globalizing societies. This was Breivik's complaint, his act of religious terrorism *cum* political manifesto articulated/written in the blood of the dozens of young liberal students he murdered. Crises "which make it increasingly difficult to determine which cultural heritage we [sic] are to cherish and preserve."[13]

Which (and whose) heritages are more *worthy* of preserving and cherishing? That/those of (to some) beautiful persons, genders, classes, ethnicities? Preservation of which/of whom would then be capable of "restoring faith" in (a) world, as with that reporter commenting on his reaction to hearing Breivik in the Oslo courtroom? Macintosh in Edinburgh, Marimekko in Helsinki, the Bauhaus in Weimar. Is the heritage of the Parthenon more or less worthily "preserved" in London than *in situ*, at and as the Parthenon in Athens? Preserved *for whom*? "The world at large" as some (even still, as of this writing) might have it, disingenuously and dangerously (we'll consider what precisely might constitute such dangers as we proceed).

If what is most deeply at stake is indeed the "historicity" of art (or *lack* thereof: is historicity fractional?). If we follow the (corporate) money, then we may be compelled to interrogate more closely and contest such exhortations more fully (and in fact more "historically") in the first place. "What time is this place (or art work)?"

But, really: *why should* (or *shouldn't*) "artworks" *transcend* (go beyond, jump over, fly away from, ignore, dispute, erase) time? Does only the British Museum (or other institutions claiming world heritage status)[14] stage timeless masterpieces? If all artworks are (potentially and in point of fact) time*less*, then of course none really are. How did we ever get sucked down into that whirlpool of a conundrum? Shouldn't conundrums be palpable enough to keep in play, to keep available to kick further down the road or at least over into someone else's yard? If art "has" a history or "is historical," it can only be defined and circumscribed by what is ahistorical, transcendent, *outside* historicity. Transcendence as the enabling mechanism for the phantasm/fiction/artifice of art's "history." Immersion in time (chronist artistry) whose *quiddity* (and surely also its *haeccity*) is strongly tethered to a co-existent and co-determined free-wheelingness.

What else could artistry's transcendence possibly mean? Is it like a transgendering? Should artworks, or perhaps artifacts in general, *know their place* in some grand Winckelmannian or Hegelian or *Opus Dei* historicist cosmogony, because any upsett(l)ing of this implied *decorum* might lead to social, cultural, or political catastrophe, or even to *time itself* being chaotic; unhinged; "out of joint"?[15] How indeed does the nature of any such cultural logic resonate with or depart from the "logic" of nature? Who *speaks* for nature and/or nature's author(ity)? Only nature's god? Who (or what) speaks (a lesser god) for culture and art? Who voices the belief in art speaking (to us) *for* itself?

In fact, this increasingly tinsel-plated (manufactured) crisis (worm-turning) in and of the historicity of art – and by implication in art's purported uses, properly or improperly, in elucidating desirable and/or undesirable identities/heritages (social, cultural, ethnic, religious, political, sexual, etc.) – may have been permanently at the core of disciplinary identity and praxis as to be arguably at one with the very mission and brief of art history as such, from before its early modern disciplinary origins in late eighteenth-century Europe. The indisciplinarity of art historical discipline.

If the (proper) historicity of a people's art were not made (decorously) legible, would the nation dissolve? Well, of course it would; it always seems on that edge (unless you *have faith*, a condition with its own edginess, its own precarious ontologies.

That discourse constituted in its historical origins a register and emblem, a marking and an ostensification, an *index*, of the multiple crises of memory and history marking the cultural and social revolutions associated with the flowering of bourgeois modernity two and a half centuries ago.[16] Nothing new there, of course, art and its "histories" was both a product of *and* a complicit producer of the newly disorienting *opacity* of the past manufactured in the wake of the social revolutions ushering in the age of nation-statism and of industrial capital, and its objects and object-worlds of the nineteenth century: that immense world of commodities marking the wealth of societies in which the capitalist mode of production – and its theological phantasms – came to prevail.[17]

This excavation is as much about what has been – and which by and large remains – *amnesiac* in the contemporary discourse on the subjects marked by these terms (again, understanding amnesia not merely as a lapse or a forgetting but as an action performed *against* a subject or a history). So in a very direct way, the book, throughout all of its Passages, is about the *specters* or ghosts haunting not a few contemporary discursive formations. It is therefore less of an historiography of an ontology or ontologies, and more of a *continuing hauntology*, standing anamorphically athwart a variety of conventional practices, theories, methodologies and epistemologies. At the same time that the book outlines a series of issues and problems and suggests certain technical resolutions (see the next chapter) – and without instantiating dangerously naïve "oppositions between" theory and practice – it also looks toward the implications of those resolutions for contemporary social practice. Indeed, what is more widely at stake in the disputes referred to above are some of the most fundamental beliefs regarding the ways in which our notions of self, subject, community, and what is commonly set apart as their object worlds in the broadest sense are *made credible*. Below, we frame and stage these questions from the perspective of the enchantments and disenchantments of not only our credulities but our incredulities and skepticisms; our beliefs and disbeliefs. Accordingly, it proceeds *askew* and apart from where a conventional historical or historiographic inquiry might be expected to start.

And it does so in a manner that takes the relationships between the scholarly and the personal as invariably inherently *porous*[18] – indeed the ghosts that haunt this text trouble and problematize conventionally *buffered* linkages between academic and biographical investigation and excavation. Along the trajectories that are staged and followed below, it will be seen that conventional or canonical distinctions between being and becoming are put in parentheses or taken as palimpsests whereby current observations or discussions are superimposed on previous matter partly erased historically (individually or conventionally), requiring some degree of stereoscopy to be rendered legible. In addition, such palimpsested renderings are not necessarily made legible univocally, but as diverse voices that do not necessarily sing harmonically. In this regard, the text is also mythomorphic – reiterating in its form the configuration and topology of what it speaks of.

Much of what continues in this book are accounts of passages both backwards and forwards in time, in relation to what is presented to the reader as the here and now of the writing that you are reading. I am working *backward* through an interlinear on some existing texts, and *forward* stereoscopically through what will have resembled a palimpsest. The consequences of that activity are what will be portrayed as its conclusions or Resolutions – which, like all such, are invitations for further dialogue. The parts or *Passages* making up the book do not necessarily resemble progressive chapters, like a unidirectional turf maze or teleology, but rather may be compared to layers of cards in a deck which are subject to being shuffled with varying outcomes depending upon how they are dealt and dealt with by the reader. I have tried to delineate as clearly as I can the complex multidimensional and multimodal space or topology of the figure being made by this book, a figure known at first glance by its boundaries. I'll talk more about that as the text progresses and the figure clarifies through its growth on these pages.

The book is (so far) more Borgesian or Calvinoesque than rectilinear or euclidean. So I'm compelled to write here (and you are invited to read) stereoscopically, as has been said of Proust,[19] and moreover in two dimensions: together with the echoes of streams of conversations extending over many years in many places, *and* together with specters from many excavated pasts which you may or may not wish to envision as stepping stones on the way to where this text-to-come is for me (and may yet be for you) in the here and now (there and then). But *what is*/shall be that *here-and-now?*

Proust's novel employed three metaphorical devices to interrupt, halt, and deconstruct/dismember the singularity and fixity of perception: *cinematography, montage, and stereoscopy.* These latter resist and arrest the continuous "flow" of time, allowing for multi-ocular framings of history and thence the reconstitution of history for purposes other than might be assumed in framing time as unidirectional and always already fixed and *on track.* A prospect not unreminiscent of Walter Benjamin's politico-epistemological project of transforming purported fixities of representation – something discussed on more than one occasion in various parts of the text below.

It may well be these two different but imbricated things: *first,* a laying-bare of what has been there all along (as sometimes said of Kant with respect to philosophy as [self-]critique), and a *second* thing which is (also to be) revealed as "there" all along – namely that which this book takes as close to the core of its subject-matter: precisely a very ancient but no less enduringly perennial particular misreading, mishearing, or *(mis)translation.*

You've not misread that; if you're wondering how any subject-matter can be expressed by (or as) a misreading or mistranslation, consider the foundation or the founding gesture of modern disciplinary formations such as "art history," which (as I've argued at length elsewhere) rests upon a *denial of the impossibility of representation.*[20] A repression necessary to the establishment and maintenance of the modern nation-state and its civility; a civility itself grounded in its re-presentability. Not to mention metaphysics and religiosity themselves – but this is merely (to anticipate/recollect) a certain necessary *grammatology 101.*[21]

Derrida called the necessity of there being "a transcendental signified for the difference between signifier and signified to be somewhere absolute and irreducible,"[22] a subject explored at length here. The point, reiterated on occasion, is that leaving *distinct and in place* the signifier–signified opposition leaves open the possibility, or indeed even the likelihood, of conceiving the "idea" as having an existence (and history or teleology) of its own, *independent* of its expression, embodiment, or representation. The material–immaterial dyadic hypothesis: the *trap* of representation. This book is devoted to the investigation of the effects and implications of this enduring metaphysical *gesture* (a word not used lightly). It is necessary in order to proceed here to contend with a number of ghosts haunting this discourse on the problematic of art-and-religion.

To reiterate: What this text is concerned with is (will continue to be) investigating what the implications of an original mis-"translation" has *itself* ostensified and resulted *in and as* our modernities. That convenient and very serviceable fiction that art, artistry, or artifice genuinely *re*-presents, re-*presences* (what are staged as and given to be seen as) individuals, communities, nations, ethnicities, times, and places; *grounding* the identity/-ies of each of these. That is, providing these fictional artifacts with functionally plausible facticities. The facticities of cogent social fictions. Which is precisely where the *amnesia* of the book's title comes in.

To put this in a certain nutshell (by in effect taking the nut *out* of its shell): it could be said that what this book is *about* – in both senses of that term, what it deals with and circulates around like a Foucault's Pendulum (its core conundrum, phenomenon or historical and epistemological event) is the oscillation and slippage between the Hebrew "name of God" and certain post-Judaic construals of that "name." If something as local as a mere modern disciplinary formation were grounded in a denial, why not religiosities and theisms themselves? I'm recalling a particular voicing of that "name" in the 1956 Cecil B. De Mille Hollywood film *Exodus* (infamous, for not a few today, for seeming to glorify/romanticize the Jewish colonization of Palestine as if the latter were a *terra nullius*, a land without people crying out for a people without land) where from a burning bush in front of Moses (played by Charlton Heston), came the booming Voice of their tribal god declaring *I Am That I Am*. A mistranslation of the Hebrew *'ehyeh 'asher 'ehyeh*, more correctly *I will be what I will be*.[23]

(The) god's declaration is that *I will be what I will be (am) becoming*. Hence the reticence about the voicing of that name, a name which should not be revealed *prematurely*. The conundrum of messianicity, a subject of concern for Benjamin and not a few others being encountered in what follows here below. So what is the difference? In short (we'll open that envelope below) the (mis)translation also marks a semiotic oscillation between *equation* (X is [literally] Y) and *adequation* (X approximates but is not necessarily *or not yet* equal to Y). In this case, a (messianic) *deferral* of an arrival, one that shall have been marked by the voicing of the *exact* Name which is to be revealed. My name is the becoming, the imperfect tense, the yet to be completed (if ever?) voicing of a (Platonic, etc.) *ti esti* – a what *is*. (The) god is perennially becoming, only (if ever) fixed and grounded by a (real) name, which is

FIGURE 5.1 Foucault pendulum, Pantheon, Paris/Pendule de Foucault du Panthéon de Paris. 2008. © Arnaud 25/ Wikimedia Commons.

the mark of time ended and completed (but I anticipate). A cosmic theo-aestheticism that maps what shall have been for what it was in the process of becoming. An identity existing in what is to come, and a question of a responsibility to what is to come.

All of which (not so parenthetically) is *homologous* to the distinction – also in space-time – between the painful mortality of things (*lacrimae rerum*) and their transcendent perfection (in divine cosmic time), as argued by the previous pope, Benedict XVI, as noted elsewhere.

As with the archive of the hauntology laid out and staged in *Passage* 4: "If we want to know what it will have meant, we will only know it in times to come."[24]

And what would happen if that name were uttered *before its time*? Would the world end? Isn't all this merely the playing out of a fictive *cosmological spatio-temporal decorum*? The core of what constitutes what this book is about concerns that "slippage"; that "mis"-translation; that oscillation or alternation – between a *religiosity* which is the instantiation of a literality; a literalist or fundamentalist equation; and the adequation that constitutes *artistry*, artifice, and art. But in order to do this, we/ you must proceed/will have proceeded not only with care, but stereoscopically, bearing in mind and baring such ghosts as may appear in what is composed by and as this text. One that deals with and confronts amnesia as the in-between of what we (still) do *distinguish* (etymologically, to *prick or pry apart*) as the fascinating dyadic artifice of *art* and *religion* that b(l)inds us.

While at the same time being amnesiac about the art, artistry, and artifice of the *and*. Which necessitates that we juxtapose an abrupt change in voice, *right here and now*.

[Close parentheses]

Notes

1 Parenthesis <*parentithenai*: "to put-in-beside": literally to *side-bar-within*.
2 An earlier version of several parts of this *Passage* appeared under the same title in *Taidehistoriallisia Tutkimuksia/Konsthistoriska Studier/Studies in Art History* 44: *Tiedeidenvalisyys ja rajanynylitykset taidehistorissa Annika Waernebergin juhlakirja* (Helsinki: Society for Art History in Finland, 2012), pp. 23–34. The publication was in honor of the career of distinguished Finnish art historian Annika Waernerberg.
3 Wallace Stevens, "The Palm at the End of the Mind," in *The Palm at the End of the Mind: Selected Poems of Wallace Stevens*, ed. Holly Stevens (New York: Random House, 1972), p. 398. See also Simon Critchley, *Things Merely Are: Philosophy in the Poetry of Wallace Stevens* (London and New York: Routledge, 2005), pp. 73–75. See also in this connection Giorgio Agamben's *The Open: Man and Animal*, trans. Kevin Attelensl (Stanford, CA: Stanford University Press, 2004 [*L'aperto: L'uomo e l'animale*, 2002]), esp. pp. 57–62, regarding Heidegger. On the (seemingly absolute) otherness of objects and things, see also *Passage* 10.
4 "Secularity" in the literal and etymological sense of the *sequential*, of what is subject to time's passage (*saecula saeculorum*).
5 Martin Heidegger, "Ce qu'est et comment se determine la physis," in *Questions* II (Paris: Gallimard, "Classiques de la Philosophie," 1968), p. 180 (my emphases). In commenting on this passage, Clement Rosset notes that "Hence the ideological complexity of the idea of nature: incapable of rendering itself, it furnishes a necessary and effective touchstone for all the metaphysical themes whose recognition depends in the recognition of an underlying nature." Clement Rosset, "The Naturalist Mirage" in *From # 1* (Rotterdam: Witte de With Centre for Contemporary Art, 1999), pp. 101ff.
6 To wit: Alexander Nagel, *Medieval Modern: Art Out of Time* (New York: Thames & Hudson, 2012), or the earlier *Anachronic Renaissance* by Nagel and Christopher Wood (Cambridge, MA: MIT Press, 2010), or the even earlier (and surely rather more theoretically canny) Mieke Bal, *Quoting Caravaggio: Contemporary Art, Preposterous History* (Chicago, IL: University of Chicago Press, 1999). No less obtuse were reviews of some of these volumes (notoriously, Hal Foster's "Preposterous Timing," *London Review of Books*, November 8, 2012, pp. 12–14), which characteristically reduce both anachronism and chronology to essentially formal, "stylistic" issues. Less attended to have been appreciations of chronology itself as both relational in nature, and marking the demonstration and staging of an ideological position *vis-à-vis* variant conceptions of staging temporality (teleology; time-less-ness, etc.). The very artifice of art historicism.
7 Foster, op. cit., p. 14. Those *grands recits* are, of course, in fact living (lurking) still or there would be no grounds for claiming their departure. Lurking in the silhouette of their absence.
8 The title and subject of a symposium held at the University of Birmingham, UK, March 26–27, 2012, organized by Matthew Rampley and featuring Grieslda Pollack, Claire Farago, Ian Verstegen, and Whitney Davis, displaying a general aura of skepticism about what might be "after" the "new" art history, as reflected in and by the remarks of speakers, moderators, and (from where I was seated, the unsurprisingly disgruntled) audience. *Plus ca change.*
9 Agamben, Benjamin, Marx, Weber, Derrida, de Certeau, Bourdieu, Jameson, Badiou, Laclau, Armstrong, Nancy, Farago, West, Adorno, Summers, Emerling, Hadjinikolau,

Arthur Evans (yes), Guattari, Barthes, Terdiman, Butler, Zizek, Ranciere, White, Levinas, Lacan, Humpty-Dumpty. . . .

10 This is a slightly modified text of Michel de Certeau's "Psychoanalysis and Its History," pp. 3–4 (my emphases).

11 In the United States, academic departments are usually called "art history departments" or "departments of art history," while in the United Kingdom, one finds departments of "history-of-art" usually without the definite article, as if the *subject* in question were actually a German compound noun.

12 Jacques Derrida, *Archive Fever: A Freudian Impression*, trans. Eric Prenowitz (Chicago, IL: University of Chicago Press, 1996) (*Mal d'Archive: une impression freudienne* [Paris: Editions Galilee, 1995]) The text was originally presented at an international colloquium held in London on June 5, 1994, entitled "Memory: The Question of Archives," which, in addition, staged our group's homage-visit to the Freud Museum at/as Freud's old home in North London.

13 As set forth in the prospectus of a 2007 projected (but never published) Dutch anthology on the uses and abuses of anachronism in the history of art. The prospectus failed to suggest any solid reasons why and for whom any such heritages should be "preserved."

14 See the discussions on heritage and public trust and corporatization in James Cuno, ed., *Whose Muse? Art Museums and the Public Trust* (Princeton, NJ: Princeton University Press, 2004), a collection of essays by current and recent directors of major Anglo-American museum institutions and foundations (most of whom have been in the same or similar or even each other's managerial position in each other's institutions in recent years: a globally drifting international super-managerial (white male, of course) shuffling-of-the-deck directorial class.

15 For earlier discussions of these issues, see *RAH*, pp. 156–179; and also Richard Terdiman, *Present/Past: Modernity and the Memory Crisis* (Ithaca, NY: Cornell University. Press, 1993); Jacques Derrida, *Specters of Marx: The State of the Debt, the Work of Mourning, and the New International*, trans. Peggy Kamuf (New York and London: Routledge, 1994), esp. pp. 95–124; Gregory Dale Adamson, *Philosophy in the Age of Science and Capital* (London: Continuum, 2002), pp. 35–154. See also Ernesto Laclau, "The Time is Out of Joint," *Diacritics*, Vol. 25, No. 2, 1995, pp. 86–96, for an important critique of Derrida's *Specters of Marx*. Compare that with Teresa Brennan, "Why the Time Is Out of Joint: Marx's Political Economy without the Subject," in R.L. Rutsky and Bradley Macdonald, *Strategies for Theory: From Marx to Madonna* (Albany, NY: SUNY Press, 2003), pp. 23–38, and, in the same volume, Samuel Weber, "Piece Work," pp. 3–22.

16 This suggestion arises from a rereading of Terdiman's 1993 book on the memory crises of early post-revolutionary Europe, which he links to the rise of capitalism. See previous note.

17 As mentioned by Karl Marx in the opening sentence of *Capital* (1867), quoting his own phrase in his 1859 *Zur Kritik der Politischer Oekonomie*, p. 3. See also *Passage 4*.

18 On this issue, see again Karl Smith, "From dividual and individual selves to porous subjects," *The Australian Journal of Anthropology* (*TAJA*), Vol. 23, 2012, pp. 50–64. Smith outlines a critique of the work of Charles Taylor, in particular the latter's *A Secular Age* (Cambridge, MA: Harvard University Press, 2007), and his earlier *Sources of the Self: The Making of the Modern Identity* (Cambridge: Cambridge University Press, 1989). We will have occasion to address these and related studies in the chapters below. Smith aims in this essay to "resolve a terminological confusion whereby individual stands for the singular human being [which] has also come to stand for a particular ideological (mis) conception better understood as individual*ism* or individual*istic*" (pp. 60–61). Smith goes on to say that "becoming a buffered self is invariably an acquired condition."

19 Notably by Roger Shattuck in *Proust's Binoculars: A Study of Memory, Time and Recognition in La Recherche du Temps Perdue* (Princeton, NJ: Princeton University Press, 1983), esp. ch. 3, "Stereo-optics of time," pp. 40ff.

20 See *Brain*, 2003, esp. ch. 1, "Haunted by Things," pp. 1–14, and ch. 3, "Holy Terrors and Teleologies," pp. 29–43.

21 Jacques Derrida, *Of Grammatology*, trans. and with an Introduction by Gayatri Chakravorty Spivak (Baltimore, MD: Johns Hopkins University Press, 1976) (*de la Grammatolologie* [Paris: Editions de Minuit, 1967]). The *first haunt* below is another text written several years ago and published in the 2007 anthology *Making Art History*, and called "Unmaking Art History." That text in turn is haunted by and is a refraction of an earlier lecture sponsored by the European Science Foundation for a symposium at the Edinburgh College of Art in March 2003, called *Conceptualising the Discipline*. Much of the thrust of the latter (which was also called "Conceptualizing the Discipline") is recuperated here.

22 Jacques Derrida "'Semiology and Grammatology,' An Interview with Julia Kristeva," republished in Jacques Derrida, *Positions*, trans. Alan Bass, Chicago, IL: University of Chicago Press, 1981, pp. 19–20. First published *in Information sur les sciences sociales* Vol. 7, 1968.

23 Verb tenses in ancient Hebrew referred primarily to perfective and imperfective aspect, distinguished later as past and future in time, so that completed action could indicate completion in the past, present or future.

24 Derrida, *Archive Fever*, p. 36.

6

GODLESS IN COPENHAGEN

Theses, corollaries, consequences

Lost in the labyrinths of recent debate about the global "resurgence" of (or the "return" to) religion in contemporary life – addressed periodically in the first three *Passages* – have been the essential roles and functions of art and artifice in the fabrication, fostering, and dissemination of religiosities and the politics claimed by some to espouse. The following considers some of the fundamental relationships between what are conventionally distinguished as *art* and *religion*, distilled into a series of theses and corollaries and consequences. *Focusing* upon their structural and semiological processes, functions, and effects, it argues for the inextricability of artistry and religiosity; their mutual entailment as obversely codependent perspectives on the nature and social functions of representation. In particular, it addresses the conundrums endemic to theist religiosities regarding the nature, social functions, and dangers of representation. Such questions are themselves of very great antiquity in the Western intellectual tradition, problematizing claims that the current simultaneous resurgence *and* critique of religion is a recent or modern phenomenon.

The contemporary attention to these questions is necessarily complementary to what religiosities (and artistries) mask, refuse, deny, or repress, namely their own ghosts or hidden and contrary suppositions. In the following, I have tried to highlight very succinctly several of the most pressing dilemmas common to religiosities of various different kinds, and so I've distilled my observations into a few basic *theses*; intended, as theses commonly are, as provocations.[1]

Thesis No. 1

All modes of religiosity may be distinguished by being either ambivalent, amnesiac, or duplicitous with respect to the fabricatedness of their own fabrications; the contingency their own artifice or artistry.

There are a number of implications or *corollaries* that follow from this, chief among them being:

a   *Religiosities are responses to circumstances perceived as prior or pre-existing and thereby determinant; as the products or effects of some condition or experience.*
b   *Religiosities are subsequent to and presuppose artistry or "art"* (religion is an artistic project or aesthetic practice), suggesting further that
c   Artistry and religiosity are either (1) *alternative responses* to some common or determining condition, or (2) *alternative ambivalences or amnesias* with respect to some prior problem or circumstance.

Religiosity and artistry may thus be seen *either* as different points on the same continuum rather than points in different conceptual/ontological spaces, *or* as indeterminate or circumstantial and situational products and effects of each other, or *both*. Some of these corollaries will be examined in some detail as we proceed.

Thesis No. 2 (also concerning the epistemological status of religiosities)

> Religiosities are fundamentally invested in the problematic of representation to the extent that they constitute positions taken with respect to what might be called the rhetoric, syntax, or semiology of signification: the nature of the relationships (structural and ethical) between an object or event and its assumed causes: the nature, so to speak of what it means to "witness."

In the case of most religious traditions, and especially of the various alternative monotheistic religiosities, this has normally entailed the explicit or implicit postulation of an *ontological dualism*, and in particular a posited opposition between what might be termed "materiality" and "immateriality"; between what is perceptually palpable or demonstrable. The positing of a dualistic ontology whereby a "material" or immanent world is contrasted with an "immaterial" or "spiritual" or "transcendent" world is not, however, in monotheist traditions, an opposition between two equal states or modes of being, but is rather marked by a hierarchy of value, whereby one realm – the spiritual or immaterial is (normally unquestionably) taken in all religiosities as transcendent and primary, or even as the origin or cause of the world of materiality. The material world as the *product* and *effect* of transcendent, immaterial forces; forces over and beyond the directly palpable. The "material/immaterial" dualism is, of course, not neutral but is already marked or articulated from the rhetorical perspective of religious faith-systems themselves: a function of religionist categories.

This realm of the immaterial is commonly personified or reified as an immaterial *force, spirit, soul, or divinity*, in which (or in "whom") is invested "transcendent" and usually unlimited, immortal, or permanently enduring or recurring powers or abilities. These latter are often invested with interventional force; with a power to intervene in and affect aspects or properties or qualities in and of the (by this logic, the produced) "material" or secondary world. The artifice or design of a transcendent designer or maker. Conversely, such reified principles or powers are often also understood to be impossibly remote, unapproachable, or even indefinably and totally *other*: the truth of otherness never being exhausted in its expression.[2]

But both conditions or properties of the immaterial principle or "spirit" are co-determined and co-constructed, and in some religious traditions oscillate and alternate: a double-bind of absolute otherness *versus* palpably powerful interventionism. In other words, any concept of an immaterial spirit or god as totally unfathomable otherness is linked and defined by an opposite transparency. Sometimes the god "hears" one's wishes, sometimes it doesn't.

What is traditionally masked in (or by) such ontologies are *both* their hierarchical structure or systematicity *and* their articulation *as a religiosity*: in other words, the very opposition between a "material" and an "immaterial" level of existence is defined *from the position of that which it purports to investigate*. The material/immaterial ontology is a preliminary philosophical hypothesis masquerading as that which it ostensibly seeks to prove. Simply by evoking the "materiality" of the world; that the world is characterized by a property of materiality or of matter, it simultaneously co-produces its ostensible antithesis; the "spiritual" or non- (pre- or post-) material world. To criticize "materialism" is to create and invoke its alleged opposite.

This thesis suggests the following *corollaries*:

a   the material/immaterial opposition is the ground or template or matrix for positing equivalent or complementary properties in *multiple dimensions*: on the level or the scale of the individual, the group, the community, the nation, the species, and so forth; and

b   these scalar transpositions or postulates are disseminated as (metaphorical) equivalences, which commonly specify (are taken to justify) a certain appropriateness; certain proper or fitting human (and other) behaviors which bear with them legal or ethical force or discipline. A cosmological modularity or *decorum*.

To which may be added that the effect of the maintenance of this duality is the possibility of imagining the belief that

i   the "immaterial" has an "independent" existence of its own (a "transcendental signified" exceeding the chain of [material] signs), and thus prior to its "material" antithesis, constituting the essence of (what is reified as) *religiosity*.[3] This semiological or epistemological artifact is the most important and powerful implication of religiosity. But it simultaneously makes possible the imagining of its *antithesis*, namely that:

ii   the "material" has an independent existence of its own, independent of and prior to any imaginary projected "immaterial" antithesis, which constitutes the essence of *artistry* or artifice.

All of which suggests a further conclusion, namely that

i   the maintenance of the duality generates a persistently uncannily "oscillating ontology," whereby "materialism" and "spiritualism" (to use the most common terms) perpetually *contend* for a position of primacy. The entire "contest" between spiritualism and materialism is, in short, a rhetorical artifice (a fairy tale).

In general, then, the maintenance of the materialism/immaterialism dualism – the belief in a realm of spirit or immateriality and its (from certain religious perspectives) lower or "derivative" antithesis, a realm of pure (or mere) matter – or *vice versa – allows for the possibility of each perspective imagining its antithesis.* Each is the ghost perpetually haunting the "body" of the other; the space of its otherness. Each "realm" or mode of being is essentially unstable or fragile, as its essence always contains its "opposite": each opposite, each "elsewhere," being what grounds and makes possible the first ontological realm.

Again, this was precisely the problem addressed 2,500 years ago by one of the most ancient treatises on artifice, Plato's *Ta Politeia* (*The Republic*), which famously (and for some moderns, notoriously) called for the banishment of the mimetic arts from an ideal city-state (*polis*); an issue which also underlies the subsequent ambivalence and/or antipathy of religiosities toward artistry or artifice.[4] Strictures against mimetic artifice, whether in terms of "naturalistic" imagery in some or all civic contexts, such as the portrayal of a reified immaterial force or divinity, or even of that force's proponent, inventor, spokesperson, "saint," or "prophet;" or against the complete visual "representation" (writing) of the name of a reified immaterial force, have been essential (even if ambivalently or inconsistently enforced) features of all monotheistic religiosities.

Perhaps the extraordinary fear – the *terror* endemic to monotheistic religiosities in the face of possible disobedience (with respect to visual/material representation), more often than not leading to ostracism, corporeal punishment, or at times in many ultra-orthodoxies or fundamentalisms, violent death, is a perfectly logical and consistent application of a systemic or structural need to *forestall or prevent even the imagining of difference.* If it were to be admitted that, for example, the structure of a certain social, political, or economic system (the state itself) were an artifact of human artistry (rather than having been "pre-ordained" [from eternity] by a reified immaterial force or divinity or deified ancestors, or by "natural" law), it would allow for the possibility of *thinking otherwise*: of imagining other forms of community, organizations of cities, economic systems or ways of life, even of different forms of human society: different ways, in short, of being "human." This is the essence of Plato's prescriptions for an ideal city-state (*polis*) which in the terms being used here resulted in what can be called a political religiosity – itself a central foundation of Augustine's distinction, many centuries later, between an ideal "City of God" and a "City of Man."

It may be readily imagined that questioning the legitimacy of certain state formations – for example the Jewish colony within occupied Palestine – amounts to questioning a fundamental religious tenet that the colonized land was a "gift" from a tribal divinity (conveniently unavailable for comment or confirmation). As Ranciere argues, commenting on Schiller,[5] Plato's proscription of art simultaneously proscribed (democratic) politics itself. But what Ranciere does not clarify is that this was an *apophatic* negation of the artifice of (kataphatic) affirmation that assumes communion; i.e., that democracy is a *property* of and is *proper to* the political.

What Plato would foreclose, again, is the very imagining of such a possibility — precisely by forming and filling up the world with delight, with art. Mapping the cosmos with a map as large as the cosmos so as to blot out thought of that which is not divine.

In other words, the terror (*theios phobos*) at the heart of many theist religiosities attests to the fundamental *fragility* of instituted and enforced systems of thought (established religions in a strict sense) in the face of possible evidence of alternative realities. If a faith community's members might be exposed to the awareness of the artifice of its religiosity — the possibility of it being not "created" by an immaterial (and thus unassailable) source or force but rather has its origins or sources in ("mortal") human invention — then the possibility also exists that *other* realities, beliefs, social systems, cosmologies, reified immaterial forces (gods), or even ideas of what is "properly" "human," might be imagined with equal cogency. The dreaded result would be the patent "destabilizing" of a given community or social contract, and the loosening of its legal bonds, leading to a vision of chaos.

The reality; the very cohesion — which is to say the (aesthetic) decorum — of an entire universe does indeed hinge for some believers on the size and shape of a scarf or the re-presentation of a sacred image, person, or object. What if the land your people now occupy really wasn't the "gift" of an immaterial divinity but was actually stolen by you or your ancestors from others co-constructed and constituted as other; as alien, sub-human, impure, etc.? While the *fact* of the "Israeli" ground may seem to some to have become the contemporary *locus classicus* of ethnic/aesthetic cleansing, even in its avowedly born-again Nazism it is of course by no means unique today in a wide variety of global contexts, as meticulously documented by Juergensmeyer and others.[6]

This antithesis to fundamentalist religiosity (and politics) is related in part to what was once characterized as a "postmodern condition" — any such "condition" being in fact a *property* of the orthodox system itself in being threatened: its co-produced and co-determined Other, which inhabits the system as its very possibility of existence in the first place.

Religiosity would thus appear *dangerously fragile at every point in its structure or system*, if it can be cosmologically disturbed or troubled if ten centimeters of (usually female) flesh were publically exposed, or if the flesh of an improperly slaughtered animal were served at a dinner table, or if the consequence of enjoying sex outside a legally sanctioned state were for one to be stoned or burned to death, or if the utterance of a disrespectful or even incorrectly pronounced or improperly written word in connection with a sanctified or hallowed person or divinity could instantly incur the wrath of that divinity or prophet or minister, or if avowing allegiance to a different religiosity or "being of" an ethnicity different than that of someone in power could legally expose one to physical violence, imprisonment, or even death.

In fact, what is specifically evoked in such instances of terror is precisely the threat to the propriety or *decorum* of a social or civic order or code of behavior – in other words, the *stylistic consistency and aesthetic harmony and/or homogeneity of an artistic fabrication*. The "truth" of any religion is tethered to the property or projected properties or "style" of "its" expression, embodiment, or artistry. Such ironies are not merely "rhetorical" but are in fact deeply *structural* – which is to say ethical, marking the mutual entailment of aesthetics and ethics; artistry and religiosity; of the "relations between" what are distinguished as subjects and "their" objects.

At base, then, it would appear that the conundrum of the "relations between" "art and religion" hinges upon alternative perspectives on the nature of signification, evoking the fundamental indeterminacy of semiosis: the fact that construction and construal cannot permanently be fixed or coordinated. There will always be an unbridgeable gap between intention and legibility: determinacy existing circumstantially and temporarily within indeterminacy. An "indeterminacy" linked, it would seem, to the survival values of signification. Matters most literally of life and death.

But there is more to this.

Thesis No. 3 (the mutually knotted [chiasmatic] entailment of the critiques)

> An effective critique of religiosity will be linked to an effective critique of art, artistry, or artifice, which in its own right constitutes a perspective or position taken with respect to signification and representation which is ostensibly antithetical to that of religiosity.

Among the principal *corollaries* of this thesis are:

a   Art (in the modernist – Western sense of "fine art") is a secondary *effect* of a position taken with respect to the problem of representation; there is no art as such except as a reified (i.e., sanctified) modernist commodity.

b   Art is not a *what* (a kind of thing) but a *when* (a position taken or a perspective *on* things) whose reification constitutes an idolatry of a certain religious or spiritualist ontology, with *scalar or dimensional consequences* (e.g., the "artist" (genius) as a *metaphor* of a "divine" creator or artificer, and so forth).

c   The modern discourse on (fine) art, which is distributed across a network of deponent discursive practices (art history, art criticism, art theory, aesthetic philosophy, and a variety or related modern disciplines and industries [tourism, heritage, fashion, etc.]) comprises a *secular religiosity* legitimizing a multidimensional coordination of social behaviors in connection with the evolution and maintenance of the modern nation-state. *Art, in short, is the obverse of religiosity in the ostensification of its fabricatedness.* Art permits us to see fiction as fiction; to see the fictiveness or contingency of the world.[7]

The point of these theses or provocations is to open up the discourse and critique of religiosity as essentially connected to and simultaneously an effect and artifact of the perspective on signification and representation (and of an ethics of the relations between subjects and between subjects and objects) of that which it denies – the discourse on and of art, artistry, and artifice. Art and religion are fundamentally *interdependent* upon each other and mutually defining, and the critique of either remains superficial and incomplete apart from or in the absence of a coordination with the critique of the other. But the point is that these are not, strictly speaking, "others," as if these (religion and art) were two autonomous and distinct entities rather than being *facets* and products of a common underlying philosophical problem.

Far from being distinct or opposed domains of knowledge-production or behavior, artistry and religiosity rather constitute *epistemological technologies* which are the products of both different perspectives on and alternative responses to a common, fundamental cognitive problem – the problem of representation (and therefore the topologies of relations between subjects and objects) as such. *Art and religion are variant yet mutually defining and co-determined answers or approaches to the same question of the ethics of the practice of the self,* of how self–other relations are to be coordinated and controlled or disciplined. The relationships between art and religion are not relationships between two random or incidental cultural phenomena; the problem of that relationship is precisely what defines and determines the most fundamental understandings of each.

It is in that relationship – how religions deal with and make possible art and artifice, *and* how artifice simultaneously deals with, produces, and makes possible religiosity in the first place – that the essence of each can be articulated and understood. Note, however, that by saying "each," one already reifies each perspective on signification – which in fact is the more general point: *neither art nor religion exist except as reifications of perspectives or positions taken on a common, more fundamental philosophical ontological phenomenon: the nature of the relationship between entities,* and, ultimately, the question of *otherness in its co-construction and constitution of sameness.*

All of which leads, then, to a fourth thesis (a final provocation).

Thesis No. 4

All the relationships considered in the first three theses constitute alternative ethical positions or implications for individual or collective behavior, as ethics – the practice of ethical relationships – is at base a consciousness of the artifice and contingency of relationships (of any kind) as such: a topology of self-and-other (implying a substantive rethinking of what is meant by ethics). Ethics, in short, as respect for otherness as otherness. Which some might voice (too precipitously) as a theological praxis, for religiosity is at base unethical, or more correctly anti-ethical.

The entailment of ethics and aesthetics (artistry) has had a number of consequences in legitimizing modern disciplines or institutions such as art history, aesthetic philosophy, established religion, and the political economies of modernity, which concern the virtual "superimposition" of objects and subjects wherein the object is seen by a subject through the screen of an erotic fetishization of another subject. The object — and in particular the (modernist) artwork — is invested with erotic agency (every object a potential love-object) and deployed as an object of sublimated erotic desire. Aesthetics (and fine art) are historically entailed with an ethics of what (from the perspective of religiosity) is framed as "idolatry" and "fetishism," a situation where in certain religious traditions, artistry and religiosity are held in uneasy balance, recalling that of an optical illusion, perpetually oscillating between alternative geometries; alternative realities.

A most basic question, then, around which both art and religion revolve, is what an object or entity or phenomenon may be said to be a *witness* to, relative to, subjects — precisely the core of the problems addressed by Plato, and which still determines and generates debates about idolatry, fetishism, and blasphemy today, 2,500 years later. But witnessing does not exist as an abstraction, apart from specific, historically active producers, objects, users or audiences: witnessing is always a complex triangulation of semiotic perspectives.

So we must be very clear about what grounds and makes possible all current religious debates in the first place — their completely simultaneous aesthetic and philosophical presuppositions and beliefs, which were prefigured in the philosophical controversies such as that exemplified in Plato's discussion about what constituted an ideal community or city-state.

In a 1975 essay by Jacques Derrida, entitled "Economimesis," published shortly before his more well-known volume *La Verite en peinture* (*The Truth in Painting*) he noted (as remarked upon earlier in this book) that "[A] divine teleology secures the political economy of the fine arts."

I have in effect been arguing here that Derrida's comment is incomplete and only half the story, and needs to be seen in relation to its complement: that at the same time it is "artistry that secures the political economy of religion." Derrida's remark referred to Kant's perspective on aesthetic practice in his *Critique* as arguing for a (very Platonic) coordination of artistry and religiosity. In observing that even though in dealing with a product of fine art, Kant says "we must become conscious that it is art rather than nature, and yet the purposiveness in its form [what Aristotle would have considered its *entelechy*][8] must seem as free of all constraint of chosen rules as if it were a product of mere nature." (Kant, 1987, 173.)[9]

But recall what was said above at the beginning of this book in reference to Henry David Thoreau about "mereness."

In other words, the artist (as a figure of genius) is imagined as producing in practice a simulacrum or exemplar of "divine" agency; an analogue to the way in which a reified immaterial force (a god) is imagined to design and produce nature itself (the material world as if it were a creation; a work of art(ifice)). A work of what was marketed as "intelligent design" in late twentieth-century American fundament-alist/evangelical Christian religious terminology. Kant's perspective on aesthetics built upon many centuries of elaborations on the proper ways in which artistry and religiosity might serve each other, a debate as old as Plato and Aristotle, not only antedating by centuries the historical invention of post-tribal monotheisms such as Christianity or Islam, but constituting the core *problematic* of each monotheist tradition.

Art for Kant shouldn't simply reproduce or re-present nature; ideally (for Kant is concerned with what constitutes the "fine arts" rather than what we've been concerned with here, namely artistry or artifice as such), art must *produce like* (i.e., in a manner *homologous* to) *nature* (and by implication, like nature's "divine artifi-cer"). The world of artifice is not a "second world" alongside the world in which we live; it is precisely the world in which we really do live. The human world is a world of art: presentation rather than imitation or re-presentation. Derrida's point was that (in Kant) the realm of the aesthetic was naturalized and given point and direction – was purposeful or *entelechal* – insofar as it could be likened to a tran-scendent "divine teleology" or purposiveness.

More generally, then, the modern invention (reification) of what is commonly taken as constituting art – that is, art as a kind of thing (a "what") – is "secured" (socially legitimized) by being imagined as homologous to divine creativity. In such an ideological framework, the "artist" (that other modernist fabrication or inven-tion) is a micro-dimensional projection of a divine persona ("genius," in its most common rhetorical rubric). The artist, the (romantic) idea of the artist-genius, was and is the *device* that pins together artistry and religiosity; the hinge linking aesthet-ics and religion. This resonates with the social and ethical position of artist or art-istry in many cultural traditions; artistry creating and defining the sacred itself, and eliding or erasing the traces of its own artistry; sanctity's dependence upon the erasure of its artistry; its fabricatedness. The finest of the "fine arts" being religiosity itself. The *Praxitelean end* (flip-side) of the equation/adequation chiasma.

In modernity, and especially with Kant and his philosophical tradition, includ-ing that of aesthetic philosophy and its concomitant network of deponent dis-courses and practices (art history, art criticism, etc.) art came to be socially sanctioned (ontotheologically naturalized) through the analogue of the "soul"; the genius, wisdom, and "spirit" of the artist, which (if exercised with a certain pro-priety or decorum, as in sanctioned "religious artistry") might itself "magnify the Lord" – even where it seems to merely magnify its own ego: romanticism as a "secular" religiosity; the entire modernist discourse of the fine arts as a secular theologism; a theology of the political ethics of the self in the service of the modern nation-state.

These very condensed observations sought to highlight the uncannily comparable (if convoluted or chiasmatically reversed) *enchantments* attending the fabrications of both religiosity and artistry – religion *as an art* and art *as a religion*: adequations, pro-jections, or mootings of possible worlds which simultaneously acknowledge and deny their fabricatedness. The preceding constitute a series of openings in an ongoing critical engagement with some very ancient yet enduringly complex questions: problems and conundrums that remain unresolved in many contemporary discussions and debates, long antedating what we understand today as "religion," "art," or "politics."

Notes

1 The following text originated as a keynote address to the international conference "Godless! Modern Criticism of Religion" (*Gødløs! Religionskritik I dag*) at the University of Copenhagen, Denmark, January 29, 2007. That lecture followed upon talks and interviews by the author in Aarhus and Copenhagen in connection with the "Mohammed cartoon" controversy sparked by fundamentalist groups in reaction to the (to be sure, patently racist) caricatures of the Muslim prophet Mohammed in the Danish newspaper *Jyllandsposten* in 2005. In those discussions, I pointed out that the controversy was not reducible either to questions of "blasphemy" or "freedom of expression," but reflected the more fundamental indeterminacies in all monotheist religiosities regarding the proper place of representation itself in civic life, the problem explicitly addressed by Plato in *The Republic*, trans. Paul Shorey (Cambridge, MA: Harvard University Press, 1935) I, pp. 243–245; II, pp. 464–465).

2 See Christos Yannaras, *On the Absence and Unknowability of God: Heidegger and the Areopagite,* 2nd edn., ed. Andrew Louth, trans. Haralambos Ventis (London and New York: T & T International/Continuum, 2005 [1986]). Articulating or *giving form* to that force or principle is commonly taken as idolatrous. Yannaras' central theme is *apophaticism*: the assumption that the truth is never exhausted in its formulation (<apo-phasis, negation). Especially interesting is ch. 7, "Apophatic Knowledge as Erotic Communion," pp. 99ff., clarifying the distinction between *eros* (yearning) and *agape* (love). See also Richard Rorty, "What is Religion's Future After Metaphysics?" in Richard Rorty and Gianni Vattimo, *The Future of Religion,* ed. Santiago Zabala (New York: Columbia University Press, 2005) (*Il futuro dalla Religione. Solidarieta, carita, ironica* [Milano: Garzanti Libri, 2004]). Rorty notes (p. 79) that in Vattimo's "Ethics Without Transcendence" in the Nihilism volume he argues that if churches gave up the attempt to dictate sexual behavior they would lose a lot of their reason for existing, for "what keeps them around is this deep, Freudianly explainable desire for purity, ritual purity." That is, as we argue here, the artifice and artistry of *decorum*.

3 Which recalls the well-known observation by Derrida – reflecting earlier observations by Benveniste, Jakobson, and others – that

> The maintenance of the rigorous distinction ... between the *signans* and the *signatum*, the equation of the *signatum* and the concept, inherently leaves open the possibility of thinking a *concept signified in and of itself,* a concept simply present for thought, independent of a relationship to language, that is, of a relationship to a system of signifiers ... leaving open this possibility ... accedes to the classical exigency of ... a "transcendental signified," which in and of itself, in its essence, would refer to no signifier, would exceed the chain of signs
>
> (Jacques Derrida, "Semiology and Grammatology," an interview with Julia Kriseva, in *Positions,* trans. and annotated Alan Bass [Chicago, IL: University of Chicago Press, 1981], pp. 19–20)

4 Issues not dissimilar to those wrestled with by the Council of Trent (meeting in the South Tyrol city of Trent 1545–63 and the Catholic Reformation over artistic license and the proper manner in which sacred imagery should be made.

5 Jacques Ranciere, *Aesthetics and its Discontents,* trans. Steven Corcoran (London: Polity Press, 2009), pp. 26–27.

6 Mark Jeurgensmeyer, *Terror in the Mind of God: The Global Rise of Religious Violence*, 3rd.
   edn., revised and updated (Berkeley, Los Angeles, CA and London: University of California Press, 2003), based on extensive interviews with perpetrators and victims of religious violence (Christian, Jewish, Muslim, Sikh, Hindu, and Japanese). See esp. ch. 3,
   "Zion Betrayed," pp. 45–60; and Ehud Sprinzak, "Violence and Catastrophe in the
   Theology of Rabbi Meir Kahane: The Ideologization of Mimetic Desire," in Mark Juergensmeyer, ed., *Violence and the Sacred in the Modern World* (London: Frank Cass, 1991),
   pp. 48–70; and Sprinzak, *Ascendance of Israel's Radical Right* (New York: Oxford University Press, 1991), pp. 220–223. See also Yair Kotler, *Heil Kahane* (New York: Adama
   Books, 1986).
7 Simon Critchley, *Things Merely Are: Philosophy in the Poetry of Wallace Stevens* (London
   and New York: Routledge, 2005), pp. 61ff.
8 Greek *entelekheia* – having a *telos* or an end, purpose, or soul *within*.
9 Immanuel Kant, *Critique of Judgment*, trans. Werner S. Pluhar (Indianapolis, IN and
   London: University of Indiana Press, 1987), p. 173.

7

SEMIOSIS AND ITS (DIS)CONTENTS

Two matters

The mess of (the) matter

By way of illustration of the foregoing theses and corollaries, consider the three following images as a compound object with three faces or facets (Figures. 7.1–7.3) and, by looking through three juxtaposed images, foreground the problems (in this case the paradoxes and conundrums) being reckoned with in this excavation. The first two images incorporate brief texts and the force or import of each is essentially tied to these multimodal entities. One deals ostensibly with art, the other with belief. The third concerns a self-conscious use of an artwork in its *hygienic* and exhortatory functions, so as to *remedy or cure* an aberrant belief at a particular time (2010) and place (Western Poland).

The first image is from an advertisement circulating online in late summer 2012 of an exhibition of artists called *In Absentia*, at Art-O-Rama, Marseilles, France, mounted August 31–September 16, 2012. Its online announcement featured this 2011 work by L.G. Williams (Figure 7.1), a parody of a Roy Lichtenstein painting of 1961 entitled "I Can See the Whole Room ... and There's Nobody in It!"[1]

The next is an illuminated double-sided notice board inserted in a brick-framed text facing both ways at the intersection of two streets (Baseline Avenue and 76th Street) at the East Boulder Baptist church, in Boulder, Colorado, on display in 2011.

What exactly is taking place in each image? What is a viewer/passerby – whether a member of the particular religious sect or not – to make of these fabrications?

Let's begin with the second. In this tableau – of a type not uncommon in some parts of the United States[2] – you are specifically exhorted here to *not* trust ("lean on") your *own* knowledge or intelligence ("understanding"). Instead you're being urged to place (lean) that trust (a firm belief in some thing or some *one* not demonstrable by your own senses except by deferring to someone else's presumed knowledge) – on an invisible or absent entity named "The Lord." *Let this* (Baptist Business) *"Lord" do your thinking for you.*

FIGURE 7.1 I Can See The Whole Room! And There's No Art in It!, 2011. Copyright © LG Williams/The Estate of LG Williams™.

Which patently ignores the obvious – that you'd have to use your own mind to "trust" or even profess "faith" in the first place. But if you can't trust your own intelligence, then how could you use it to *en*trust your own understanding to this "Lord" entity? The presumption is that "leaning upon" your own intelligence (by implication imagined in this billboard as existing in its own right, prior to or distinct from its embodiment or expression) would likely result in your *falling over* that abstracted mentality. So it's to your advantage to lean on some *thing* that is presumed/believed/asserted as *being there* in the first place to lean upon, even if you can only <u>*verify*</u> *its being there by* <u>*believing*</u> *(trusting) it's actually there in the first place* (in such a case, demonstration or proof is not merely *in* the pudding: it *is* the pudding itself).

A self-justifying demonstration: the proof of what is believed is supported solely by the act of *avowing* belief; the actual *practice* of *believing*: by the belief itself, in other

FIGURE 7.2 East Boulder Baptist Church sign. Photograph taken by the author.

words. A common exhortation to believe in a phenomenon promoted as real by the authority vested in a human institution designed to promote belief in what cannot be accounted for except by acting/believing what is being promoted: taken "on faith" rather than demonstrable by (your) reason or intelligence or understanding. A trust justified by the authority of those human persons promoting the belief in a superhuman force or strong power, "trust" being an index of strength and power.[3]

A credulity which, as we shall see, is as old as Plato's attempt to justify the artistry, the design and organization, of his ideal or utopian city or community by *denying* its own artistry or constructedness, situating the entrusting authority in belief in its (ideal) naturalness in those individuals holding power – a king or lord or aristocracy surely in itself a *sign* (index, symbol, expression, representation, embodiment, etc.) of divine favor (from Latin *favere*, to show kindness to). Like Blanche Dubois in *A Streetcar Named Desire*, who had to lean or depend upon the kindness of strangers to survive in a cruel world, we too must rely on the favor of the (i.e., *their*) lord. Pragmatically, one should depend or *lean* upon a cadre or class of rulers themselves entrusted with the task of *correctly* interpreting the "will" of the god (or gods); in a cosmos or universe claimed to be *its* (or *their*) divine creation.

The cosmo-spatial or metaphysical metaphor ostensified by the East Boulder Baptist church's public signage is in fact quite *spectral*. The tableau's legibility depends on accepting the juxtaposition and linkage between (what are distinguished in advance as; *asserting* in the place of demonstrating or proving as) distinct or separate or opposed and antithetical ontological domains – the *material* or corporeal or palpable and the *immaterial* or spiritual or ghostly. *Lean* your understanding (staged abstractly as distinct from "its" expression) on an *im*material entity or phenomenon. As a "thing," entity, force, immaterial phenomenon you can *bend toward* as if to some *thing* or some person. An object-lesson in how to practice believing (*mode d'emploi*). A metaphorical topology to be sure.

But, of course, metaphor is never innocent, nor is it ever *dis*interested, invariably *staging* and *orienting* understanding and investigation as well as prefiguring the results of any inquiry.[4]

In addition, our church-business advertisement is an apt illustration of the multifunctionality and multimodality of signifying practices wherein a variety of forms and meanings (intended and unintended) are staged in concert, serving disparate ends for multiple audiences, as well as amplifying and strengthening any message or communication. A single and seemingly one-dimensional artifact or utterance will not uncommonly manifest and evoke multiple functions and orchestrate multiple modalities in projecting signification. Indeed, as we shall also see below, communicative and social praxis is invariably multimodal and multifunctional – a situation rendering the isolation of particular modalities or functions abstract and fictive – not that such abstractions have no real consequences; indeed quite the opposite.

The Baptist tableau is also a classic illustration of the rhetorical device of *syllepsis*, whereby two terms – one "literal" or material (bodily *leaning*) and one "metaphoric" or allusory ("the" [im-material, meta-physical][5] *Lord*), – *precisely in being made syntactically adjacent*, in that juxtaposition, and by that syn-tactility, appear to imply (and causing viewers to infer) causal connectivity. (*Con*)-*nectere*: to bind (together) physically. An allomorph or echo of "religion"; (*re-ligio*; a lashing or re-binding or binding-back-together; constituting a *bond* of obligation; a ligature; [<*ligare*]). As G. Flaxman once put it in relation to the cinema screen, which ostensifies the fantasy or illusion that "Mind and matter *exist on the same plane and consist in the same material*,"[6] exemplifying in another register the irony of the artifice, the artistry or the constructedness of *syllepsis* and the consequences of taking syntactic structure as a literal re-presentation/expression/embodiment *of* (a) truth.

Fostering as real the non-material – material duality or division, in effect, makes it possible to imagine the former (spirit, soul, mentality, intelligence, idea, will, intention, etc.) as ("itself") capable of engendering or producing the latter. The shape of the palpable universe as somehow the *product of* a non-material mentality, will, or "design," is a tactical reversal of the commonplace notion that immaterial fancies are the product of human brains: the sylleptical or (syn)tactical obversal designed to engender and foster believing.

This touches on what is the essential *conundrum* of fundamentalism, as we shall see elsewhere below – no less than that of the religiosity/*secularity* distinction. The local Baptist tableau is by no means an innocent or disinterested fabrication, but an ideological *manifestation* of faith; an object-lesson in *how* to believe (and not merely believing in "a dozen impossible things before breakfast") *and* how to *dis*believe;

believing as essentially a relational praxis, tethered inexorably to its antithesis (denial or *dis*belief); its shadow or penumbra.

The conundrum ostensified here in believing in antithetical things has two co-present facets or valences. (1) First, the necessity to distinguish (as absolutely distinct and separate) ontological domains of materiality and non-materiality. Such an antithesis, however, is not symmetrical, but (in linguistic or semiological terms), asymmetrically *marked*: that is, a distinction between an unmarked state (the material) and a state marked or sited as superior or prior or generative (the immaterial or non-material or "spiritual"). The material as the effect or product or artifact of the spiritual. What this asymmetry also marks is the point of view or positionality of the viewer/enunciator. (2). The second aspect of the conundrum is this: Having established (postulated [as if] real) a distinction and absolute division between "the" material and "the" immaterial, their distinction is inflected by an opposite movement toward assuring that the non-connection between the two is nonetheless breachable, but properly. The two are to be juxtaposed in a fitting manner whereby the nature of the immaterial must be materially accessible – by those with a *sanctioned sylleptic authority* to do so, a conundrum in its own right. What is visible or palpable must be juxtaposed with its proper or sanctioned legibility. If a text is to be justified as the "word" of a god or prophet, care must be taken so as to "read" such words correctly. But the words don't read themselves; they must *be* read; they must elicit a reading. Which of course they do by virtue of manifesting (a) *lack*; the engine of desire.

In other words, it must be a self-justifying system, a perpetual motion machine, whose "guarantee" is in the *exercise* of properly sanctioned authority; a particular voice. In and by the act of *reading authoritatively*. Trust not in your own understanding but lean on "the Lord," etc. By instantiating reliance on higher authority as the key to genuine understanding and the key to avoiding confusion (by thinking by/for oneself), the roadside sign is a small local echo of a widespread political movement (not unique to North America) to stage, channel, constrain, and discipline belief. For example, the recent attempt by one provincial legislature (the bottom state of Texas) to outlaw "critical thinking" in schools because it leads/has led children to disobey those to whom they should properly give (lean) their trust (parents, teachers, or political or religious powers upon whom [it is believed by those holding or desiring power] they must lean or place their trust). (Who knew Plato was a Southern Baptist?)

What underlies all this – and what is reiterated, mirrored, and echoed below in various dimensions – is the problem of the inevitable disconnection between signifier and the signified (noted again recently by Agamben),[7] or, as it is often termed here, the *indeterminacy* at the heart of signification or semiosis. In a sense this is the *burden* of signing; the price to be paid for language as a sign system, a system of communication built upon difference, and this is no less the case than for any other system of signification in any medium or modality. Founded in difference and deferral of fixity or resolution. If you make a distinction between what is expressed and its expression, however voiced (representation, expression, embodiment, etc.), precisely *how* and at whatever level such ligatures "between" them might be staged are inevitably political, moral, ethical, social, and economic matters. There have been many ways in which this conundrum has been engaged with historically, for these are hardly unique to our modernities.

In the case of Western religious traditions, the related artifactual problem of *translation* is central to any understanding of religiosity, as we will see below. In Western Christianity, whose sacred texts (or most of them) were in languages not native to Europe, the problem was and remains acute, but the scale and dimensions of the problem are no less present where the "other" language is one's own in the distant past (ancient Greek to modern; Sanskrit to Hindi, ancient Hebrew or Aramaic to modern spoken variants; the Arabic of seventh-century Saudia to modern spoken Arabic, or to Persian, Turkish, etc.).

One of the central issues of concern here is precisely the orienting of under-standing in diverse and apparently antithetical ways by semiotic practices or epistem-ological technologies conventionally gathered under the (modern, Western) denotations of "religion" and "art," whose very distinction is the product of histor-ical evolutions in semiotic strategies and tactics. Oriented, moreover, toward very particular social ends: the justification of the concept of the European nation-state and its citizen-enablers.

But let's hold all this in abeyance for a while: what of the first image above (Figure 7.1)?

It seems to be ostensibly concerned with "*artistic*" rather than "religious" prac-tice – and its staging of what is visible *and* what is invisible *as* art. Two things are immediately striking about the picture. First, the nature of what is proclaimed as being seen or recognizable *as* "art." Meaning, in the case of what is (presumably) being *not* seen through the peep-hole held open by the finger of the viewer – namely, any (works of) "fine art," that is, artwork as a kind of modern thing or type of marketable product or commodity. Just imagine! There's no art, not a single artwork, in this whole place! There's also no religion to be seen – but just because its not visible doesn't mean (as we'll see) it is not a force with palpable effects.

However, what is stated as *not visible* (to the looker) *as art* is of course the "whole room" (that is, that thing that is devoid of art; that has "*no art*-work(s) in it"): *the room or space itself* as an artifact (artwork/work of artistry) in its own right. The viewer is looking into the space without *seeing* the artifice of the made/built environment; the architecture *in which* no artwork is visible. Undressed or unadorned space; bare or *mere* space; an "empty" room. An artistry or artifice.

The emptiness of the room does *not* call attention in this image to what is visible as an instance of artistry *except ironically* – the presumed *point* of the captioned image of the artist (L.G. Williams). An evacuation of the space of art in favor of the (denied; overlooked) art of space. You can't see the forest for the trees – that is, you can't see the forest because there are only trees (or space) *in* "it," so there must then not be any such *it* visible or palpable. What is called into attention is the indispen-sible role of the spectator in the carpentry of signification.

Several things here recall some of what was noted above about the multimodality and multifunctionality of semiosis or signification. In addition, there is a conundrum

or paradox bearing a similarity to what is avoided in the *conative* or exhortatory artifact of an ecclesiastical *syllepsis*. In both cases, what is being staged is a lack of understanding or a denial of the artistries that underpin what is being proclaimed. *Both
practices are sylleptic, and each in its own way is* zeugmatic – juxtaposing (conventionally) appropriate and inappropriate entities or phenomena.

But where exactly was the "religion" (in)visible in that room, but not, as implied
earlier, any less palpable? To contend with that implication, we need to perambu-
late over to a third image and the intriguing remarks of its patron and sponsor, a
parish priest in the small western Polish town of Swiebodzin, the Reverend Syl-
wester Zawadzki. The object in question is the new (2010) 108-foot statue of
Christ, even taller (with its crown on) than the famous statue of Christ with out-
stretched arms overlooking Rio de Janiero (Figure 7.3).[8]

FIGURE 7.3 Colossal Christ Statue, Swiebodzin, Poland. Photograph taken by the author.

The statue is sited facing the town of Swiebodzin, the alleged hotbed of secularism, and stands very tall as its "remedy" or cure. *"I hope it will become* [its] *remedy,"* the priest Zawadzki says. Rather than a "tourist attraction" – which of course it instantly became, adding to the church's income, simultaneously establishing a venue for pilgrimage and veneration. It may be asked how a statue can *cure* a malady: Is this an instance of what used to be called art therapy? Sympathetic magic? Can any artwork serve therapeutic ends? But explicitly foregrounded as the dominant functionality in the artifact's multifunctional semiosis is its *conative* function here; that aspect of a communication oriented directly at a (potential or actual) addressee or audience. It coexists with the artifact's referential, aesthetic, emotive, phatic, and allusory functions.[9]

So is the power of the cure a property and effect of what are colloquially and loosely called the particular "stylistic" properties of an object? So that, for example, an Apollo *Belvedere* statue might cure (an ancient Hellene) more thoroughly and effectively by contrast to a poorly crafted image of some other deity – our statue of Proteus, for example. Or an image of "lesser" divinity, say Pan.

Hygiene as a religio-aesthetic instrumentality or social functionality. But is this (not to mention the practice of genital mutilation/modification/artistry – see below) a case of art "as" (a) religion, the religiosity or the "spirituality" of or in artistry, or the artistry or artifice of belief and believing? Or all of these, given that we seem to be considering here – however summarily, and in anticipation of later *Passages* that weigh the interrelations of multifunctionality, multidimensionality, and multimodality – the seemingly inescapable *multiplicity* not to speak of the motile *indeterminacies* of signification?

For the moment we need to press this conative exhortation further, and consider what is being said by the reverend Zawadzki. *The* remedy for *"this* secularism" – that is, the local instances of secularity or the material*ism* so poignantly exemplified by the mores of the town of Swiebodzin *toward which the statue is faced*. Should we imagine that citizens of the town, in the midst of shopping for groceries, would be reminded (looking over their shoulders, say) by a gigantic Christ looming above, or momentarily glimpsed crossing a street, that the god (The Lord) is watching them flaunt their (promiscuous) secularity in broad daylight? What kind of remedy is this: just looming/intimidating/guilt-inducing; that is, *mere* (though given the scale a grandiose) *ostensification*.

Curing by *reminding*; reminding the citizen of the lessons learned (or not) in church as children. What would prevent the citizen from deflecting that "remedy" by focusing on the clumsy (or fine) modeling of the huge (and, as we suggest, multifunctional) statue? What appears to be happening is a linking, a juxtaposing, of a material work of artifice with a set or system of values – as *embodied* by another material object – the town of Swiebodzin, whose citizens are allegedly ensnared in a fetid swamp of secularism. Is Fr. Zawadzki not practicing sympathetic magic, holding up an image with the power to smite enemies of (a) truth; enemies (witting or unwitting) of the religious system embodied by a (fetish) object replicating an incarnate(d) divinity as if *to embrace*, and by embracing, in that very symbolic embrace, *cure* the sin(s) of secular materialism?

But: surely this priest is practicing a form of *idolatry* (or even fetishism) in attributing, or seeming to attribute, to this statue an inherent power or force *to* cure that is not unlike the power or force attributed to the Buddhas of Bamiyan by the Taliban who dynamited those gigantic stone images because they were "idols" fostering idolatry, yet of course (as noted before) in doing so revealing *themselves* as idolaters, projecting power and force into the objects.

It should also be noted in passing that this artistic remedy, this life-like (however gigantic) image is "realistic." It closely appears to resemble Christ (that is, it conforms to a certain style in Western religious image-making of a Christ-type). It is crafted according to the protocols of Western "optical realism," which itself is *a visual instantiation of the metaphysical illusion of the transparency of language*. The rise of optical "naturalism" in art enlivened and promoted during the Catholic Reformation (and marking a historical confluence of a series of aesthetic, social, and epistemological developments) to foster and strengthen belief by making palpably and stunningly real the lessons of the Christian religion, was the basis of what was to become naturalistic artistry. The latter as the *afterlife* of religious practice, an allomorph of secularity – an allomorph of theomorphism ... as religiosity's afterlife in (Western) modernity. Throughout the history of Western Christianity there were numerous instances of the use of "realistic" imagery to cure, convert, proselytize, convert, or strengthen in their faith individuals, communities, states, or whole peoples.

The misery of matter, or the perfidy of the palpable

There is no material, no materiality, without art. Nor any "cultural materialism" of any stripe. Artifice, artistry, is the core of what is construed as materiality or materialism.

In the summer of 2010 in Paris the Centre Pompidou held an exhibition called *The Promises of the Past*. It was a poignant and rather haunting look at some of the avant-garde artwork made in a variety of media in post-war Eastern Europe before the fall of the Berlin Wall in 1989. The works on display were examples of the ways in which art flourished as an oppositional or subversive activity in several Eastern European countries. The wall text near the entrance consisted solely of the phrase "the idea of art is to change and improve the world" – a simply stated *manifesto* about the function or idea of art being to change the world for the better. But at the same time, of course, it also implies the opposite: that art *may* also change the world for the *worse*. In addition, isn't it the case that if artistry is at base a valence of palpability, isn't it the case that the idea of the material is to change and/or maintain the world for both better or worse?

Yet the assumption common to either declaration is an understanding that however defined, art was an intervention, inflection, or intrusion into social or civic space that affected existing perceptions and social habits precisely by its *being there* in that world. Its very being manifesting or ostensifying something about that world. I use the term *ostensify* very deliberately in contrast to the word *signify*, for very particular reasons which I'll try to clarify later. What we call works of art don't signify in the conventional sense of the term.

The mid-twentieth century American poet Archibald MacLeish, in a poem called *Ars Poetica*, put it this way: "A poem should be palpable and mute as a globed fruit." It then sets out ways to imagine what a poem should be: "dumb as old medallions to the thumb; Wordless as the flight of birds; motionless in time as the moon climbs; equal to: not true," ending with "*A poem should not mean / But be.*"

But can *art* not mean but simply and *merely* be? Art as non-representing?

There are two major themes here: the *historicity of artifacts* and their *modes of signification*: how they don't only mean but *are*. And I will try to clarify how the oscillations between avowals and disavowals of meaning constitute the essential connections and distinctions between what we call art and religion.

First, the question of historicity is related to what I'm going to call the *funicity* of artifacts, adopting a term originally coined by MIT materials scientist Cyril Stanley Smith[10] after an old story by Jose Luis Borges entitled *Funes the Memorious*, about a man who was unable to forget anything. Funicity is an inbuilt quality of materials that permanently "remember" their original time and place of creation, so that, for example, any piece of rock bears traces of its original geomagnetic orientation. The art historical practice called connoisseurship – itself a mode of *geomancy* in its own right – entailed the ability of an investigator to identify the locus in time, place, and personality of the *facture* of an artwork, enabling the adept practitioner to situate its historicity and by extension its calibrated stylistic identity – style itself being a mode of relationship among entities.

Such an ability was practiced to great commercial success by art historians such as Bernard Berenson, who in the first decade of the twentieth century claimed that the "truth" of the personality of an artist was directly and fully "palpable & ergo legible" in the material of an artwork without appeal to other evidence. Of course, Berenson was writing in the midst of swirling controversies stirred up by Freud and others who were endeavoring to demonstrate that the "truth" of a personality was never fully legible in what was palpable about a person but only existed in its deferred or delayed or indirect and hence ultimately indeterminate articulation. I'll return to this in *Passage* 9.

The most fundamental belief within the history, theory, criticism, and museology of art is that art "has" a history; that an art object (however defined) is believed to manifest or ostensify its position in space and time – its funicity – and has thereby an assignable "address" in the unfolding historical narratives of individual biography, or of the social fictions of ethnicity, nationality, class, gender, or race. And the most basic art historical task has always been to render the visible *legible* – readable, that is, in the language or vocabulary of historical development itself, of historicism.

The second problem needing attention is one that contemporary art history, theory, and criticism have been less successful in reckoning with, particularly if art is considered a "secular" modernist practice. This concerns the perennial conundrum of art itself as a theological praxis built around avowals and disavowals of signification. This is a complex and not easily articulated phenomenon, but is none-theless fundamental to the very idea of art as it has evolved in the West over the past half-millennium.

As epistemological technologies, histories of art reconfigured time as succession; as narrative deferrals of signification wherein the past is only legible as the preface to eventual resolutions that – existing outside of time – never palpably arrive. Like messiahs, avatars, or democracy. Or they arrive only as *specters*, interrupting specularity by desynchronizing time, as Ernesto Laclau once put it in his aptly titled text *Time is Out of Joint*. What seems to beg for fuller attention in current musings about categories of historical interpretation is the need to address the problem of art itself – by which I mean "art" as *the* central problem or conundrum of contemporary knowledge-production. As phantasmagoria, art is neither exactly "within," "of," "proper to," "out of," "beyond," or "apart from" time, but, as a mode of artifice itself, *art is precisely what which calls attention to the fabricatedness of any form of time-telling* (or social, cultural, and political identity-crafting), therefore occupying a time which is quite literally "out of joint." Art, in short, as the neither-in-nor-out, and the neither-material-nor-immaterial, constitutes the *specter* of modernity.

The ghost is already *built into* the structure of the machine which we imagine it to merely inhabit, and its existing is constitutive of matter which is never mere as such, having, as Deleuze notes, a certain "vagabond" quality, as Bennett also observes.[11] Or a *drifting* identity, as noted above by Kroker.

Expanding upon attention to artifice also sets a groundwork for a reconsideration of the relationships between artistry and religiosity by revealing the latter as practices designed and/or destined to *disremember* the artifice of their own fabrications, instilling often legally binding "faith" in the non-fabricatedness of their own fabrications. The age-old conundrum of any book or monument which hegemonic powers claim is sacred or the true voice or index of an immaterial entity or spirit, compelling obedience. This is not uncommonly a matter of life and death: believe in the reality of what faith reveals, or die. By contrast, art(ifice) – and this is the fundamental distinction between art and religion – is precisely that which gives the lie to fundamentalist literalisms, calling attention to facture and fabrication (of any kind) *as such*. If we forget this radical and terrifying power of art (which hegemonic power works tirelessly to ensure we forget, using the tools of artistry against us – Plato called this the *theios phobos* or divine terror of art) we ensure our own servitude.

I'm speaking here, of course, not of ghosts which are "immaterial": A ghost is an entity that disobeys what are imagined (at a given time and place) to be the laws of physics, but rather of *specters*, which are both material *and* immaterial and reducible to neither, troubling the distinction itself. There is an (un)avoidable uncanniness of art, as well as its modern allomorph, its Siamese twin sibling separated at their joint birth, the *commodity*. (Recall Marx's insight about the uncannily theological/mystical nature of the commodity.) Art's spectral thingness, as the most uncanny human "thing" of all, is inextricably linked umbilically to its (disciplinarily) unknown sibling. Moreover, neither sibling is adequately comprensible without reckoning with its other; without its desire for the other, palpable in its very muteness.

Artifacts commonly persist in myriad ways, some seemingly forever, like the pyramids at Giza, whose sempiternal availability continues to afford countless interactions, construals, and metamorphoses of judgment, sense, and subjectivity. Endless opportunities for being *signified*. Objects of minimal temporal extension and material duration may also be no less sempiternal in their effects and challenges, so that, finally, bracketing anachronism as a problem apart from diachrony as a whole, with all of its variants, makes sense only insofar as it foregrounds the potentially multidimensional *affordances* of any artifact; any fragment of the humanly made or the humanly appropriated environment. The human *Umwelt* is multitemporal in its spatial duration or object (im)permanence. Virtually every humanly used world is a spatio-temporal hybrid of dynamically evolving palimpsests haunting its present and former selves; which *palimpsesting itself* conjures into existence. But then if this is "all hybridity" there is not simply no hybridity but more importantly the hybridity–purity double-bind is itself deeply problematized and must be re-excavated back beneath the foundations of the side chapels of multiculturalism, gender, and postcoloniality within the temple of identity. What I referred to earlier as the temple of entelchy.

In the end, in reckoning with art *in-and-out-of time*, we must reckon with the uncanniness of what art creates, engenders, transforms, *and* problematizes: that "divine terror" (*theios phobos*) induced by artifice itself; by Plato's joint admiration for and fear of that which at the same time fabricates and renders problematic a state's hegemonic realities, not to speak of our own identities.

To imagine that art exists in-or-out-of time is, of course (like any *abstraction*) ideologically driven: an avant-gardist (and thereby at base religionist) phantasm designed to serve (and creatively foster) political ends in compelling belief – for example, in a community's heritage or patrimony, or an individual or community's identity, as if such things materially existed, rather than being the articulation of a (sometimes not-so-secular) theologism that disremembers the origins of its own artistry.

I mentioned earlier that I'd try to clarify what I meant by suggesting that art/artistry doesn't "signify" or *mean* but rather *ostensifies*. There's been an enormous literature spanning the last half-century addressed to the question of how art signi-fies, and I plead guilty to having in the past played a part in adding to that enormity of the "semiology" of art. But the failure to elaborate convincing semiologies of art (architecture is another matter) lay less in its failure but in the misrecognition of its success; a misreading of the significance of art's semiotic character. I've come to reconsider that tradition in a different light more recently, in no small measure by taking up the question of the relations between art and religion.

Looking at the problem of how art signifies from the standpoint of artistry as a facet of artifice more generally in its problematic intertwining with religion has made it apparent that (first) the historical career of art history as an instrument for perpetuating a notion of art as representation or expression was an essentially reli-gious enterprise designed to perpetuate the distinction and juxtaposition of signifier and signified so that the latter might be imagined to exist in its own right, precisely a simulacrum of the problem of the soul in monotheist religiosities.

To put this perhaps more succinctly, art history was an instrument of a meta-physical semiology which is theologically grounded, since its underlying brief is to justify art (or any human artifice) as the material embodiment of immaterial abstract ideas (mentality, ethnicity, spirit, soul, time, style, etc.). Artworks materially *signify* what is purported by the structure of the system itself to signify. But if you focus on the broader picture of artifice as such, what is revealed is that neither art nor religion have an existence apart from their antithetical positions on the nature of signification itself.

This, again, is precisely why the (mimetic) arts had to be prohibited: you cannot predictably control how any artifice will be construed without management. For Plato what was most deeply at stake was what we would term the aesthetic homogeneity of the artifice of the state: its decorum, in fact. But underlying any decorum is the problem of the essential indeterminacy of signification: the permanent gap between construction and construal.

Art history is thus grounded in the conundrum – at once theological and semiological – of decorum. Which is why religions are aesthetic artifacts the contingency of whose fabricatedness must be managed. So Derrida was half-right: If it is the case that a divine teleology secured the political economy of the fine arts, then the obverse is equally cogent – that it has been *aesthetics*, broadly construed, that has always "secured" (or seemingly grounded) the political economy of religiosities or "divine teleologies."

Religiosities (and artistries) are fundamentally invested in the problematic of representation to the extent that they delineate and promote positions taken with respect to the rhetoric, syntax, or semiology of signification: the nature of the relationships (structural and ethical) between an object or event and its assumed cause: the nature, so to speak, of what it is to "witness."

In the most general sense, artistries and religiosities constitute positions taken on putative relations (congruencies, disjunctions, concordances, and homologies, etc.) between objects or entities and individual or collective subjects. In the case of many, if not most, religious traditions, and especially the various alternative mono-theist belief systems, this has normally entailed the "belief in" (i.e., the fabrication of) an *ontological dualism* – a posited opposition between what might be termed *materiality and immateriality*. The positing of a dualistic ontology whereby a "material" world is contrasted with an "immaterial" or "spiritual" and even "transcendent" world is not, however, an opposition between two equal states or modes of being, but is rather marked by a hierarchy of value, whereby one realm – the spiritual or immaterial – is (normally unquestionably) taken as transcendent and primary, or even as the origin or "cause" of the world of materiality (seen or staged as its "effect"). The "material/immaterial" dualism is of course not neutral, but is already articulated from the rhetorical perspective of religious faith systems themselves: a function of religionist categories. As is the opposition between the "religious" and the "secular," the latter being a theological category, referring literally to the succession of ages – temporalities, histories – in contrast to atemporality – the timeless nature of the divine.

Commonly this realm of the immaterial is idolatrously personified or reified as an immaterial force, spirit, soul, or divinity, in which (or in "whom") is invested transcendent and usually unlimited, immortal, or permanently recurring powers or abilities. These latter are often invested with *interventional* force; with a power to intervene in and affect aspects or properties or qualities in and of the produced secondary ("material") world. Conversely, such reified principles or powers are often also understood (even in the same sectarian faith system) to be impossibly remote, unapproachable, or even indefinably and totally *Other*. But both conditions or properties of the immaterial principle or "spirit" are co-determined and co-constructed, and in some religious traditions oscillate and alternate: a double-bind of absolute otherness *versus* transcendently powerful interventionism. In other words, any concept of an immaterial spirit or god as totally unfathomable otherness is linked and defined by an opposite complete transparency. Sometimes the god hears one's wishes, sometimes he, she, it, or they don't, won't, or can't.

What is traditionally masked in (or by) such ontologies are *both* their hierarchical structure or asymmetry *and* their articulation *as a religiosity*: in other words, again, the very opposition between a "material" and an "immaterial" domain of existence is defined *from the position of that which it presumes (claims) to investigate*. The material/immaterial ontology is a preliminary *philosophical hypothesis masquerading as that which it ostensibly seeks to prove*. Simply by evoking the "materiality" of the world; that the world is characterized by a property of materiality or of (mere) matter, it simultaneously co-produces and constitutes its ostensible antithesis; the "spiritual" or non- (pre- or post-) material world. To criticize "materialism" is to create and invoke its hypothesized opposite.

I'd like to change direction and summarize these theses in what I hope is a more succinct series of corollaries. These would be as follows.

1   The material/immaterial opposition is the ground or template or matrix for positing equivalent or complementary properties in *multiple dimensions*: on the level of the scale of the individual, the group, the community, the nation, the species, and so forth.

2   These scalar transpositions or postulates are disseminated as (metaphorical) equivalences, which commonly specify (are taken to justify) a certain appropriateness; certain proper or fitting human (and other) behaviors which bear with them legal or ethical force or discipline. A cosmological modularity or *decorum*. Articulating the cosmos as if it were the "artifact" of a super-human or divine artificer.

To which may be added that the *effect* of the maintenance of this duality is the possibility of imagining the belief that

a   the "immaterial" has an "independent" existence of its own (a "transcendental signified" exceeding the chain of [material] signs), and thus prior to its "material" antithesis, constituting the essence of *religiosity*. This semiological or epistemological artifact is the most important and powerful implication of religiosity. But it simultaneously makes possible the imagining of its *antithesis*, namely that:

b   the "material" has an independent existence of its own, independent of and prior to any imaginary projected "immaterial" antithesis, which constitutes the essence of *artistry* or artifice.

All of which suggests a further conclusion, namely that

c   The maintenance of the duality generates an uncannily "oscillating ontology," whereby "materialism" and "spiritualism" (to use the most common terms) perpetually contend for a position of primacy or transcendence. The entire "contest" between spiritualism and materialism is such a rhetorical fabrication.

In general, then, the maintenance of the materialism/immaterialism dualism – the belief in a realm of spirit or immateriality and its (from certain religious perspectives) lower or "derivative" antithesis, a realm of "pure" (or mere) matter – or *vice versa – allows for the possibility of each perspective imagining its antithesis*. Each is the ghost perpetually haunting the "body" (or the "soul") of the other; the system of its otherness. Each is the unconscious of the other. Each mode of being is essentially unstable or fragile, as its essence always contains its "opposite," each opposite (each "elsewhere") being what grounds and makes possible the first ontological realm. In the Western Christian tradition, the problem of the *eucharist* – the sign that when consecrated ceases to be a sign or representation but *is the divine body* – is the hinge on which the semiotic possibilities I've just described revolve.

So the final irony is that the *eucharist* – pure *ostensification* – only exists because of and in relation to what it is defined by: signification. The realm of historicity and temporality; the "space" of the signifier/signified.

This makes it clear that the distinction and connection between art and religion is that neither has an independent existence of its own, because *neither is an "it" but a relationship to when and how things signify or ostensify*. Each exists primarily in terms of the contrast with its opposite – what Ranciere in another context once referred to as *partage*. But Ranciere never considered the parallactic base from which partage itself arises, nor did he contend with the fundamental modernist *parallax* that is artistry-and-religiosity.[12]

I've tried to suggest that (art) history, as a signifying practice, as the investigation of artifice in terms of how it *signifies*, is at base not secular but religious (or rather it demonstrates that secularity is a religious fabrication). If, as Judith Butler recently argued, we accept that secularization is a way that religious traditions "live on" within post-religious frameworks, then we're not really talking about two different frameworks, but two forms of religious understanding, intertwined with one another in various modes of *avowal and disavowal*.

This is precisely where what we call art comes in. If we construe artistry as representational or expressive, or as symbolic or indexical with respect to mentality, style, identity, spirit, and so forth – in short, *as signifying (rather than as ostensifying)* – it involves a fundamental disavowal of its own fabricatedness and constitutes a reiteration of a metaphysics of signification which is a continuation of the religiosity from which it evolved in the sixteenth century. A "secularism" that perpetuates religiosity in a post-religious environment.

And as a secularism in its root sense, as an articulation of its being of the ages or in temporality, it will always be subject to waves of fashion in decorum, of what is fitting at a given time for given social needs and hegemonic and/or oppositional desires. Attempts to "theorize" rhetorical distinctions between historicities by transforming them into distinctive features or modalities of artistic practice are essentially circular and largely serve the art historicisms of the past two centuries and their romantic dreams of scientificity: the games of science and the games of meaning: the games of the science of meaning.

Notes

1 © The Estate of L.G. Williams, Hollywood and Vine, Los Angeles, CA 90036. The work is a parody of a 1961 painting by Roy Lichtenstein, "I Can See the Whole Room … and There's Nobody in It!" which sold for $434.2 million at Christie's in New York in November 2011, originally bought by the seller for $2 million in 1988.

2 And somewhat unusual in much of the rest of the world; see below for similar conservative Christian proselytizing using different means.

3 The term *trust* itself entered Middle English from Old Norse *traust* or *treysta*, a mark or expression of power or strength.

4 Jacques Derrida, *Writing and Difference*, trans. Alan Bass (Chicago, IL: University of Chicago Press, 1978 (Paris: Editions du euil, 1967), pp. 16–17.

5 I use the term metaphysical in the sense of F. Mathews' *For the Love of Matter: A Contemporary Panpsychism* (Albany, NY: SUNY Press, 2003), as cited by Deborah Rose, "An Indigenous Philosophical Ecology: Situating the Human," *The Australian Journal of Anthropology* (TAJA), Vol. 16, No. 3, 2005, p. 296. Mathews' analyses of several aboriginal belief systems argues that *metaphysical claims* are "claims concerning the way the world is independently of our contingent experience of it."

6 G. Flaxman, ed., *The Brain is the Screen: Deleuze and the Philosophy of Cinema* (Minneapolis, MN and London: University of Minnesota Press, 2000), p. 23 (my emphases).

7 Giorgio Agamben, *The Man Without Content. Meridian* (Stanford, CA: Stanford University Press, 1999), trans. Georgia Albert (*l'uomo senza contenuto* [Milan: Quodlibet, 1994]), p. 15.

8 The reverend is quoted as saying "I hope this statue will become a *remedy* for this secularization" as reported in the *New York Times* on December 12, 2010: "Poland, Bastion of Religion, Sees Rise in Secularism": www.nytimes.com/2010/12/12/world/europe/12poland.html (accessed December 12, 2010).

9 The six-part multifunctional model of signification elaborated by Roman Jakobson is usefully summarized in his "Closing Statement: Linguistics and Poetics," in Thomas A. Sebeok, ed., *Style in Language* (Cambridge, MA: MIT Press, 1960), pp. 350–377. See also Roman Jakobson, *Coup l'oeil sur le developpement de la semiotique: Studies in Semiotics*, Vol. 3 (Bloomington, IN: University of Indiana Press, 1975), Ian Verstegen, "A Semiotic Profile: Donald Preziosi," *Semiotix*, Vol. XN-8, 2012, and *RAH*, pp. 143–155, with bibliographies on visual and architectonic semiologies and their twentieth-century evolution.

10 See Cyril Stanley Smith, *A Search for Structure* (Cambridge, MA: MIT Press, 1981), pp. 327ff. See also Smith's "The Texture of Matter as Viewed by Artisan, Philosopher,

and Scientist in the 17th and 18th Centuries," in *Atoms, Blacksmiths, and Crystals: Practical and Theoretical Views of the Structure of Matter in the 17th and 18th Centuries* (Los Angeles, CA: William Andrews Clark Memorial Library, University of California, 1967). See also Jane Bennett, *Vibrant Matter: A Political Ecology of Things* (Durham, NC and London: Duke University Press, 2010), pp. 58–61, and n. 39, p. 139, with reference to Heidegger and Deleuze and Guattari. Bennett's fourth chapter on metals in fact mentions Smith's work on the artisanal epistemology (my terms) of metallurgy.

11 See above, *Provocations*, on Henry David Thoreau on the attention to mere matter, and Jane Bennett, op. cit., ch. 3, "Thoreau, Dead Meat, and Berries," pp. 45ff. She writes that "The activity of metabolization, whereby the outside and inside mingle and recombine, renders more plausible the idea of a vital materiality … a vitality obscured by our habit of dividing the world into inorganic matter and organic life" (p. 50). See also: Gilles Deleuze, "Metal, Metallurgy, Music, Husserl, Simondon" and "Sur Anti-Oedipe et Mille Plateaux: Cours Vincennes – 27/02/1979," www.webdeleuze.com (accessed May 2, 2013).

12 Another aspect of *parallax* (gendering) is examined in *Passage 9*.

8

THE ROMANCE OF THE EUCHARIST AND THE PHYLACTERY

A spectral messianicity is at work in the concept of the archive and ties it, like religion, like history, like science itself, to a very singular experience of the promise."[1]

I've been concerned above with time, with the chronicity of the discursive formation of artistry, and with anachronicity. All of which presupposes a concern with the archive; with the archival, and with the spectral messianicity of the archives which haunts any activity of recounting. So when exactly does artistic activity become *archival*? Is it (if it is an "it") a distinct mode of artistry; a particular *kind* of thing? Or is archival artifice a way or using various kinds of materially diverse things in similar ways, or for common or similar purposes, palpably distinguishable from other (non-archivic) artistries? And if the latter, then exactly what kinds of purposes or functions might be signaled by archival uses of things; or by the *fevers* or *impulses* or *tendencies* promoted by some as archival?

If a certain criticality is claimed to adhere to archival objects or processes, then by implication there would then have to be archival activities that were *non*-critical; that were possibly amnesiac with regard to their criticality, into which, perhaps, might be injected "criticality" as a special ingredient or quality; as a distinguishable artisanal *perspective*, or as an *impulse* or a *tendency* (caged or otherwise) *within* artistry? We've been here before: nearly a decade ago the current director of London's south bank or modernist Tate once referred to his new museum just prior to the latter's opening as a "zoological garden of caged tendencies." Which could suggest that there must then also be artistries that are without "tendencies," uncaged or (historically) untethered and critically neutral or impulse-free. Undecorous, even. There are surely some who would wish to believe so, even at this late date, in and out of the museum, and on both sides of the Thames and Hudson.

Or might it be the case that as epistemological technologies, as practices productive of knowledge, archives are *by definition* critical, whether by intent or effect? And in a similar vein, are museums and collections critical artifacts, by virtue of their removal of objects from overt economic circulation, rendering them *available* for new or different (or newly laundered) semiological affordances? If that were the case, what then would prevent us from attributing qualities, reflexes, tendencies, or impulses of criticality to any or all forms of artifice, either essentially or as a function or effect of their social and cultural contexts or positions?

Is an archive, then, a what or a when? If we wish to believe that criticality (or redemptivity or messianicity) is a property or impulse *of* artistry or artifice, either generically or with respect to particular forms of artistry, then are we not left with perpetuating a dubious – and, some would claim, rightly, a dangerous separation of reified essences from their "expression" or re-presentation.

Wallace Stevens had something to say about that, as does/did not a few others both before and after. Which – as not a few, myself included – have argued, *keeps theocracy on the table.* A quivering, quavering specter. The haunting, daunting specter of the distillate or reification of the process of religiosity, that is, "religion."

It becomes evident very quickly that a more than superficial interrogation of archival artistries entails an obligation to engage with the promises and conundrums of artistry or artifice as such, and of course (and no less importantly) an obligation to engage with the ethical implications and conundrums – the interwoven affordances and constraints – of living in a world of artifice (i.e., living in *the world*). Historically, archival and museological practices have worked to *reduce* the conflictual pluralities of history, identity, and memory to phantasmatic uniformities and narrativities. There are a number of prefabricated templates for articulating these practices: among the most commonly evoked master narratives in the Western tradition have been those of Greek fatalism, Judaic and/or Christian redemptionisms, bourgeois progressivisms, and Marxian utopianisms,[2] or some combination of two or more of these, as famously (or notoriously) the case with the interrupted project(s) of Walter Benjamin, not to mention those of not a few others.

What is most deeply at issue here is the problematic and deeply contested nature of artifice itself, the critique of which in the West is in fact as old as Plato, and the earliest documented writing we have on the origins and purposes of art and representation, as we'll see shortly. At the same time, what might be claimed as critical archival practice is itself of great antiquity, and virtually coterminous with the western aesthetic tradition. To wit (among others) The *Lesche* of the Knidians at Delphi, the first museological artifact in Europe.[3]

The concept of the archive as a mode of artistry – which is to say as an *epistemological technology*; as an instrument for the production, regulation, and distribution of knowledge – has been widely recognized as an important aspect of modernity. In its various forms, and ranging across the entire spectrum of the arts and sciences, archival institutions and practices have been the exemplary means by which the world and its objects have come to be systematically ordered and classified; to become *knowable.* Modern and contemporary archival practices are the successors to various traditions of staging and formatting knowledge-production that began with the "arts of memory" in Greece 2,500 years ago, referred to on occasion in the *Passages* above.

Governed by rules of perspective, partition, exclusion and inclusion, both spatial and temporal, by articulations of process and structure, and by the establishment of internal hierarchies, archives have invariably been multidimensional, multimodal, and spatio-temporal in character, involving processes of framing which historically constituted the matrix of distinct (and nominally autonomous) intellectual disciplines, institutions, and practices.

Archival institutions (as with other exhibitionary complexes) are geared to the production of knowledge *by explicitly positioning or juxtaposing knowing subjects within their domains, either corporeally or virtually, as operators of the archival machinery.* Knowledge emerges as the *symptom* of a desire for resolution which is both continuously produced and contained or frustrated – but ultimately not exhausted – by the internal structural logic of the system.

It may be useful to distinguish what I have come to believe have historically been two principal dimensions (or tendencies, or impulses) of many archival practices, which I'll call the *eucharistic* and the *semiotic*. The *first* constitutes the staging of desires for deciphering truths or origins that transcend the arbitrariness of signs – for which the bitter necessity of interpretation is lived as a kind of *exile*. The *other* impulse, no longer primarily oriented toward origin, affirms artifice, arbitrariness, and hypothesis, and strives to pass *beyond* humanism, the "human" being the name of that being which, throughout the history of Western metaphysics has dreamed of the plenitude of presence, of reassuring foundations, of origin and of the end of play.[4]

These two orientations upon the ontology or *quiddity* of the archive, building upon the foregoing paraphrase of Derrida's (1967) text, are (in his words) "irreconcilable, even if we live them simultaneously and reconcile them in an obscure economy." But it is not a question of choosing; any consideration of the archive evokes the need to address the "common ground" (*sol commun*) of two irreconcilable modes of interpretation; the need to reflect upon what in fact keeps in play these two perpetually oscillating perspectives: the distinct principle of affordance of any unresolvable oscillation, any (not merely optical) illusion. This is more than simply a distinction between the factual and the fictive. To put it simply, this is a terrain where distinctions between the aesthetic and the theological – as well as what are nominally projected as the technological and the spiritual (Benjamin's unresolved paradox) – are most radically problematized. Historically, archival and museological activities have worked to stage that very conundrum, more often than not by disguising it as non-problematic; as if it presented an either–or choice.

This goes well beyond the question of archival activity: it is, in effect, the problem of art, artistry, or artifice, grounded in the presumption of (or desire for) representation, expression, and embodiment, that has underlain several historical master narratives referred to earlier in this book. Among the names for this "obscure economy," this *lived simultaneity of irreconcilability*, as I've argued elsewhere is the modern discourse of visual studies/art history. Or, more specifically, that modern matrix of deponent and co-dependent professions and institutions (including art history and criticism, aesthetic philosophy, museology, etc.), which from their early modern beginnings were destined to be permanently in thrall to their foundational conundrums and contradictions; proactively *keeping them in play* in a perpetual, virtually metronomic motion whose alternating agonistic energies generate the warm illusion of disciplinary progress and of a definable object-domain for its putative subjects. Art history, theory, and criticism, not to speak of visual studies more generically, occupy the "common ground" defined by what Michel de Certeau also once characterized as the *irreducible antitheses* between history and psychoanalysis;[5] that *topos* unfolded by their juxtaposition that was discussed above.

The deeper and more pressing reason for deconstituting this *topos* (the conundrum evoked by the term "representation") is the problematic *(dis)connection between* art and religion (artistry and religiosity), arguably the key philosophical problematic of the present time and the target (the image projected from the surface of the puzzle) of these passages. One not entirely *ignored* by the modern (disciplinary) discourse on the (fine) arts, as noted in various places above and below in this text: perhaps it's more correct to say it has been mostly *sideswiped* institutionally and professionally.[6] I'm referring to what lies beneath the familiar representational impulses commonly voiced under that rubric, namely the "spirituality of art" (spirituality as a specific quality or impulse or effect (*haeccity*) of the more generic *quiddity* of artistry) and/or the "artistry of spirituality" (artistry as a property or quality of effect of spirituality). Duns Scotus had not a little to say about this.[7]

The distinctive opposition and epistemological oscillation is in fact that which exists precisely *within and as* the two antithetical construals of art or artifice itself, *one of which is commonly called religion.*

Let's recall Derrida here for a moment:

> The question of the archive is not ... a question of the past. It is not a question of a concept dealing with the past that might already be at our disposal, an archivable concept of the archive. It is a question of the future, the question of a response, of a promise and of a responsibility for tomorrow. The archive: if we want to know what that will have meant, we will know only in times to come. Perhaps. Not tomorrow but in times to come, later on or perhaps never. A spectral messianicity is at work in the concept of the archive and ties it, like religion, like history, like science itself, to a very singular experience of the promise.[8]

Which, as I've been suggesting, is precisely the problem summarized in the coextensive and antithetical modern inflections of the term *art* referred to earlier – art as a kind of thing, or as a way of using any thing. In my reading of Derrida's text, one important effect of any archive (or museum or collection) is *to imagine futures that will not actually start until* after *we've stopped imagining them*, held in suspension as we necessarily are in museological space-time. As if in amber. Us, that is: it's not just the exhibits that are framed on a pedestal, or behind glass, but the perusers, choreographed and circulated about and by those spaces.[9] Unimaginable afterlives (us and them) whose fervent projections encatalyze fevers which will not abate until after one ceases obsessing. (And about which, Derrida, in a different register, once termed "the logic of the supplement.")

Recall Walter Benjamin's remark in his *Work of Art* essay (p. 266): "It has always been one of the primary tasks of art to create a demand whose hour of full satisfaction has yet to come." Creating, of course, an anxiety, more or less unabated, for ground and anchorage; for a final (true) horizon that really will (finally) stop receding as we approach it: a motility and mutability that we long to arrest with the power of the bare word – the *mot juste*; the artifice; the artistry of the/a "horizon." But as we have seen, that full satisfaction that never arrives; that transcended point, is the engine of the movement of desire; that which tethers desire as perpetually unfulfillable (transcendent divinity).

The time of redemption, that is; or even, depending upon the tradition, for messianic *embodiment*. Archival activity is perforce the staging of a future perfect tense, or as Lacan put it about two decades before Derrida's *Archive Fever*, "the future perfect of what you shall have been for what you are in the process of becoming." That ideal plenitude and asymptotic resolution of which any given history of art, any museology, any theology, will always be a fragment. That art historical or museological plenitude which never quite arrives or comes through the door, of which all our critical interventions are deponent and fragmentary.

Do museological artifacts, then, *dream* of transcendence? Of being slotted into their proper places in a geometry of plenitude?

What is at stake here, again, is the ontological status of *artifice as such*, which evokes the relation of artistry and religiosity: the primal juxtaposition of what I'm calling the semiotic and the eucharistic. Which, and following upon what I said earlier, impacts upon any sense of the "criticality" of any artistry, and not only explicitly archival tendencies or impulses.

It's important to be clear that none of these problems are specific or unique to our modernities. In fact, they are quite ancient within the various intertwined and partly co-constructed Western traditions. To repeat what has been noted above, in the earliest documented speculation in the Western tradition on the nature of artistry or artifice and its social, political, and religious affordances, Plato evoked a deep ambivalence about the *uncanniness* of art – the ability of art to *simultaneously fabricate and problematize* the hegemonic (political and religious) powers imagined to be materialized, embodied, or "represented" in and as a people's forms and practices. This is the ambiguity of *artifice* as such[10] in not simply reflecting but in fabricating the world in which we live, the precise problem addressed in *The Republic*.[11]

Art itself – and especially what Plato called the representational or mimetic arts – deeply problematizes seemingly secure oppositions between what we might want to ideally contrast as fact and fiction; history and poetry; reason and emotion; the sacred and the secular; contrasts that are the circumstantial and mutable *effects* of human artistry.[12] As I argued above, what art, artistry or artifice created (for Plato), then, was not some "second world" alongside the everyday world in which we live – a phantasmatic or fictional world of "fine art" as upper class entertainment (the modern arm of art historicism); what art creates *is* the actual world in which we really do live our daily lives.

The "divine terror" that Plato also said art induced *in the soul* of the ordinary citizen *was the terrifying awareness of precisely this paradox*: that works of art don't simply "imitate" but rather *create and open up* a world, keeping it in existence, as Heidegger famously put it in discussing the ontologically creative potential (which is to say, the criticality) of artworks in his essay "The Origin of the Work of Art,"[13] where the experience of art was taken to be fundamentally "religious" in nature, or more precisely as problematizing many conventional distinctions between the two. What was at issue for Heidegger (no less than for Plato and many philosophical and religious writers at various times) was the truth or falsity of artistic fabrication: Is a work of artistic creativity an imitation of some ideal essence or immutable truth or transcendent reality? Is an archive or a collection always a fiction, whether personal or collective? And what would a "true" archive consist of? Hayden White succinctly termed it some two decades earlier in his explications of the rhetoric of historicism: What are in play are "the fictions of factual representation."[14]

The basic paradox is essentially this: Once staged or embodied, objects open themselves to alternative readings, which elicits a need for control and rectification. Artifacts appear in social spaces delineated by the coordinates projected by the opposition between decorum and indecorousness, the latter being a failing or a sin and subject to corrective discipline. In the fantasy worlds of theocratic or fundamentalist religion or politics, however, these are no benign abstractions, but matters of life and death: believe in the reality of our artistic fictions, or you will die.

What Giorgio Agamben had not long ago also called "art's original (terrifying) stature" echoes what for Heidegger was an openness to the experience of its *uncanny thingness* or *quiddity*: the *awesome authenticity* of artifice characterizing the Greek experience of art's spiritual or psychic power. Every artwork (or archive) the *mooting* of new realities; every object or image or collection therefore a potential catalyst of redemption. For both Agamben and Heidegger, then, the modernist age of the aesthetic (lasting from the mid-eighteenth century to the end of the twentieth century) had approached its limit. As Agamben has also noted, this would demand the radical abandonment of the early modern invention of aesthetics and its institutional progeny.

Plato was concerned with what he saw as the fundamental dilemma of social and political life; about what should constitute an ideal society or polity in the face of the very dangerous powers of artistry to both create *and* problematize or ironicize manifestations or expressions of hegemonic political or religious power; art's power as both gloriously seductive and terror-producing and alienating – emblematized in antiquity by the face of the Medusa. The representational arts, he argued, should ideally be employed to articulate and give *proper or appropriate expression* to a political order and its social structures; its hierarchies of individuals and groups mapped onto the space-time continuum of the artifice of the state. A world in which what is materially fabricated decorously evokes some "true" or "natural" order or *cosmos*, promoted (by those in power, of course) as "truly" constituting that world. A polity that would ideally express, embody, re-present, and promote an ideal unity, purity, and homogeneity of purpose (commonly projected as having been lost or even stolen); a built world that *embodies* individual and collective yearning for such aesthetically ideal worlds.

Plato was very clear that by its very nature, art itself fundamentally problematized the seemingly irreconcilable distinction between fact and fiction – fatal to a civic order grounded in (the artifice of) truth-staging. What he saw as necessary for an ideal state was that it be taken as *truly real* and securely *grounded* in an *im*material or spiritual or sacred (and it's necessary to add, unaccountable) order – i.e., *as if such an order really were natural*, rather than an aesthetic, political, cultural, or philosophical *hypothesis*. In other words, in effect, *its artistry or artifice must literally be amnesiac: bent toward erasing the evidence of its own fabricatedness; its own ficticity*. It must be *seen* to be on the side of "fact" rather than of "fiction" (as historians claimed); on the side of Real History (as the Marxists claimed); of a "true" Nature (as scientists claimed), or of independently pre-existing forces, gods, or spirits (as theologians or theists claimed). On the side of ontology, in fact.[15] "Proper" art must therefore *deny or mask its artistry and artifice* – that essentially Praxitelean gesture underlying all theocratic religiosities or spiritualities, erasing the traces of their own brushwork. An order where the law of the community *really was* the (actual) "word(s)" of the god(s), as properly interpreted by those properly ordained to correctly interpret – namely, of course, those holding or desiring power.

This is precisely what is most deeply at stake in any discussion of the putative relations of artistry (archival or otherwise) to something being promoted by hegemonic power as transcending mortality or secularity, as sacred or spiritual or eternal or superior to matter. Such claims have always had profound (and often dire) implications for the life and death of individuals and communities. It has consistently been the case that such claims are linked to political and legal systems of discipline and enforcement, in many societies around the world, and across many different religious belief systems and political cultures, and not only those linked to the various competing monotheisms.

In conclusion I'd like to reiterate that the more fundamental oppositions on all these fronts may not be between art and something "external" to it, whether politics, science, history, or religion; rather, the opposition or distinction, as I said much earlier, is internal; *within artistry itself*; between two paradigms of meaningfulness; between two semiotic or aesthetic paradigms or two antithetical construals of the idea of art. The one (what I termed the *eucharistic*) being idolatry or fetishism, namely, a literalization of representation, and the other (what I called the *semiotic*) its anti-essentialist antithesis, namely, the foregrounding of the contingency and situatedness or mediatedness of all human fabrication or artifice. In Plato's theocratic utopia, these differences were mapped onto hierarchical distinctions in *class*: it was necessary for the ordinary citizen to believe the hocus-pocus; the aristocracy, while observing the forms of belief, knew better.

The irony, of course, is that socially and historically these two states more closely resemble alternating poles of an optical illusion: co-constructed states, neither of which exists independently of the other. Which brings us back to Derrida's irreconcilabilities, both in his *Archive Fever* text of 1997 and in his earlier *Writing and Difference* essays three decades earlier.

This suggests further that instituted religions are not infrequently in effect *the legalization and social disciplining of an idolatry in denial of its own artistry; its own fabricatedness.* What is at stake are alternative modes or methods of reading or witnessing – one that affirms the arbitrariness of signs and symbols, and the other which perpetuates a metaphysical essentialism or literalism; a fetishism of the sign. In recasting the problem of art and its "history," the problem of the archive stands at the juxtaposition of the antitheses I've been talking about. One way of construing artistry is as the *process* (and perhaps the word impulse is not without merit in this context) of highlighting, foregrounding, or calling attention to the contingency and situatedness of any projection claiming independence of its expression.

Artistry, as the apparent antithesis of religiosity, is a process of ironicizing the *idolatry* of essentialism. Which is precisely what, in attempting to project a theocratic utopia, Plato was explicitly aware of in recognizing that any proper and effective politics, any proper or true religiosity, entailed the suppression of the artifice of its own fabricatedness.[16]

It is at this level – a re-engagement with the conundrums of representation itself, with what I've called "Plato's Dilemma" – that the recent discourse on archival artistry needs to be more explicitly articulated if it is to more than cosmetically contribute to the ongoing rethinking of (art) historical and critical practice. Far too much is at stake today socially, politically, and ethically to *not* continue the emergent project of radically transforming our critical visual practices in effective and substantive ways rather than decorously or cosmetically. Any such impulse (archival or otherwise) would surely be worth attending to.

I'd like to insert here an image of one of the most remarkable *archival performances* in the history of Western artistry, and one which thrust those who experienced it into the very center of the conundrum about artistry and religiosity that I spoke about at the beginning. Figure 8.1 is of what remains today of the famous Gallery of Maps in the Vatican, designed by the Dominican scholar Egnazio Danti and inaugurated by Pope Gregory XIII in 1581.[17]

If knowledge emerges as a *symptom* of desires that are simultaneously produced and constrained by the internal logic of an archival system, then in the Gregorian Gallery there was, in addition to the sequence of maps representing the world as seen from the perspective of the central spine of the Italian peninsula, a quite amazing object (or indeed, an *objet petite a*). To walk through this gallery was to kinesthetically recapitulate the world order beyond; a remarkable precursor of the modern museum, and a not uncommon instance of an epistemological technology clearly grounded in the ancient Greek and Roman arts of memory.[18] This cartographic archive, however, incorporated one artifactual device that was in a sense the catalytic engine of the entire experience. This was an anamorphic mirror at the

FIGURE 8.1 View of the Gallery of Maps, sixteenth century, Galleria delle Carte Geografiche, Vatican Museums, Vatican State. Photo credit: Nimatallah/ Art Resource, NY.

climactic cartographic, historical, political, ideological, and religious end of the gallery. As the visitor approached this point at the end of the gallery, the image of a chalice suddenly appeared suspended in space, above which was also suspended a *eucharist*. This holy *trompe-l'oeil* was reflected up from a blurry (anamorphic) image painted on a panel in the floor.

Having progressed through the political and religious history figured perspectivally along the walls of the gallery, the visitor is then magically confronted with an image of the eucharist, the embodiment of (the body of) Christ, floating in real space-time, an image literally produced by the spatial movement of the visitor. The meanings of the various Old Testament biblical sacrifices, depicted along the gallery walls and ceiling, achieve their overall climactic resolution in the ultimate sacrifice, that of *Christ, as embodied in, by, and as the eucharist*. The anamorphic mirror and pavement image no longer exist, although there are very clear and reliable contemporary accounts of this remarkable artifact.[19] There are ancient precursors of this archival practice (which space doesn't permit examining here),[20] where the *perspectival resolution* of a visual conundrum triggered by a visual (architectonic) anomaly also depends upon the bodily movements of an observer, recalling the definition of an archive earlier as *incorporating* the material or virtual presence of an operator.

The magical appearance in mid-air of the eucharist (the "object" of desire) in the Vatican Gallery of Maps is materially *evoked* by the forward movement of the visitor. There is an uncanny resemblance between all this hocus-pocus and the Lacanian notion of the "*objet petite a*," which (as is usually forgotten) was Lacan's own abbreviation of the ancient Greek word *agalma*, or "statue." A term used not for any statuary, but for statues of the gods. The virtual presence of the eucharist enacts the gaze of the observer, enacts the trajectory of the viewer's desire, throwing the three-dimensional entity back toward the viewer. As Lacan says, "the objet a in the field of the visible is the gaze."[21]

What of the *phylactery* (Figure 8.2)? (Greek *phylax* < *phulassein;* to guard/protect).

Foucault described archives as built around emptiness or lack. Can an *absence* itself be a document? An archival event? Can an empty space or passage in a museum (one thinks necessarily of Liebeskind's Berlin museum with its contrived void-gallery intended to ostensify and thereby *evoke* a specific ethic absence, or the empty sunken area beneath Manhattan's demolished World Trade Center) formed so as to be *read unambiguously* (as if) documenting a specific absence? What kind of semiological relationship is the equation of emptiness and absence? How might the sign or mark of evacuation or removal signify? Is a circumcised penis – a genital mutilation that, in and the marking of an absence, claims to denote a distinction and a subject-position, an identity – a monument or a document or a troubling of that very distinction? A calling into question of the non-fabricatedness of the distinction

Is this *mark* of an erect (and "naturally" unsheathed) penis visible on/as an organ in a flaccid state the *sign* of incipient arousal? A token of an arousal to come? How is a sign of future potency an archival marker of ethnicity? Of ethnic religiosity?

FIGURE 8.2 An IDF soldier prays with phylacteries, 2006. © Yoavlemmer/Wikimedia Commons.

The marker of potency, inscribed (or, in fact, excised) onto/from a currently non-potent or quiescent state of an organ, of the desire or anticipation of future power? Is this merely the adopting, at the behest of an invisible god, as essential to a compact with, a compacting and juxtaposing of oneself to, that entity that/who is by definition immaterial, of the sign of a current or previous enslaving power, adopting a practice indigenous to their enslavers (the late-Pharaonic dynasty Egyptians), as a mark of future power and independence of those enslaved? A liberation *to come* and a *message* to all ages.

A phrase from Derrida's 1994 Naples text *Archive Fever* (written, as he put it, "on the rim of Vesuvius"): "A spectral messianicity is at work in the concept of the archive and ties it, like religion, like history, like science itself, to a very singular experience of the promise."[22]

Derrida's explicit omission of "art" from practices "tied to a very singular" promissory experience might seem puzzling, for surely an archive is an artistic fabrication which may not only be likened to these other promissory institutions or professions, but may in fact be seen as constituting the very *modus operandi* of their realization. So are their singular promises themselves *secondary inflections* of artistry itself? Are history or science or religion culturally specific *modes* of artistry or artifice? And what of that one form of artistry that Derrida does explicitly contend with, the body art of genital mutilation serving a key ethnic archival function in reminding an ethnic group of its former "bondage" in a country, Egypt, where circumcision was indigenous to the native population? What do archives and their "fevers" share with genital artistry that might be relevant more than locally to artistry as such? Are unmodified body parts *not* archival or unavailable for archival functions? Is archival artistry distinct or detachable from "its" embodiments or expressions?

As is so often the case where an interrogation of a text (Derridean or otherwise) may become a catalyst for the re-examination of one's own basic assumptions about a particular issue, I find my own reading leading to a reframing of some general questions – the first of which might well be this: If the concept of the archive is tethered or tied to promissory experience, then *when exactly does artistic activity become archival?* That is, as archivally promising as Derrida would see "religion, history, or science" to have been. Are archives distinct forms or modes (or even "fevers" or "impulses") of/as artistry, religiosity, scientificity, historicity? Is an archive a particular *kind* of thing? Or is archival artifice a way of using various kinds of possibly quite diverse things for common or similar purposes? And if the latter, then exactly what kinds of purposes or functions might be signaled by archival uses of (any) things; or by the *fevers*, tendencies, or *impulses* promoted by some as archival?

Derrida ties *genital artistry* to its externalization; its exhibitionary economy (its pub(l)ic face). Juxtaposed to his all-too-brief discussion of what he terms the *enigma of circumcision* as an "archival act" is the following "however":

> I must put it aside here [this question of the enigma of circumcision], not without some regret, along with that of the phylacteries, those archives of skin

or parchment covered with writing that Jewish men, here, too, and *not* Jewish women, carry close to their body, on their arm and on their forehead: right on the body (a meme le corps) like the sign of circumcision, but with a being-right-on (*etre-a-meme*) that this time does not exclude the detachment and the untying of the ligament, of the substrate, and of the text simultaneously.[23]

We need to press Derrida further here, and superimpose his juxtapositions. Derrida astutely "re-members" circumcision by suggesting its obverse and twin – the application of the *phylactery*, the skin inscribed with text, *onto the skin of the circumcised male but elsewhere*. Let's think these together for a moment. Here we have a transferral, a translation, one might say (both displacement *and* condensation), of severed skin into text; and not without some echo, one might also say, of that superimposition of Word and Godhead at the opening of Genesis ("In the beginning was the Word and the Word was with God and the Word was God") which begs the question as to what exactly *comes first*. Which is, of course, the essential question, after all, of the archive as such, that question that always remains the same: What/who *comes first*? (the question of the *arche* or origin or beginning, or, literally, the first [thing]: *"en te arkhe ein o Logos"*). In archiving was the Word. In the beginning was the *(be)foreskin*.

But the true new beginning, repeated in every generation, was its replacement (but, note, *elsewhere* on the body) by a new skin of text. The skin of text as a scrim on the forehead (and/or left arm – the arm that generally [it is presumed] does not write), a reminder of the pact; a promise. How can the re-presencing of an absence be a promise? The mark, perhaps and not so incidentally, of that modernity that is the reification of an *amnesia* about the past in the present. What and exactly how does it *conjure*?

Derrida *puts aside* this question of circumcision – the *removal* of a portion of skin – and of the *phylactery* – the *application* of a piece of skin (parchment, paper); a leather box, a *tempietto*, within which are letters, thereby *covering with writing* the body of the genitally altered male – "with some regret" as he says. Yet he never returned to this question nor did he address that regret. But the need remains to focus on the double question of who (or what) *is* the "artist" in this archive; the *archontic principle* of an archive – aside from the god or its representative performing this *briss*-artistry, a subtraction which is displaced so as to serve as a promise to the future, and I'd like to consider the archive as the marker of loss – and, equally, a mark of mourning. And a mark of sexuation, of gendering, as itself, as Judith Butler once put it, the mourning of a loss which was effected in order to think its loss and to act, to en-gender, to perpetually repair the rift. A *vow to the future* to repair what cannot again be whole. And a reminder to *keep the (letter of) the law*.

That is, to foreground its *artifice*. A rift it (gender) perpetually and futilely instantiates and re-creates. (A whiff here of an early Hellenic myth explicating gender division as two halves perpetually in search of an original singularity.[24]) A transcendently full *trans*gender, A Levantine inflection of the ontologies of gender origins articulated in Greek religion as the hermaphroditic, and of the perpetual and futile attempt to re-join what "nature" (*sic.*) has rent asunder. Which links this problem to the problem of art and artistry itself.

Derrida rightfully insists that archival activity is directed not simply or merely to the past, but to the future. Which raises for us what I'd like to suggest is the key question of the archive in relation to art, artistry, and artifice. Is any artifactual activity that is tied to a *promise* either by intent or construal *archival*? Is any artistic act the conjuring or (as it's being articulated here) the *enchanting* into being of a world: a virtual or spectral world that is (by nature) caught up in the kinds of conundrums and irreconcilable double-binds that Derrida's extraordinary text is itself so poignantly caught up with?

We must now (fittingly) consider (anew) this locus or site of gendering; that parallactic paradox.

Notes

1 Jacques Derrida, *Archive Fever: A Freudian Impression*, trans. Eric Prenowitz (Chicago, IL: University of Chicago Press, 1996), p. 36.
2 One of the more lucid explications of this issue was that of Hayden White: see his *The Content of the Form: Narrative Discourse and Historical Representation* (Baltimore, MD: Johns Hopkins University Press, 1987), pp. 150ff., and his more recent essay in *The Art Bulletin*.
3 See *Passage 9*.
4 Jacques Derrida, *L'ecriture et la différence* (Paris: Seuil, 1967), p. 427.
5 Michel de Certeau, "Psychoanalysis and its History," in de Certeau, *Heterologies: Discourse on the Other*, trans. Brian Massumi (Minneapolis, MN: University of Minnesota Press, 1986), pp. 3–16.
6 That is, not engaged with head-on; an avoidance that is the product and effect of not asking certain questions.
7 See Brad S. Gregory, *Unintended Reformation: How a Religious Revolution Secularized Society* (Cambridge, MA: Harvard University Press, 2012). Jonathan Sheehan, "When was Disenchantment? History and the Secular Age," in M. Warner, J. Van Antwerpen, and C. Calhoun, eds., *Varieties of Secularism in a Secular Age* (Cambridge, MA: Harvard University Press, 2010), pp. 217–242, observes (p. 225) that a book similar to Gregory's, namely Charles Taylor's *A Secular Age* (Cambridge, MA: The Belknap Press of Harvard University, 2007) "is not a history. Rather, it documents a set of contrastive categories."
8 Derrida, *Archive Fever*, p. 36.
9 Recall the remarks in the opening *Passages* regarding materiality and "vibrant matter," "dividuality," etc.
10 See the synopsis of the theses in D. Preziosi, "Enchanted Credulities: Art, Religion, and Amnesia," *Xtra*, Vol. 11, No. 1, 2008, pp. 1–7.
11 Plato, *Republic*, trans. Paul Shorey (Cambridge, MA: Harvard University Press, 1953), esp. 1: pp. 243–245 and 2: 464–465. Much of the bulk of the discussion is carried out in book 6, esp. at the end, with the consideration of the contrast between the intelligible and the visible (pp. 511ff.).
12 With regard to history, see Hayden White, "The Fictions of Factual Representation," in White, *Tropics of Discourse* (Baltimore, MD and London: The Johns Hopkins University Press, 1978), pp. 121–134.
13 Martin Heidegger, "The Origins of the Work of Art," in Heidegger, *Poetry, Language, Thought*, trans. A. Hofstadter (London: Harper & Row, 1971) (*Der Ursprung des Kunstwerkes, Einfuehrung von Hans-Georg Gadamer* [Stuttgart: Reclam, 1960, 1967]); Friedrich Nietzsche, *The Will to Power as Art*, trans. D. F. Krell (London: Routledge & Keegan Paul, 1981).

14 White, "The Fictions of Factual Representation," pp. 121–130.

15 As in the conviction that an ordered system of a world being described – for example the cosmological order in the *Summa* of Thomas Aquinas – actually is that world rather than a hypothetical approximation, like any articulation. The latter would be artifice as *adequation* – an imputed or virtual likeness – rather than as *equation* or identity. On the semiotic structure of this and related categories, see *Brain*, esp. ch 8, "The Limits of Representation," pp. 137–151.

16 There is a very long history of these questions in philosophy, theology, in art and in the sciences which became submerged by the modern institutionalization and professionalization of disciplinary knowledge. I should make it clear that such insights are of course not new or modern, but are indebted to a long-standing distinction, made originally by Aristotle and carried further in the Western Christian theological and philosophical tradition, between *equation* and *adequation* (*aequatio* vs. *adaequatio*). Within that tradition, the distinction was emblematized and (literally) embodied in the ironic realism (the artifice) of the *eucharist*, made quite explicit in the willed (and legally enforced) belief that *at the moment* when a priest intones the words *hoc est corpus meum* (this is my [Christ's] body), that piece of (properly consecrated) bread *really is* the body of Christ and not just an arbitrary or contingent sign or symbol. The artifice, in short, of non-artistry or facticity. This opposition was made quite explicit in early modern theories of language and signification, notably in the philological system formulated in the 1660s by the religious order of the linguistic theorists of Port-Royal, who postulated that, whereas all signs were contingent and arbitrary, every sign standing for, in place of, or pointing to something else (*aliquid stat aliquo*), this entire system dialectically depended upon and revolved around *the one "sign" that was not a sign*: the eucharist. (An echo of the hypothesis that a non-material entity had been *literally* embodied [not just symbolized] *by and as* the person of a young and distinctly unorthodox rabbi – an epistemologically and semiologically similar thesis. The artifice that the existence and life of Jesus had *performed*: the artifice of the-self-as-non-artifice.) There is an uncanny resemblance between all this hocus-pocus and the Lacanian notion of the "*objet petite a*," which (as is usually forgotten) was in fact Lacan's own abbreviation of the Greek word *agalma*, or "statue" – which, however, will be pursued elsewhere.

17 See Francesca Fiorani, *The Marvel of Maps: Art, Cartography and Politics in Renaissance Italy* (New Haven, CT London: Yale University Press, 2005), esp. part II, "Maps as Sacred Art: The Gallery of Maps," ch. 7, pp. 171–208, and fig. 7.2., p. 173.

18 On which see Mary Carruthers, *The Book of Memory* (Cambridge: Cambridge University Press, 1990) and *The Craft of Thought* (Cambridge: Cambridge University Press, 1998), and Francis Yates, *The Art of Memory* (Chicago, IL: University of Chicago Press, 1960).

19 See Fiorani, op. cit., pp. 1–12, 224–229; see also Lucio Gambi. *The Gallery of Maps in the Vatican*, trans. Paul Tucker (New York: Braziller, 1997), for a complete inventory of the illustrations. See also *RAH*, ch. 4, part 5, "*Hoc Est Corpus Meum*," pp. 102ff.

20 The organization of the Propylaia of the Athenian acropolis, for example, where the asymmetric anomalies of the facades are resolved into bilateral symmetry in the movement upward and forward by the visitor. The point of resolution is also the first place where a pro-Athenian and anti-Spartan political tableau becomes visible. This "apparatus" is diagrammed and discussed in detail in the final chapter of *RAH*. The visitor is suddenly fixed in place mid-way up the steps toward the Propylaia and it is only at that point that the (otherwise inexplicable) asymmetrical façade on the north appears bilaterally symmetrical. That part of the building housed a pinakotheka or picture gallery with images of the history of the city. If the visitor then turned around facing west, the first clear view of the Bay of Salamis appears, the site of the Athenian naval victory over the Persians (in contrast to the Spartan claims of victory). The dramatic visual manifestation of this political claim by Athens is presumed to have been a catalyst for the Second Peloponnesian War with Sparta.

21 See Antonio Quinet, "The Gaze as Object" in Richard Feldstein, Bruce Fink, and Maire Jaanus, eds., *Reading Seminar XI: Lacan's Four Fundamental Concepts of Psychoanalysis* (Albany, NY: SUNY Press, 1995), p. 106; and Jacques Lacan, *The Four Fundamental Concepts of Psychoanalysis*, ed. Jacques-Alain Miller, trans Sylvana Tomaselli (New York: Norton, 1977). See also Peter Schwenger, *The Tears of Things: Melancholy and Physical Objects* (Minneapolis, MN and London: University of Minnesota Press, 2006), pp. 35ff.
22 Derrida, *Archive Fever*, p. 36.
23 Ibid., p. 42.
24 Discussed in *Passage* 9 ("Art, religion, and the parallax of gender.")

9

ART, RELIGION, AND THE PARALLAX OF GENDER

The cleft of Delphi[1]

What follows deals (as if as a case study) with the interpretation (and to move from a temporal register to a spatial one) of one large historical artifact: the remains of the ancient Greek sanctuary at Delphi (Figure 9.1). It is concerned with the problem of reconciling disparate bits of evidence in a variety of media about the origins, nature, functions, and historical evolution of that remarkable object.

FIGURE 9.1 View of Delphi. Photograph taken by the author.

It is equally concerned with the fabricatedness – the artistry – of what has conventionally been taken as *evidence* itself. Among the phenomena being considered are (1) the ancient traditions classified in modernity as "mythological" or "religious"; (2) the archaeological record (the "facts on the ground," so to speak, whose facticity is itself the product of hypotheses about their significance and function); and (3) the writings of ancient users of and visitors to this extraordinary place.

The written tradition spanned over a millennium of recorded observation and commentary, while the archaeological record at Delphi is some three millennia older than the remains visible today.

The written tradition included the famously exhaustive description of Delphi by the Greek traveler Pausanias, and his very detailed discussion of two major but no longer extant mural paintings by the most famous early classical Greek artist, Polygnotos (a name meaning "multiply-knowing" or "polymath"). Depicting some 70 figures, the paintings covered the walls of a picture gallery (*pinakotheke*) at the top end of the sanctuary of Delphi, built as a clubhouse or *lesche* by the city-state of Knidos (Figure 9.2).

Polygnotos' two murals only survive in Pausanias' descriptions. One, known as the *Iliupersis* (the perishing or destruction of Troy) on the walls to the right of the building's entryway on the southern facade, dealt with the aftermath of the Trojan War and the departure of the conquerors to their homes in Greece. The second, known as the *Nekyia*, to the left of the entrance, dealt with Odysseus' visit to the Underworld (Hades) and the many souls he encountered there in attempting to find his way home. Pausanias' descriptions attempted to reconcile Polygnotos' paintings with the texts of Homer and other ancient authors he was presumed to be illustrating, as well as his comments on the artist's skill at portraying the emotional and ethical character of the figures depicted.

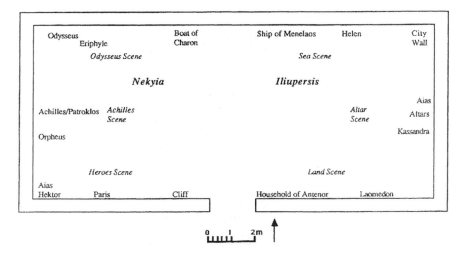

FIGURE 9.2 Plan of Lesche of the Knidians gallery. Drawing by the author.

The text is in fact the first extant piece of extensive critical writing about a specific artwork in the European tradition. Most of the post-classical commentary on Polygnotos' artistry has been concerned with its fidelity or lack thereof to Homer's *Iliad* and *Odyssey*.[2] Arguably the most famous picture gallery in the ancient world, the Knidian gallery was visited by *individuals* from around the world, and by the time Pausanias wrote about the paintings they'd been on view for some 600 years. He spent more time describing these paintings than he spent on the entire rest of Delphi itself.

The differences between the literary tradition about the events depicted by Polygnotos and the images themselves are emblematic of our understanding of Delphi itself, as there are striking differences between the historical and religious narratives concerning the foundation, evolution, and functions of the sanctuary, *and* the scientific or archaeological record of the Delphic monuments. One of my reasons for walking us through the thicket of these contrasts, contradictions, and conundrums is a conviction that an attempt to reconcile these dissonant artistic and scientific phenomena may have wider implications for the interpretative missions and methods of the modern disciplines of art history and archaeology.

Specifically, I will argue that Delphi and its monuments are less well understood if we take them (as is still natural in modern disciplines such as art history) to be primarily representations, reflections, embodiments, or expressions of the mentality, personality, ethnicity, or gender of their makers. Such a perspective on how artistic phenomena signify was common in the age of Berenson, who is once said to have considered that artworks provided sufficient evidence *in themselves* from which to securely deduce the biography of an artist – a tendency I've described elsewhere as the conflation of *artists and/as their works*.[3]

But what exactly would be alternatives to unproblematically construing artworks as representations, expressions, or indices? To pursue that question, we would need to interrogate the historical grounds for modern Western distinctions between art, science, and religion, attending closely to what preceded our modern ideas about art.

Such a task is well beyond my intentions here,[4] although what I will be discussing may be read as having implications for such a project.

Pausanias was a Greek native of the non-Greek region of Lydia on the central western coast of Turkey, who lived in the time of the Roman emperors Hadrian and Marcus Aurelius in the second century CE. He was what we might call a cultural geographer, an historian of religion, and an observant amateur naturalist who visited Syria, Palestine, Egypt, and Rome itself before recording his famous travels throughout mainland Greece.

His text, known as the *Pariegesis* (literally "a leading around") was a detailed *guide* to all the regions of the country, yet it was mostly unknown until early modern times. The *Pariegesis* was preserved in a single manuscript recorded in 1418 in the Florentine library of Niccolo Niccoli (1364–1437), one of the chief learned men in the company of Cosimo de' Medici. It was deposited after Niccoli's death in the library of San Marco, but was mostly ignored until the late nineteenth century and the accelerated archaeological interest in Greece, when the ancient site of Delphi was finally excavated after the medieval village of Kastri beneath which it was buried was destroyed by an earthquake, its inhabitants moved to a new village built by the French excavators several kilometers to the west.

Pausanias' text came to prominence among modern classical scholars who were learning that as a guide to the many ancient Greek monuments being uncovered at the time, it turned out to be a more reliable description of the remains of Delphi than the commentaries of the then-influential German classical philologist Ulrich von Willamowitz-Moellendorff. As a visiting fellow at Magdalen College in Oxford, Willamowitz delivered two lectures in June 1908 about historical writing and the figures in Pausanias' Polygnotos, alleging the superiority of literary accounts of ancient Delphi over any actual paintings that might possibly be unearthed by the (French) archaeologists then working at Delphi. Willamowitz (a notoriously vociferous critic of his own former schoolmate Friedrich Nietzsche) claimed that the truth regarding personal character was entirely deducible from textual sources – a view consonant with those of his contemporary Bernard Berenson.

The title of this *Passage* refers to a phenomenon I became aware of during my research residencies in Greece: something marked both in the archaeological record and in a variety of puzzling references in the extant ancient literature. There seemed to be two interrelated phenomena.

The *first* was what appeared to be the increasing marginalization or erasure of the monuments and sites of female ceremony, celebration, worship, and divination at major ancient religious sanctuaries, and their full or partial replacement or obliteration by the monuments and rites of male divinities. Familiar at the two most famous Pan-Hellenic sanctuaries of Delphi and Olympia, the changes at the majority of Greek religious sanctuaries took place over several centuries, accelerating in the sixth century BCE, just before the classical period.

The *second* phenomenon was the very striking difference in the ways in which male and female monuments and places of worship were spatially organized, approached, accessed, and ritually used: their antithetical yet co-existing topographies. These contrasts were echoed elsewhere, and indeed the sites of male and female ceremony constituted two entirely different worlds in ancient Greece, where parts of the same landscape were used quite differently by each group.

In the Greek religious ("mythological") literature, these archaeologically palpable distinctions in the uses of a sacred site were articulated as the effect of primeval "contests" between male and female gods for control of a place. The differences in spatial topography as reflected in the architectonic complexities of sacred places have to this day garnered little notice and less formal investigation, especially within the academic disciplines of classical art and architectural history and archaeology. There has been, in effect, a kind of historiographic firewall between literary and art historical traditions of interpretation; between visible "facts on the ground" and the mythic history, which floats like an independent and impermeable bubble in mid-air. Apart, of course, from what have been taken as legible or embodied in Greek painting and sculpture.

The most famous of those gendered divine contests was that between the goddess Athena and the god Poseidon for hegemony over the Athenian acropolis. As figured by the sculpture of the west pediment of the Parthenon itself, each divinity was required to produce a miraculous artifact, for the cleverest of which their fellow Olympians would award a prize: dominion over the Akropolis and by extension the city and its territory (Attica). Poseidon struck the rock with his trident and there spewed forth a spring of seawater, presumably a forecast of future Athenian hegemony over the seas. Athena did the same with her spear, and an olive tree sprouted out of the rock. Their fellow divinities gave the prize to Athena, deeming an olive tree (the first ever seen) rather more useful than a spring of salty water. And as every modern tourist will attest, Athena's olive tree is still standing, having been miraculously rediscovered by the Greek tourist agency about a century ago. And the town was named Athenai, not Poseidonia.

Struggles between the genders were played out poetically, politically, architecturally, topographically, gymnastically, and onomastically in the foundation myths of many Greek sites. With few exceptions, virtually every site said to have originally been sacred to a female divinity was gradually transformed (as the archaeology and literature records) into a major site for the worship of a male god.

How exactly are we to *read* such apparent contrasts, dissonances, and transformations? Are we to take the mythological traditions as coded *exegeses* (interpretative artifacts in their own right, to be sure) of subsequent complexities and seeming contradictions? While we can say with some confidence that traces of the monuments and sites for the celebration of female forces or spirits were indeed in later times marginalized, obscured, or obliterated wholly or in part, the situation is by no means straightforward. The question of the *gendering* of a place arises with special poignancy in looking at the extraordinary artistry of the sanctuary of Delphi – the place regarded by all Greeks as the center of the world; the navel (*omphalos*) of the Earth. Let's look at it more closely.

The name in both ancient and modern Greek is, like Athens, *plural*: "the Delphis," or the *clefts* (in the mountains; in Mount Parnassos), the site of the famous Castalian Spring whose health-enhancing, mildly sulfurous waters gushed forth out of the mountain then and now. One speaks even today of going *stous Delphous* (to the clefts); to the healing springs in the clefts. It is one of the most magnificently situated of all ancient sanctuaries, and, in a country where the land has been hallowed for millennia in so many ways, Delphi surely stands out as one of the most breathtaking sacred landscapes anywhere, every inch of whose ground is the site of a recorded legend. It's spread out on the steep southern slopes of Parnassos, with a view southward out toward the Gulf of Corinth and the Peloponnese (the "island" of Pelops) beyond.

Delphi was a major site for the worship of Apollo; *Phoebos* or shining Apollo; one of the most interestingly gendered of ancient Greek divinities. Apollo, the twin brother of the goddess Artemis, was quite simply the spirit or god of intellectual *brilliance* (as was she). Apollo's temple was at the same time the site of the (female) Delphic *oracle*, a dispenser of wisdom to whom petitioners came from all over the

Greek world and beyond. The oracle was a young priestess with the ceremonial name of *Pythia*, by tradition a pre-pubescent girl, thought today as working under the influence of hallucinogenic drugs. She was known for her enigmatic and famously ambiguous answers to written questions submitted on small lead tablets to priestly intermediaries, who after submission returned answers written on lead tablets to petitioners.

She famously answered questions with another question, or when presented with two choices, opted for a third – for the querulous wordy Greeks, the quintessential sign of human intelligence. Her name is related to the word for snake, *python*. Speaking snakes slither sonorously through more than one ancient belief system; you might recall there's a tree-dwelling one in Judaic creation mythology, similarly entwined with (in that Levantine version) the recently gendered/divided beings Eve and Adam. Gender as a *deponent* character of human beings.

By classical times, the *pythia* uttered her responses in the *adyton* or sunken crypt at the rear (west) end of the rectangular temple of Apollo, a building sited at the upper climax of a ceremonial procession route up the steep hill. The *pythia* or oracle was seated at a tripod, in which or below which a fire burned, probably to heat the herbs and/or drugs whose vapors inspired her prophetic pronouncements. It is thought today that the *adyton* was built over or reconfigured a natural cleft (*delphos*) or cavern in the rock from which emerged sulfurous fumes. The girl underwent ritual purification in the nearby Castalian Spring prior to her prophesies, in a large (vaginal) cleft (the *delphos*) in the mountain a short walk east of the Apollo temple.

The temple stood on a large platform reached in classical and later times by a winding paved pathway (Figure 9.3) flanked by small treasure-houses donated by city-states from around the Greek world, each holding offerings in support of the sanctuary's upkeep, and of the pilgrims from each region, each building vying with those around it in its architectural refinements, cleverness of orientation and siting, and wealth of decoration, which commonly included sculptures or reliefs depicting the famous victory of city-state *X* over city-state *Y* (whose own treasury was next door, proclaiming its subsequent victory over city-state *X*). These buildings also served as clubs or rest houses for visiting citizens and pilgrims from those cities.

One such clubhouse or *lesche*, erected by the citizens of the city-state of Knidos, was literally off this beaten path of intercity machismo. It stood apart from them all at the upper end of the sanctuary at the time; I'll return to it in a moment.

Most of what we appear to know about the early history of Delphi comes from attempts – the recorded structural intuitions of the ancients themselves – at synthesizing disparate legends about the sanctuary. Many of these seem to have been exercises in historical etymology and onomastics: attempts to explain the origins of various personal and place-names. One of the accounts of Delphi's founding has Apollo slaying a serpent (*pytho[n]*) – from which the name of the oracle was taken. The earlier name of the site, according to Pausanias, was in fact Pytho.

Apollo had to atone for this murder – seen by some moderns as a poetic hieroglyph of the conquest of an indigenous (perhaps matrilineal or matriarchal Minoan

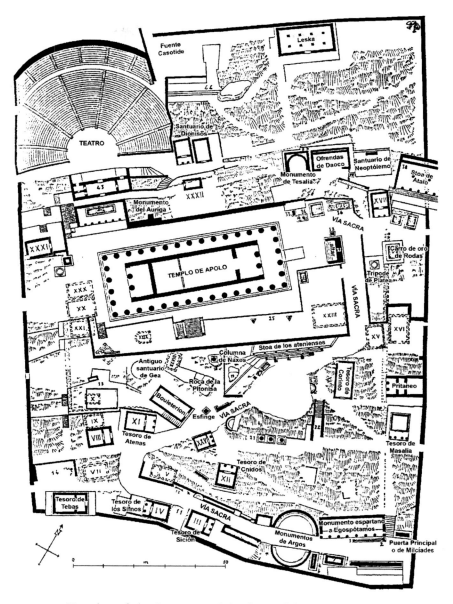

FIGURE 9.3 Site plan of the Sanctuary of Apollo, Delphi (source: P. de La Coste-Mabinière: Au Musée de Delphes. Recherches sur quelques monuments archaïques et leur décor sculpté [Paris: E. de Boccard, 1936], Wikimedia Commons/Public Domain.

or Mycenaean) people by later patriarchal Greek-speaking colonizers. One of the foundation myths of the place held that it was founded by shipwrecked Minoan (Cretan) sailors, rescued by dolphins who conveyed them to land near the foot of Parnassos on the shore of the Gulf of Corinth. (The) Apollo was exiled for nine years to northern Greece, an event commemorated by a festival (the *Stepteria*) in which a simple hut of reeds and thatch was built in an open field by an especially beautiful young man, who, playing the part of Apollo, burned the hut in which stood an image he made of himself as a token of his ritual purification.

This odd story is commonly taken as a euphemistic version of memories of an original human sacrifice – the ritual sacrificing of a young boy-Apollo – in a purpose-built cremation hut. A simulacrum of scape-goating, a practice not unfamiliar in not a few non-Greek traditions.[5]

Apollo's twin sister – the equally brilliant and beautiful Artemis (the Roman Diana) – also had a place at Delphi, but by classical times a very minor one, when she was powerfully overshadowed by her twin brother. I could go on for some time evaluating the conflicting etymologies and pseudo-etymologies of the many names associated with the place. The ancient Greek words for dolphin, cleft, vagina, and womb are *allomorphs* or *homonyms* of each other, and you can see something of the ways in which the syncretisms of various ancient *etymologies* (on which see the *Provocations Passage*) represent attempts at unifying what by hindsight came to seem conflicting and contradictory historical and mythological memories. An art (or science) of *parallax*.

I've been dwelling on these diverse foundation-myths to give you an idea of what I'll call the ancient practice of *parallax* – parallactic artifice: the process of bringing to bear a number of dissonant or partly overlapping phenomena which in and by their superimposition appear to generate (are made to form) a single image or vanishing point. The art of interpretation as an exercise in speculative geometry: as *topological epistemologies*.

What you may also hear in what I've been discussing is a very palpable oscillation or *gender ambivalence* or *transvalence* amongst ostensibly male and ostensibly female persons, spirits, divinities, ceremonies, genealogies, and practices in and at this complex, multidimensional artifact, which was at the center of Greek and Roman historical consciousness for centuries before Pausanias arrived there.

But how exactly would Parnassos have been "gendered?" Of course the body of the earth is always suggestively and metaphorically "gendered" in relation to more or less palpable similarities to (as *iconic signs*) and structural intuitions about organic bodies and their parts. But this is only part of what was being *enacted* (not, strictly speaking, "re-presented") by the artifice of the Delphi compound itself. A better question should perhaps be *how was Parnassos parallactic?* The short answer is that it was parallactic *in and as the artifice of Delphi* itself: as a *Gesamtkunstwerk* or a total, multimodal, multidimensional, and multivalent orchestration of objects, images, texts, and performances in space and time.

What does any of this have to do with Pausanias' account of the painting of Polygnotos? I suggested earlier it was *emblematic* of the artifice, the *Gesamtkunstwerk* of Delphi itself: How might that have been the case? The short answer is that it ostensified and embodied dissonance on multiple levels: (1) with regard to the ambivalent links – the *indeterminacy* – between visual and verbal signification; (2) with regard to the relative positions, connections, and disconnections between male and female figures portrayed; and (3) with regard to the portrayal of relations between space and time. Let's consider the painting itself – and I'm aware of the irony of saying this, since the only trace of what was perhaps the most famous ancient Greek mural painting is in its ancient description: *nothing whatsoever* (except a few traces of colored plaster in the *lesche*'s ruins, of unknown provenance) remains of the work itself. Attempts to render its legibility visible have occupied generations of classical scholars (Figure 9.4).

Pausanias describes Polygnotos' painting as a large mural in two parts. The subject to the *right* of the entryway is the aftermath of the destruction and capture of Troy (*Ilion*) by the (Mycenaean) Greeks. That to the *left* of the door is Hades, the realm of the Underworld, with Odysseus consulting the soul of the seer Tiresias about the proper route to take to his home back in Ithaca, off the northwest coast of the country. Odysseus, Pausanias writes, appears in both paintings – first, to the right, in the chaotic aftermath of Troy's destruction, where sailors, women, and many children are depicted clambering into ships while a single warrior is shown still putting Trojans to death. Untouched is Helen, the ostensible catalyst of the Trojan war, seated alone (like a statue [*agalma* – the Greek word for statues of divinities][6] as Pausanias tells us), apart from the chaos of the ruined city. An occasional abandoned child is depicted clinging to a ruined Trojan altar whose gods have fled.

The illustration of Hades, on the left, is a kind of catalogue of the many individuals one might meet there (Sisyphus, perpetually trying to roll his boulder back up the hill, etc.). The only figure that appears in *both* halves of the painting is Odysseus – earlier, seen as leaving the ruined Troy on the right of the door, and later, the only "live" soul in Hades on the left.

The painting depicts what would have been familiar to a contemporary audience who knew these stories from early childhood. This would have been a *talking gallery*: a series of images intended to be *spoken of* in referencing stories already familiar from childhood, and scenes to explicate to those unfamiliar. Pausanias describes the episodes or vignettes as far as we can tell beginning from the gallery's door, reading outward in opposite directions, that is, counter-clockwise, but it is difficult to tell the exact narrative order to the paintings themselves. He also doesn't tell us how the two parts of the painting joined around on the far (north) wall, only that immediately to the left of the ships departing Troy is another water-scene with the Underworld spirit Charon rowing figures of the deceased across the waters of forgetfulness (*Lethe*) to the Underworld.

The Aegean is juxtaposed with or blends into the waters of the stream of *Lethe*: the waters of *forgetting*; amnesiac water: *a-letheia* or "non-forgetfulness" being the ancient Greek term for "truth" as "non-forgetting" – an *etymology* favored by Heidegger and critiqued by Blanchot as ignoring the disobedience or indisciplinarity

FIGURE 9.4 Reconstruction of the Lesche mural. Wikimedia Commons/Public Domain.

and historical contingencies and drift of verbal signification (see the *Provocations*). A *dissonance* in or disruption of (Euclidean) space-time.

All the figures were labeled in the painting, as on many contemporary ancient Greek vases, and in many respects the entire painting seems a magnified version of one of those expensive painted classical gift vases which depict vignettes of the Homeric epic poems of the *Iliad* and *Odyssey*. In fact, a recent attempt to reconstruct the painting in its entirety in the space allowed by the size of the excavated remains of the building[7] argued that this might be accomplished by synthesizing two bits of apparent evidence: by analogy with the depiction of similar scenes found on contemporary vase paintings, and by a textual analysis of the syntactic structure – prepositional and adverbial parts of speech – in Pausanias' text. By taking literally that when Pausanias says figure X is above, below, beside, or nearby figures Y and Z, we should reconstruct the figures in that fashion, taking care that the resultant composition fits the actual spaces and wall surfaces. This meant adjusting to the wall surfaces of the building the 70 figures of men, women, children and animals mentioned by Pausanias, plus two boats, a tree, and a couple of cliffs.

All that remains of the great mural is what Pausanias *said* Polygnotos depicted, and three small pieces of blue-painted plaster a couple of centimeters long found in the ruins which *may* have come from the walls or floor of the ancient gallery. Pausanias was more interested in how Polygnotos' painting conformed to or contradicted canonical interpretations of the Homeric epics.

So where does this pursuit of Pausanias' Polygnotos at Parnassus leave us? We may wish to say that the painting is an index or is "emblematic" of what is notable about the *Gesamtkunstwerk* itself that constitutes Delphi, where several different bits of evidence can be brought to bear. But then this may not be the point of what is to be learned here in this remarkable place. As far as we can tell the gender dissonance embodied in the sanctuary's *monuments* is not reflected in Polygnotos' *painting*, however you parse Pausanias' prepositions.

However, like any built environment, Delphi was a *four-dimensional* artifact, whose significance unfurled in its performance by the visitor and user in space and time. It was realized and legible architectonically as two distinct yet co-terminous juxtapositions of monuments, buildings, and pathways. Two topologies in one topography – or rather, a topography *realized and articulated dyadically*.[8] One is the processional avenue beginning at the entrance to the sanctuary on the southeast corner and rising in a zig-zag fashion along a route marked by the treasuries, votives, and monuments of the various city-states, climaxing at the entrance to the uppermost platform marking the precinct of the temple of Apollo.

While you can trace this in the plan of Delphi, what you would have actually *seen* and felt in antiquity as you walked up through this crowded route, beyond and behind which you might get occasional glimpses of parts of the temple, *it is only when you are up on the temple platform itself that you can see that great building fully and completely*. What was visible in pieces is only now fully seen. And that view is truly spectacular: *everything else in the sanctuary disappears down below, and the great luminous*

*temple of Shining Apollo appears suspended in air, its gleaming columns and walls a simu-
lacrum of the character of the god himself. The house of the god's image, floating in air.*

Pure religious theater. A stunning and brilliantly contrived revelation. A revealing in plain sight of what shining Apollo instantiated and ostensified.

What could a god *in the air* be heard or read as saying-by-showing (recall Benjamin)? Q. How exactly is a sky god *legible*? *A*. Through its performativity; the
poetics of walking the sanctuary.[9]

And yet: Apollo's temple was *superimposed over and disrupted* an earlier sacred
landscape centered on worship of the earth mother (*Gaia*), now (in classical times)
marginalized and occluded by the Apollo construction. The center of the Gaia
sanctuary is preserved in/as a *precinct* just south of the Apollo temple platform and
it has several extant associated monuments. The *omphalos* or navel of the Earth is
said to have been located here.

But in the goddess' precinct *the chief "monuments" were natural landscape features*
– a rock said to be where the original speaking *oracle* sat (before being re-housed in
Apollo's temple); a round, leveled dancing area (*khoros*); a place devoted to the
muses, those (female) spirits of various human arts, crafts, and sciences; and another
sacred rock, associated with the goddess *Leto*, the *mother of the twins* Apollo and
Artemis, who also had a sacred precinct on the Cycladic island of Delos (around
which it is said all the Cycladic islands revolve). In contrast to the unidirectional,
climactic topology of Apollo, we have *here* a multidirectional web of sites evocative
of *facets* of the goddess: topography as syntax, legible and evocative in and as their
ritual performance. In and as their materiality; their *embodiment*.

I began this *Passage* by repeating a hypothesis framed years ago as a doctoral student
about the increasing "maleness" of this and other ancient sanctuaries, based on my
observation (originally supported by voiced intuitions of my mentors)[10] that traces of
the worship of female divinities in those landscapes were gradually obscured or obliterated – a process, according to the ("scientific") archaeological data read together
with ancient texts, that took several centuries. Returning to this material today suggests that my old hypothesis (and their intuition) was premature: this was *not an erasure
but a superimposition, a palimpsesting* rather than a replacement. A leaving in place and
retaining a fertile and dynamic dissonance and tension. Generating significance not
unlike the poles of an electric current. Perhaps rather like "gender" itself in ancient
Greek society, as many (and not only Foucault) have long conjectured. Never exactly
harmoniously meshing, nor exactly related as figure and ground, *but always partly out
of synch in their simultaneity; existences defined precisely by their dynamic juxtaposition.*

So, finally, what might this imply for the enterprises of interpretation? Parallax
is not a stereoscopic fixing upon a final or singular signification, but an artifice
calling attention to its own fabricatedness, and enhanced by the potential motility
of the point dually pointed at. It implies for one thing that a model of interpretation
whose aim is to decode or decipher what are taken as signs or expressions or representations – that old Berensonian bias, perhaps, but not only his – will always be
an abstraction out of the multimodal circumstances in which any image or object
appears and functions.

Like a Delphic Apollo, a reification floating in mid-air, seemingly untethered to the earth below. Dazzled by the shining god, the divine artifice of singular and fixed interpretation, it is much too easily forgotten that Apollo had a twin sister whose "temple" was indeed the very earth (*gaia*) itself, on which airy Apollo is grounded. The very stuff of grand opera....

It may well be that what came to be realized or ostensified at Delphi were two asymmetric modes of *embodying/practicing* a landscape – Apollo and Gaia/Artemis – which were not fully or distinctly legible *apart* from each other; whose existences are functions and effects of the relationship itself. Like art and religion, as we have seen here. What Delphi appears to ostensify is that the sacredness of a place is what cannot be fully (or literally or directly) read, fixed, or captured singly or finally. Hallowed ground as enigmatic signifier, simultaneously encouraging *and* negating the phantasm of a "secret" beyond both linguistic and material form; of the existence of signification outside its material "expression."

A desynchronizing of *space* recalling *the specter's desynchronizing of time* as noted earlier and throughout this text.

Precisely the enigma that in fact elicits desire itself, and the paradox of the seeming separateness of artistry, scientificity, and religiosity, *art and religion*, which I suggested at the beginning of this book were effects of distinctions between such artifice that acknowledges its fabricatedness, and that which stages its artistry as Praxitelean; as art*less*. Distinctions that have been voiced in certain modernities, as noted throughout this text as *art and religion*.

The challenge today is to reckon deeply and widely with the fact that what art creates is no "second world," no *hetero*topia within the realm of daily life, but the very world, the very tops in which we really do live. The modes of practice we might create that build upon that awareness may be better able to voice and foster links with diverse forms of knowledge-production, whether conventionally referred to as artistic or scientific or philosophical or political. Or religious.

We are today (a mere 40 years after Berenson – a mere blip in time) *realizing* such vividly imagined new syntheses of art, science, and philosophy.[11] Or more correctly, re-animating as syntheses what were taken by hindsight as distinct.

Notes

1 An earlier version of this chapter was presented under the title "Pausanias' Polygnotos and the Parallax of Parnassos" at a conference in honor of Martin Kemp in Oxford in 2010, concerned with "the results of 40 years of progress in approaches to art and science since Berenson." I discussed one instance of transformed approaches to interpretation in one field – archaeology – that both bridges and troubles conventional distinctions between art and science. Or, as I considered in my paper, that more fundamental distinction between artifice that acknowledges its fabricatedness, and that which alleges its art to be artless – a different topology foregrounding and clarifying relations between art and its fraternal twins, science and religion.

2 An issue discussed above in the opening (*Provocations*) *Passage* of this text with respect to the problem of etymology and of the *etymon* ("On Etymology"), following the section "On Method."

3 See *RAH*, ch. 1.
4 See *AINT*, *passim*., for an indication of the directions such an inquiry would take.
5 There are a few (rare) tantalizing and highly disputed traces of what may have been human sacrifice at some very late Minoan (early Mycenaean) sites on Crete.
6 On Lacan and *objet petit a*, the *a* standing for *agalma*, see *Passage* 8.
7 M.D. Stansbury-O'Donnell, "Polygnotos' Iliupersis: A New Perspective," *American Journal of Archaeology*, Vol. 93, 1989, pp. 203–215; and M.D. Stansbury-O'Donnell, "Polygnotos' Nekuia: A Reconstruction and Analysis," *American Journal of Archaeology*, Vol. 94, 1990, pp. 213–235.
8 At least minimally; I suspect that most likely there were several palimpsested fractal topographies realized by gender, perhaps by fractions of variously mooted gender.
9 Michel de Certeau once compared to the experience of walking in a city to a "long poem" orchestrated by a walker in his essay "Walking in the City," from his book *The Practice of Everyday Life*, trans. Steven Rendall (Berkeley and Los Angeles, CA: University of California Press, 1984), pp. 91–110.
10 One of those pedagogical ploys academic advisors impose upon their students to do the actual fieldwork to possibly verify their intuitions. Often successful.
11 One of whose pre-eminent practitioners and most vivid imaginers was the person (like Polygnotos the multiply-knowing) to whom the aforementioned conference in Oxford was dedicated, and where the paper upon which the present *Passage* was drawn was presented in an earlier version.

10

THE TEARS OF THINGNESS AND THE AMNESTY OF AMNESIA

Sunt hic etiam praemia laudi;
Sunt lacrimae rerum et mentem mortalia tangunt.
Solve metus; feret haec aliquam tibi fama salutem.
Virgil, *Aeneid 1.461ff.*[1]

The tears of thingness

The previous *Passage* ("Art, religion, and the parallax of gender"), dealt in part with a complex multidimensional and multitemporal wall painting on the walls of the most celebrated picture gallery in antiquity, the *lesche* or club-house of the citizens of the city-state of Knidos, in the Greek sanctuary of Delphi on the slopes of Mount Parnassos. The large mural spread over the four walls of the gallery depicted on one side the destroyed city of Troy, the *Iliupersis*, and on the other side the *aftermath* of the Trojan War as seen through the eyes of Odysseus, one of that band of conquering Greeks traveling westward across the Aegean (and through the underworld) on his way home on the island of Ithaca, on the west coast of main-land Greece.

This *Passage* begins with *another aftermath* of that War, but seen through the eyes of some of the defeated Trojans also wandering across the sea in search of a new home, in particular the Trojan prince Aeneas, carrying his small son and aged father, and accompanied by some of his retinue. The lines of the poem quoted above are the words of Aeneas, who sees in a temple in the citadel of Carthage on the north coast of Africa a mural of scenes of the Trojan War seven years earlier depicting the key figures in those battles, including the slain Trojan king Priam. Aeneas' words reflect his own deeply emotional encounter with a painting of the destruction of his homeland, here in an alien city on a strange continent where he and his entourage have sought temporary refuge. The poem says that even here, in this strange land, the praiseworthy has its rewards, yet there is a sadness about things: the *mortality of things touches the mind*. But let go of your fears; this fame of yours will bring you some deliverance and calm.

Sunt lacrimae rerum.[2] There was always a certain *sadness* about modern institutions such as "art" or "religion." A sadness about their *insufficiencies* in doing justice to the premises of their promises.

The following quotation images are catalysts for refocusing attention on the historical wrangling with the *problem* that is religiosity's artistry and artistry's religiosity. The sadnesses of religion: why religion *always fails by not living up to the dreamwork of its aesthetic brilliance and splendor*. Unless, of course, you really believe that it truly does (live up, that is). Perhaps the insufficiencies built into religiosities are a tactic for eliciting sympathies by seeming to *almost* succeed, thereby evoking and eliciting (the desire for) belief even more strongly. Never underestimate the brilliant double-speak of martyrdom (or of planned obsolescence).

To introduce the subject I'd like again to set out several things to jointly think with about art as a religion and religion considered as one of if not the finest of the fine arts.

1   The first is an *encomium*, one made recently by Bernard Carr, Professor of Mathematics and Astronomy at Queen Mary College, University of London, writing about his PhD advisor in the 1970s, Stephen Hawking, and one of the many tributes made by his colleagues and admirers around the world on the occasion of his seventieth birthday in Cambridge on January 8, 2012. Carr said that

> Stephen's discovery in 1974 that black holes emit radiation due to quantum [*that is, palpably material*] effects was one of the most important results in 20th century physics. This is because it unified three previously disparate areas of physics – quantum theory, general relativity, and thermodynamics. Like all such unifying ideas, *it is so beautiful that it almost has to be true*, even though it still had not [yet] been experimentally confirmed. The renowned physicist John Wheeler once told me [Bernard Carr] that *"just talking about it was like rolling candy on the tongue."*

Q. So is the "truth" of science a property and function of its purported beauty?

2   The second is a *lament* voiced some three decades ago by British architectural critic and historian Robert Harbison in a delightfully eccentric book called *Eccentric Spaces*. "Art," he wrote, "is troublesome not because it is not delightful, but because it is not more delightful: we accustom ourselves to the failure of gardens to make our lives as paradisical as their prospects."

Q. But do we ever *really* just settle for the gardens we cultivate? How precisely *could* art become *more* delightful? (Are there built-in limits to or quantifiable quota for aesthetic delight?) Sounds like a come-on. . . .

3   Let's superimpose upon our *encomium* and our *lament* a strong *claim*, this one made
by the Bavarian art critic Joseph Ratzinger, whose day job was (until recently)
being Pope Benedict XVI, and a theoretician of art cited frequently and most
recently in a conference held several years ago in Cork, Ireland, devoted to what
is being claimed now by some Catholic theologians to be a "New Reformation"
in the liturgy of the Catholic Church (in fact, strictly speaking it should be called
a *Counter*-Counter Reformation, but then who am I to question the pope?).[3]
Throughout Benedict's large body of writing on aesthetic philosophy, he consistently claims that *art incites not delight or pleasure but <u>pain</u>*. Art is very deeply painful.

But whereas Harbison claimed that we consistently "accustom ourselves" (or not)
to the insufficiencies of artistry to transform our lives by invariably failing to
conform to or confirm the promises of artistry or artifice, Benedict goes under the
radar, so to speak: He claims to explain exactly *why* art's insufficient delight is
painful. This is because its beauty manifests or *calls attention to its own finitude or contingency – thereby allowing for imagining, desiring, or evoking its antithesis; its Other.*
Which is the artifice or fiction – my words, not Benedict's – the artistry, that is, of
transcendence; of something permanent or genuinely fixed and time*less*. The timeless
sacred as opposed to the timely, transitory, or *secular* or profane: what is mortal and
by definition subject to the sequential ravages of time.

As a good (neo)Platonist and determined anti-modernist and vehemently anti-
postmodernist whose words at times seem to have been ghost-written by neocon-
servative British aesthetic philosopher (the erstwhile specter haunting that gathering
at Cork) Roger Scruton, Benedict claimed to harness and rein in the secularity and
consequent transitoriness of artistry whose beauty he finds disappointing by tethering and securing it to what Derrida called a "divine teleology," by rectifying and
bringing art (back) into proper alignment and orientation – the word Benedict used
(as noted earlier in this text) was *Gleichschaltung* – the aligning together or re-
aligning of all facets of human experience.

Divine – or more accurately *preternatural* – decorum: the stagecraft of a conjoint
decorum of the spiritual and the material. The insufficiencies of art are to be celebrated, Benedict claims, *for their capacities to evoke a vision of the more real, more genuine
alternative other-world of the spiritual* or *im*material. Disorder as evocative of the ideal
immortal divine order of the cosmos. The papal cosmetology of cosmology. Suf-
fering the pain caused by insufficient artistry is a penance we must and *should endure*
because it very palpably cries out for (a) god.

This may indeed sound all too familiar to those schooled properly in their cat-
echisms or catechism-equivalents (Mao's little red book; Ayn Rand's *Fountainhead*,
Book of Mormon, Scientology, etc.), and those familiar with the myth of Narcissus
and/or Lacanian psychoanalytic theory – for Ratzinger's *transcendent "real"* is indeed
the Lacanian order of the *imaginary*. The "real" of the human is rather its vulner-
ability and mortality, which the imaginary – the order of the promise; of messianicity; of the perfect(ed) world to come; of the techno-sublime – keeps the reality of
our mortality at a distance and in abeyance.[4]

For Harbison the insufficiency of art was a sign or *symbol* of disappointment; for Benedict, it is staged on the contrary as a *real index*; virtually a contact-relic or arrowed inevitability; a pointing at and (by heavy-handed implication) touching the divine. The "truth in *pointing*," evoking Derrida's famous argument in his handsomely impertinent *The Truth in Painting* (1976).

Recall Hannah Arendt's observation about the deepest source of the aggressiveness of totalitarianism being the lust for power or profit, but rather the urge to make the world consistent.

An alternative mode of semiosis, postulating a real direct link between a signifier and (what is consequently constructed as) what "it" signifies: its referent; its referee. In contrast to a symbol, as a hypothetical, mooted, arbitrary, and context-specific connection between (what are distinguished as) signifier and signified. Equation versus adequation. Which may give us an insight into the *semiological aestheticism*, the artistry lurking in the shadowed badlands of theocratic politics. As Nusselder puts it:

> The myth of Narcissus illustrates that the will to be similar to the image and to eliminate the tension caused by the "real self" can lead to self-destruction: Narcissus drowns. Lacan discusses this aggressive trait of narcissism as the action of "narcissistic suicidal aggression" ... In it, the subject tries to resolve the aggressive tension caused by the disparity between its (limited) embodied self and its (ideal) image by directing the aggression against the (real) being that does not correspond to the image.[5]

The perverse logic of the fanatical fantasist ("Tea," or Narcissist) wing of the old US Republican political party, hell-bent on dismantling democracy itself in every possible way because such a country no longer conforms to its image of what it is supposed to be (but palpably is no longer). A logic not dissimilar to that motivating Anders Breivik, the mass-murderer of Oslo, discussed above in *Passage* 3 ("Perambulations"), or that of the Talibani who dynamited the colossal Buddhas of Bamiyan, or for that matter, any apartheid-enabler, Inquisitor, or political theocrat, ancient or modern.

Again, consider the remarkable and remarkably convincing sleights of hand that replace one mode of artistry *not* with something different from or outside artistry, that might independently guarantee it, but *by another artwork*: the designation or artistry (or that even better art) called *transcendence*. (Literally, that which *climbs across, over* and beyond [what is, *by the act of climbing over*, thereby crafted by designation *as*] the palpably "material".)

Artless artwork. As Ratzinger himself said, "Anyone who has heard one of Bach's great *Thomas Kantor* cantatas *knows that faith is true*." A breathtaking sleight of hand.

Are those enchanted by (enchained to) *Lady Gaga* (or whatever currently hot *X*) the children of a lesser god?

4 To all of what has now been mentioned (encomium, lament, and claims) I'll add a fourth thing: the artistry of perspective and of *panopticism*. Italo Calvino

dramatically staged a nest of dilemmas (or knot of conundrums) throughout his remarkable book *Invisible Cities*, and perhaps most starkly in his account of the imaginary city of *Eudoxia*, one of the places the protagonist of Calvino's remarkable anti-novel, Marco Polo, describes to his host/captor, the Chinese emperor Kubla Khan, when exhorted to describe to the blind ruler the delights of all the cities of his immense and diverse empire. Which all turn out, as the reader becomes aware, to be facets of Marco Polo's memories of the different identities of his own native Venice, masquerading as increasingly exotic and more and more impossibly surreal cities in Asia.

> It is easy to get lost in Eudoxia: but when you concentrate and stare at the carpet, you recognize the street you are seeking in a crimson or indigo or magenta thread which, in a wide loop, brings you to the purple enclosure that is your real destination. Every inhabitant of Eudoxia compares the carpet's immobile order with his own image of the city, [with] an anguish of his own, and each can find, concealed among the arabesques, an answer, the story of his life, the twists of fate.
>
> An oracle was questioned about the mysterious bond between two objects so dissimilar as the carpet and the city. One of the two objects – the oracle replied – has the form the gods gave the starry sky and the orbits in which the worlds revolve; the other is an approximate reflection, like every human creation.
>
> For some time the augurs had been sure that the carpet's harmonious pattern was of divine origin. The oracle was interpreted in this sense, arousing no controversy. But you could, similarly, come to the opposite conclusion: that the true map of the universe is the city of Eudoxia, just as it is, a stain that spreads out shapelessly, with crooked streets, houses that crumble one upon the other amid clouds of dust, fires, and screams in the darkness.

Chaotically crooked democratic Athens in contrast to the new contemporary planned cities and colonies in the Hellenic Mediterranean and Levant. Calvino's deceptively simple tale calls attention not merely to something fundamental about the ways in which we imagine cities and architecture and the stagecraft of art in modern life; it also points to something that lies at the heart of modernity itself, as what I called at the beginning of this book a *paratheistic* practice: the *theological dream or aesthetic fiction* of some true panoptic perspective or position or site from which the confusions and complexities of things could be revealed in their true underlying essence or ideal form; in the *Idea*, that is, of what they appear to be desirous of.

A perspective that would fix things in place and keep them from flying away – which is, as Michel de Certeau put it, that remarkably enduring fiction that "like a proper <u>name</u> ... provides *a way of conceiving and constructing space on the basis of a finite number of stable, isolatable, and interconnected properties*." Properties, that is, of certain objects and forms understood as – or imagined *as if* – containing, conveying, or re-presenting some truth(s). The splendid fiction of the body as the "temple of the spirit," for example; of the body as a veritable site of *entelechy*, as Aristotle put it regarding the *psyche* or *soul* as the center point or enactive force or principle of *that which is thereby distinguished as* what "bodies" it forth; its embodiment. An inner fiction projected as the *reality* of what one "is" and would wish moreover *to be seen as*. Which is precisely what the aesthetic fiction of the soul or spirit or psyche or persona is designed to do and be. That panoptic modernity whose cogencies were always and still remain grounded in amnesiac religiosities engineered as a concerted action *on and against* the past; causing us to forget so as to (re)formulate a present we desire to inhabit *as if it were the product of what we might have wished to be descended from*, as Hayden White once poignantly put it.

But the point of Calvino's *Invisible Cities* beyond the implication that any city is an imaginary version of what one takes as real, is that reality itself is already an inverted image; already a representation. The "home" that one imagines all these allomorphs, all these "cities" described to the emperor by Marco Polo, to be inversions of, is itself unreal: a phantasm; a veil tossed over the real, beneath which is not what seems to be hidden, but (a) nothing. A nothing thrown back in one's face. Thrown back upon the artistry, the artifice, of "understanding itself" – revealed as preternaturally porous.

Calvino's *Eudoxia* in his catalogue of "invisible" places calls to mind a contemporary echo and instance:

5   Marco Polo lived 1,000 years too soon to have walked around the modern Chinese megalopolis of Shanghai. For the citizens of contemporary Shanghai there is an uncanny *allomorph* of the temple in Calvino's *Eudoxia*: a gigantic wooden *model* of the city on the top floor of a building in the city's central square, the *Museum of the City of Shanghai*. Visitors walk along a metal walkway above and surrounding the giant-scale model, and each visitor can recognize his or her neighborhood or house or street panoptically, in their *true* (i.e., cartographic; Euclidean) relations to each other. It's a monumental-scale model (paradigma) of this vast and diverse city of 20 million citizens, and an extremely popular exhibit, always (at least whenever I was there) crowded with visitors jostling to find their place; their home base; in the massive urban puzzle model and to *see* the relations of all places to all others. To (re)find themselves by having a visualizable address in a city massively reinventing itself all the time.

In this multistory and multitemporal (past/present/future) Museum of the City the monochrome wooden model represents the city at *present*; it is twinned with the other major exhibit on the building's top floor, a 3D Cinemax mini-theater that takes visitors seated in a futuristic vessel on a fanciful flight to the brilliantly colored Shanghai of the *future*. The antithesis of the monumentally monstrous and monotonous city outside the museum.[6]

As you (virtually) swoop over and above that city-yet-to-come, you see off to the side an image of what the city looks like today (a photo rendition of the wooden model you just walked around next door) now dissolving and being left in the darkness as you fly forward in time. That future city in fact being presently brought into being outside the museum by the hundreds of high-rise construction cranes you can see on every horizon outside. The lower stories of this museum houses photo, film, and print archives documenting the city's *past*.

For the inhabitants of Marco Polo's *Eudoxia*, the panoptic point of resolution was the temple carpet within whose geometrical patterns and motifs one imagines delineated the *true* relationships among complex things, events, people, or emotions. But one could substitute for that carpet many apparent substitutes – museums, universities, sciences, philosophies, religious dogmas, histories – the historical "truth" of buildings, cities, social relations, ideologies, etc. The tale of *Eudoxia* is so *familiar* precisely because it articulates something fundamental about the ways in which we envision understanding itself in our post-Enlightenment modernities: as the revelation of the truth of something from some privileged and particular perspective. Like the staging of a papal desire for a counter-counter-reformation and the rectification and re-orientation (*Gleichschaltungen*) through artistry of *what is thereby and consequently articulated by contrast (that is, co-produced) as its twin(ned) dis-order.*

Artistry as constitutive of religiosity – and *vice versa*: as obversely parallactic.

The amnesty of amnesia

Amnesia is commonly understood as a complete or partial loss of memory. Today the term is taken as a mental (cognitive or psychological) disorder of *individuals*; the inability of a single person to remember things. It is also commonly applied to material personifications such as institutions, professions, groups, or incorporations of individuals.[7]

But in its Greek origins[8] the term referred to communal or civic matters; specifically to collective juridical or political matters. Amnesia was a *variant* of the term *amnestia* – referring to a sovereign act of oblivion or forgetfulness that was *granted* with regard to past crimes of an individual or group, often concerning political crimes. As Landzelius notes, tethering his etymology to a first amnesiac of this kind, namely the Athenian general and political leader Thrasyboulos who, in BCE 403 "after restoring democracy to Athens, pushed through legislation that obliterated the juridical remembrance of the misdeeds of those associated with the regime of the Thirty Tyrants."[9] In other words, they were granted an "amnesty" that *erased the legal record* of past misdeeds; of things the city-state wished to collectively obliterate. A particularly *proactive* use of amnesia in the *polis*, as the sanctioned erasure of an erasure. An absolution.

As Christine Boyer put it in relation to the fashioning and function of urban space,

> A panoramic flow of unstable visions offer[s] a new accounting of memory disturbances: those of amnesia, paramnesia, hypermnesia, for example, all

narrat[ing] not only an increased medicalization of disturbances at the end of the 19th century, but revealing as well a growing anxiety and need to establish a normal relationship between the present and the past.[10]

Modernity can be understood in this regard as a collective amnesty of things past: a "placing in oblivion such things thus made past (objects as well as practices) in a way that amounts to a continuously reiterated collective amnesia."[11] The product of this amnesia is a matrix of institutions and practices assigned with the role of (selectively) remembering *and* forgetting.

The latter is a deeply political activity in the *pushing* of certain objects and practices (and indeed, certain peoples – e.g., those now to be distinguished as "primitive") *out of the present*, erecting borders between what is and is not relevant to remember of the past in the present. Acts of reification, in other words, turning parts of the present into *absences* in the present. Kicking things not merely down the road but into another space-time; another dimension.

"Being," as Merleu-Ponty once asserted,[12] "is synonymous with being *situated*." To be sited is to be cite-able. Reification is linked to alienation chiasmatically: another modality of parallax.

In the aftermath of art and religion

Following a recently co-authored book called *Art Is Not What You Think It Is*,[13] some might have expected to be reading here its (or *a*, or *the*) sequel or *aftermath*, describing (finally, at last!) what art *really really is*, or that a new book advertised as this one has been as dealing with "art and religion" might have been expected to be subtitled something like *Religion* is (also!) *not what you think it is*. Both expectations would not have been far off the mark, for in fact one of the aims of the present book was to demonstrate that any study that claims to investigate "relations between" two fictional entities can only itself be a fiction (the sum of two fictions is a third fiction, not a *non*-fiction; a further work of artistry and artifice in its own right, like that of facticity).

The conundrum of magical thinking, both ancient and contemporary.[14]

The first expectation, that the present book is the former's *aftermath*, will be met in and by what follows here – taking that term quite literally as that which follows a particular event; its upshot or consequence(s). But while the term might seem related to measurement (*mathesis*): the measuring or accounting for something afterwards, it is in fact connected to something more prosaic – *mowing*: *-math* (*maeth*, in Old English, from Old High German *mad*), refers to a new growth of grass after or following a mowing, which may itself be grazed, re-mowed, or plowed under. What something looks like after having been mowed or mowed down and matted.

But *Art Is Not What You Think It Is* did consider what art "is," from the standpoint (among other things) of it not being a *what* but a *when* and consequently a *how*.[15]

This aftermath or after-mowing; this plowing-under, however, comes not only after *Art Is Not*, but also after a book published in 2006, an earlier "aftermath" with the explicit title *In the Aftermath of Art (Ethics, Aesthetics, Politics)*, a collection of earlier published essays framed and followed by a long critical commentary by Canadian art historian and critic Johanne Lamoureux.[16]

In her commentary she says that what was done (my assembly and re-collection of texts) was rather like what Mary Shelley did in *Frankenstein* – injecting the gothic into the phantasmagoric story of the neoclassical origins of art history, and dis-membering and *recognizing the fragmentary morbidity of the material at hand*: the body or corpus, the *corpse* of "art history," a stitching together of deponent parts, put together so as to project the fiction of a unity, an illusory wholeness or singularity. A discipline or dis-ciplining of bits and pieces with disparate histories, trajectories, and uses:

> it is important to understand that (t)his title [*In the Aftermath of Art*] does not act as an invitation to cultivate the transparence of a discipline that would be perfectly and absolutely instrumentalized; or to the contrary, of denouncing the false opacity of it. It is rather an affirmation of the necessary lucidity of the historian's eye, sensible at the same time to the *artifice of the montage* and to the underlying conditions that render it possible. "To see through," *in the same way that one could "look through" a painted window by Magritte*: in other words, to connect, beyond the disciplinary confines of art history, with the conditions and operations that inscribe a larger epistemological configuration in it, and in relation to which it only possesses a little autonomy, if not the same phantasmatic autonomy that its colleagues are also imagined to possess.[17]

The book's title was not what would lead readers to discover once again that the Emperor has no clothes, but rather it would allow them to observe that *his body is stitched-together*. As Lamoureux noted, "the scars are telling and the seams are tight. There will be no perfect fit." That aftermath brought together a series of texts in no teleological or linear order, intended as resources of things to think with and reckon with by readers, rather than delineating a fictional teleology or progressive unfolding of a particular principle or "take" on art. A collection or reading together in any way the reader might fancy.

Taking the idea of an "anthology" literally, in its derivation from *anthos* or flower, a collection of flowers to be assembled by a viewer into another arrange-ment. In fact a re-inscription that transcribes and alters it (the artifice of the collec-tion) in ways that no deliberation can fully anticipate or control. The method of *that* aftermath has also been that of *this*.

In other words, and in addition, the present very *haunted* text – as with one of the aftermaths of that aftermath (*AINT*) – refused to efface the signs of its own artifice; the traces of the processes of re-membering its (own) sewing (back) together; its own fabricatedness, rejecting the duplicity/decorum of *erasing* the scars of its legibilities, its (if anything remains of its) Praxitelean decorum. Scars as fissures (*Ursprungen*[18]) in a text which would serve as springboards or passages to move one's reckonings forward.

In fact, this may be said to be the very subject of what this book (*this* "aftermath") has become, within the frames of the connections/oppositions between two reifications; two fictive phenomena, namely "art" and "religion," staged *as if* ontologically distinct, for the sake of argument, as they say. Art permits us to see fiction as fiction, to see the contingency of the (human) world. As Wallace Stevens put it in *Adagia*, "The final belief is to believe in a fiction, which you know to be a fiction, there being nothing else. The exquisite truth is to know that it is a fiction and that you believe it willingly."[19] Fiction is/as the truth of truth. The "supreme fiction" of the fiction, the artistry, the artifice, of fact.

It has been with a reckoning with Stevens' conundrum, the paradox of the fiction of absolutes, that this investigation has evolved through its various *Passages*, as in fact was said at the beginning of this book, repeated here and now in the aftermath of what the book has become.

It is not that art produces illusion or "is" illusion, that it's a *mere* copy of what is imagined as perfect, as is commonly believed Plato believed: artistry competes not with some palpable *thing* in what (for example) Ranciere called the "distribution of the sensible."[20] More importantly (as I think Plato appreciated) art, artistry, and artifice *trouble* that which is beyond appearance: the *transcendence* of the sensible.

If "art," in short, is not a kind of thing but a process of bringing to sensibility the artifice of transcendence, is religion, then, the complementary antithetical (chiasmatic) process of masking the artifice of transcendence and of manufacturing anxiety (fear and terror) in the face of *inconsistency*?

Notes

1 Book I, lines 461–463. Literally: "Here, too, the praiseworthy has its rewards; *there are tears for things and mortal things touch the mind*. Release your fear; this fame will bring you some deliverance." The epic poem about the founding of Rome, *The Aeneid*, was written *c.* BCE 29–19 by the Roman poet Publius Vergilius Maro (BCE 70–17). Book I of the poem may be accessed online at: www.thelatinlibrary.com/vergil/aen1.shtml.

2 See Peter Schwenger, *The Tears of Things: Melancholy and Physical Objects*. (Minneapolis, MN and London: University of Minnesota Press, 2006). Ch. 1 ("Words and the Murder of the Thing") originally appeared in *Critical Inquiry*, Vol. 28, 2001, pp. 99–113.

3 See D. Vincent Twomey SVD and Janet E. Rutherford, *Benedict XVI and Beauty in Sacred Art and Architecture: Proceedings of the Second Fota International Liturgical Conference, 2009* (Dublin: Four Courts Press/New York: Scepter Publishers, 2011). The volume examined the fundamental principles guiding the church in determining which works of art are truly "signs and symbols of the supernatural world."

4 Andre Nusselder, *Interface Fantasy: A Lacanian Cyborg Ontology* (Cambridge, MA: MIT Press, 2009).

5 Regarding the "promise" of technology, and the techno-sublime, see ibid., p. 96:

> We need beliefs (of our own immortality) to keep (anxiety about our own finitude) at a distance. Technology incorporates those beliefs, as is most clearly expressed by the transhumanist quest for immortality (cloning, freezing the body, downloading our mental self in a computer, and so on).... Technological possibilities can seduce us to such an extent that we imagine the constraints of the real being eliminated (the addict who only lives online – the realized fantasy). Problems arise when we imagine we can use technology to fulfill the promises that belong to existence itself: for

example, when we think that psychopharmacology is the solution to each and every psychic problem; or when people get addicted to their life on the screen because they feel so much better than in "real life."

See also Jacques Lacan, *Ecrits* (Paris: Seuil, 1966), pp. 174, 187, on the myth of Narcissus.

6 Punctuated, in my limited experience walking that city, by two exceptions: a score of international celebrity-architect-designed high-rise buildings (all looking like 1930s Hollywood *Flash Gordon* sci-fi movie sets), and occasional reconstructions of old traditional brick neighborhoods and "little Chinatowns": theme-parked "traditional" zones.

7 Note the distinction between American and British usage of singular and plural voice in reference to the latter. Americans would say "The BBC reports (singular) that…" while British would say "The BBC report that…" (pl). Perhaps the currently legally enshrined position in the US that corporations are "individuals" is in part a reflex of syntactic ideology.

8 Caution: see the *On Etymology* section of *Provocations* at the beginning of this book and the discussion there on Blanchot and Humpty-Dumpty through the medium of Leslie Hill. Landzelius' contentions about the links between amnesia and amnesty bear thinking about further.

9 Michael Landzelius, "Amnesia as Depoliticized Absence," within "Spatial Reification, or, Collectively Embodied Amnesia, Aphasia, and Apraxia," *Semiotica: Journal of the International Association for Semiotic Studies*, Vol. 175, 2009, pp. 46ff.

10 Christine Boyer, *The City of Collective Memory: Its Historical Imagery and Architectural Entertainments* (Cambridge, MA: MIT Press, 1994), pp. 24–25. See also Richard Terdiman, *Present Past: Modernity and the Memory Crisis* (Ithaca, NY: Cornell University Press, 1993).

11 Landzelius, "Amnesia as Depoliticized Absence." See also my remarks above in *Provocations* on the linkage between the origins and ends of (what is sited as) what I might now call an "etymological decorum"; regarding Blanchot's critique of Heidegger's political agenda regarding the use of (imaginary) linguistic origins justifying present situations.

12 Maurice Merleu-Ponty, *Phenomenology of Perception*, trans. Colin Smith (London: Routledge and Kegan Paul, 1962; 1989 reprint), p. 252.

13 Donald Preziosi and Claire Farago, *AINT*, whose title was a response to an invitation to write a book on "the idea of art" for Blackwells' "Manifestoes" series of volumes in various academic fields.

14 And the self-made double-bind of believing that what is "after art" is *not* more, better artistry, whether analogically or digitally. We've been there before: most recently, the lamentably naïve and ahistorical *After Art* by David Joselit (Princeton, NJ: Princeton University Press, 2013), yet another re-upholstering of tatty old disciplinary machinery.

15 One of the key issues addressed in that book – the problem of *indexicality* and its pertinence to issues of artistry and religiosity – was further developed by Claire Farago, "Towards an Archaeology of the Index," in *Taidehistoriallisia Tutkimuksia/Konsthistoriska Studier/Studies in Art History, 44: Tiedeidenvalisyys ja rajanynnylitykset taidehistorissa Annika Waernebergin juhlakirja* (Helsinki: Society for Art History in Finland, 2012).

16 D. Preziosi, *In the Aftermath of Art: Ethics, Aesthetics, Politics* (London: Routledge, 2006), pp. 131–154.

17 Ibid., p. 151.

18 The reference is to Heidegger's 1935 *Der Ursprung des Kunstwerkes/The Origins of the Work of Art* (Stuttgart: Philipp Reclam, 1967), with introduction by Hans-Georg Gadamer. See also Sam Weber's discussion of this point in his essay "After Deconstruction," in Samuel Weber, *Mass Mediauras: Form, Technics, Media* (Stanford, CA: Stanford University Press, 1996), pp. 129–151, where he notes (p. 149):

> The "real" begins to emerge as an *after-effect* of the possible rather than as its actualization or implementation. And the possible begins to look more like the *origin* – the *Ursprung*, the primordial *crack* – of the "real" than its deficient anticipation … one could say that *possibility defers the real* instead, as previously thought, of *deferring* to it (that is, submitting to its authority).

19 Wallace Stevens, *Adagia*, in *Opus Posthumous* (revised, enlarged, and corrected edition), ed. Milton J. Bates (New York: Knopf, 1989), p. 189. See Simon Critchley, "The Twofold Task of Poetry," in *Things Merely Are: Philosophy in the Poetry of Wallace Stevens* (London: Routledge, 2005), pp. 57–60, esp. pp. 58ff. "Poetry," Critchley writes, "reveals the order which we impose on reality," allowing the contingency and fictiveness of the world to be palpable.

20 See Jacques Ranciere, *Aesthetics and its Discontents*, trans. Steven Corcoran (London: Polity Press, 2009) (*Malaise dans l'esthetique* [Paris: Editions Galilee, 2004]), pp. 34–35. In speaking of a Greek statue of a divinity, the fundamental problem of Ranciere's attempt to relate art and politics came to the fore. He said

> The statue, like the divinity, holds itself opposite the … subject, in other words it is foreign to all volition, to every combination of means and of ends. It is closed in on itself, that is to say inaccessible for the thought, desires and ends of the subject contemplating it. And it is by this radical unavailability, that it bears the mark of man's humanity and the promise of a humanity to come, one at last in tune with the fullness of its essence. This statue, which the subject of aesthetic experience cannot in the least possess, promises the possession of a new world. However, from another angle, the statue's autonomy pertains to the mode of life that is expressed in it.… [It]'s autonomy is in effect a result: it is the expression of the comportment of the community whence it issues.

He goes on to say:

> [T]he Greek statue is art for us because it was not art for its author, because, in sculpting it, the author was not making an "artwork," but translating into stone the shared belief of a community, identical with its very way of being.
>
> (Ibid., p. 35)

Yet nowhere did Ranciere deal with the evident problems raised by the (admittedly translated) terms *mark* ("mark of man's full humanity"), *translation* ("translating into" stone), or *expression* ("expression of [the] comportment"). The "living power of the community" is seen as being "nourished by the sensible embodiment of its idea" (p. 37). In short, his general project of articulating the relationships between politics and aesthetics (discussed *en passant* earlier) is shorted or short-circuited by its uncritical attention to the implications of its rather conventional modes of signification.

As noted on occasion in the present text, the ancient Greek term for the statue of a *divinity* is *agalma*, a term Lacan referred to in connection with his *objet petit a* – the "a" standing for *agalma*. The *objet a* is desire's cause, "the things one drops of oneself into the world in order to be a subject forever desiring their irretrievable return." See Juli Carson, "On Critics, Sublimation, and the Drive: The Photographic Paradoxes of the Subject," in Parveen Adams, ed., *Art: Sublimation or Symptom* (New York: The Other Press, 2003), p. 99. In the same volume, see Graham Hammill, "History and the Flesh: Caravaggio's Sexual Aesthetic," p. 56: "In Lacanian theory, the *objet a* is *not the desired object*: exactly the reverse. The *objet a* is desire's cause, and, *if anything, desire's objective is to obscure that cause.*" A Praxitelean practice.

In contrast, see Charles Shepherdson, "History and the Real: Foucault with Lacan," *Journal of Postmodern Culture*, Vol. 5, No. 2, 1995; or Carolyn Dean, *The Self and its Pleasures: Bataille, Lacan, and the History of the Decentered Subject* (Ithaca, NY: Cornell University Press, 1992). Or, for that matter, this book and others referenced above.

11
CODA

Coda. A concluding passage, often in music, the function of which is to bring a composition to a cogent and well-proportioned close. From Latin *cauda,* "tail." Etymologically unrelated to caution, but one must take heed and be cautious of allowing the tail to wag the body of the text (as was often said of Beethoven's seemingly interminable symphonic *codas*).

I will be brief. This book's final *Passage* dealt with the sadness and insufficiency or mortality of things and with what lay beneath and was productive of such tears: the awareness of their fabricatedness; that they were stitched together, however Praxitelean they may have seemed in erasing the signs of their facture.

And that *Passage* ended with the word *inconsistency*: a term evocative of Hannah Arendt's discussions of totalitarianism[1] and the attempt to account for its aggressiveness as rooted less (or not merely) in the lust for power and profit and more deeply and fundamentally in ideologically driven desires to *make the world consistent.* Who else shares in ideologies of decorousness? Art critics? Designers? Ethnic cleansers, house cleaners, city planners, historians, politicians, imperialists, manifesto writers, cartographers, parents?

Consistency (from Latin *sistere,* to stay or stand [firm], ult. from Latin *stare*). Related to existence, subsistence, persistence, resistance, desistence, assistance.... And the root is related to place as well, as in consistory (from Latin *consistorium,* a place of assembly (religious or political); a well-ordered place or site.

Returning us to the theme (consistency, decorum, fittingness, and their allomorphs in space and time) that emerged in many places in all the *Passages* above; one considered most explicitly a variety of phenomena such as the *eruvim,* the *phylacteries* (t(e)fillin), the *eucharist,* and the question of blasphemy, idolatry, and images of the prophet Mohammed, which evoked earlier Christian ambivalencies about artistic representation or expression (iconoclasm versus iconophilia) of god.

What exactly linked such disparate things? The book was haunted from the outset by juxtapositions of disparate events and phenomena, and pursued a investigative trajectory/epistemological excavation on multiple fronts.

Juxtaposed were:

1   The *eruv* (pl. *eruvim*) (see Figure 1.1): the delimitation of a place or site within whose boundaries some activities, and in particular the carrying of certain items, may take place. The delimitation in effect transforms parts of what may be common public or civic space into a place consistent with the strictures of Jewish law regarding what may or may not be properly performed in such spaces. Where crossing boundaries constitutes a *transgression* of (a going across or beyond) the law. It is both heterotopic and, by implication, heterochronic, in that it simulates in space what applies to sanctioned activities carried out at periodic moments.

2   A *phylactery (t(e)fillin)* (see Figure 8.2) materially connects the forehead and left arm of a religiously observant Jewish male to the Torah during morning prayer, specifically to fragments of the holy scripture which are contained in two small square leather boxes on the forehead and left arm (facing the heart). The spatial tableau is also legible as a simulacrum of the Hebrew letters *shin*, *daleth*, and *yod*, which together form the divine name *Shaddai*. A religio-semiological tableau, as a symbol of comportment: metonyms orchestrated together as a metaphor of standing-with or consistency with the law.

3   The Christian *eucharist*, a piece of bread which at a specific ceremonial moment (and only then) does not merely stand in for, signify, or *re*-present the body of Christ, but is believed to *be* the latter at the exact moment when a priest pronounces the words *Hoc Est Corpus Meum* "This is My (i.e., Christ's) Body." It is a heterochronic artifact whose identity with the (no longer present) body of Christ is the one sign that is *not* a sign: the one and only exception to the semio-religious distinction between signifier and signified.

4   Plato's proposed banishment of mimetic artistry from an ideal city-state was *inconsistent* with his proposed cure for the mimetic inadequacy of art, namely, the transformation of the state itself into a decorous object or artifact in its own right as itself mimetic of an (imagined) divine or cosmic order. In other words, the ideal state would be a human simulation of a transcendent cosmology. Transcendency, to put it bluntly, articulated not merely as *better art(istry)*, but as perfect artifice; the "artifice of eternity."

5   "Trust not in your own understanding" as one local Baptist church's advertising board insisted, but rather in the (one and only *true*, of course) "Lord" – the artifice/embodiment of a transcendent (and ambivalently accessible) force or power. Transform your mortal life into an embodiment of a decorous moral life, a simulacrum/artifice of eternal life, where your body is *legible* as a temple of (what is *thereby distinguished as*) your unique, and *individual/non*-divisible, singular spirit or soul. Where, in short, everything is decorous; in its *proper* place. Where your soul doth *magnify* the Lord. Recalling the echoing pottery

urns placed at various strategic positions in a Greek theater to amplify the voice
of actors.

6   Evoking – and returning us to – the central *Passage* (No. 6) above; the still,
patient, quiet center of the book; its core *theses* (from Greek *tithenai*, to place,
put into place or position: a pro-positioning). Which, seen cartographically
(that is, from above, from the eye of a bird or a god), is that from which all
things surrounding (its corollaries [from Latin *corollarium*], diminutive of *corona*
[crown or garland] or circumferential inferences) *followed*, spreading outward
like ripples in a pond. Ripples staged as passages in a narrative composition.

The theses articulated the interrelated theoretical and epistemological status and
the consequences of the dis-position-ing of "art" and "religion," recasting that
conventional opposition or distinction in relation to the underlying problem of the
ambivalence, amnesia, or duplicity, as well as the accordance with/acceptance of
the fabricatedness and contingency of their fabrications. In effect, different positions
on the same epistemological/semiological continuum. All of which renders the
reified ontologies of artistry and religiosity problematic and available to critical
reckoning with inconsistency in potentially more productive ways.

As discussed in the text, the Danish cartoon controversy, ignited in September
2005 by deeply insulting portrayals in the Danish newspaper *Jyllandsposten* both of
the prophet Mohammed and of Muslims or Arabs more generally, linking all of
them to aspects of terrorism, brought to the surface fundamental and sharply diver-
gent political, religious, and social attitudes toward the nature, functions, and
responsibilities of artistry and representation in the contemporary world. Such differences were commonly reduced in both the popular media and in academic discussions in many countries as resulting from essentially incompatible or irreconcilable
beliefs in "Islam" and "the West" on the relationship between art and religion in
public life – crystallized as a debate between "individual freedom of expression"
and the strictures and prohibitions of religious dogma.

Lost in those debates were two things. First, the intensity of racial and ethnic
antagonisms embodied in the portrayals – dismissed by some as "mere (culturally
and legally permissible) satire," and by others as a racist political and religious
crusade by "the West" against Islam. The second thing lost was something that
became central to the inquiry pursued by the text above – an inquiry itself crystallized in the controversies unfolding in the wake of the cartoon controversy. *Passage*
6 was an attempt to recount what the miscommunications following the cartoon
controversy evoked: an urgent need to pursue in depth what lay beneath these
"miscommunications"; namely, exactly how and why and under what conditions
what in one society are or have been distinguishable as art and religion can be
*in*distinguishable in another. It also sought to bring to the fore the diversity of
Muslim opinions toward imagery or iconism in general, within which *insulting*
imagery is but one variant. In short, it was not imagery *per se* that was the source of
the reactions, but one functional or performative mode of signifying: not aniconism
as such, but one dimension of semiosis (negative phaticism).

The book's investigations had as their chief aim a further understanding of what motivated and made possible such concordances and discordances; such compatibilities and incompatibilities; such consistencies and inconsistencies. What was clarified in the course of these investigations was, among other things, the *situatedness* of all such relationships: their determinacy within and with respect to a broader set of possibilities (indeterminacy).

In short, their motivations. Leaving us, finally, with the question of *ethics* and the need to acknowledge artistry and religiosity as alternatively (and, in certain social, cultural, and theological contexts, antithetically) ethical processes: a distinction between ethical and *an*ethical perspectives on witnessing what is and is not (to be) acknowledged; between remembrance and its repression. And since artistry and religiosity exist only in relationship to each other, ethics and its antitheses are chiasmatically entailed.

Once again, and finally, the need to deconstitute their epistemological topography remains, here and now, the most pressing.

Whether this *coda*, this concluding passage, has brought the preceding composition, this book, to a "cogent and well-proportioned close" remains to be seen in the ripples that will continue.

Beginning here and now.

Note

1 Hannah Arendt, *The Origins of Totalitarianism* (New York: Harcourt Brace Jovanovich, 1951, 3rd ed. with new prefaces, 1973).

INDEX

Page numbers in **bold** denote figures.